GLOBE
LIFE SCIENCE

Mary C. Hicks

•

Bryan Bunch,
Senior Author and Editor,
Globe Science Series

GLOBE BOOK COMPANY
Englewood Cliffs, New Jersey

EDITOR

Jenny Elizabeth Tesar

CONSULTANTS

Nancy T. Davis, Science Department Chairperson/Teacher, 8th Grade Science, Valley Springs Middle School, Arden, NC

Wayne R. Schade, Ph.D., Science Coordinator-Secondary, Austin Independent School District, Austin, TX

Sid Sitkoff, Ph.D., Professor of Science Education, University of California, Berkeley, CA

Barry Wiesenfeld, Assistant Principal, Marie Curie Junior High School, New York, NY

AUTHORS FOR TO DO YOURSELF

Thomas Covotsos
Burton Goldfeld
Jack Rothman
Jean M. Squires

Second Edition 1986

© 1985 by GLOBE BOOK COMPANY

Printed in the United States of America

10   9

ISBN: 0-87065-796-8

Table of Contents

UNIT 4 DIGESTION AND TRANSPORT

UNIT 5 BREATHING AND MOVEMENT

UNIT 6 BEHAVIOR AND CONTROL

UNIT 7 REPRODUCTION IN SIMPLE ORGANISMS AND PLANTS

UNIT 8 REPRODUCTION IN HIGHER ANIMALS

UNIT 9 HEREDITY AND CHANGE THROUGH TIME

UNIT 10 PROTECTING HEALTH

To the Student

Welcome to *Globe Life Science*.

Globe Life Science is different from other science books you have used. Each lesson starts with a question that will be answered in the lesson. The question is followed with **Exploring Science,** a story of one of the many interesting or exciting parts of life science.

After that, you start the lesson itself. Here is where you will learn about the ideas of life science. We stick to the ideas that are most important. You will not need to learn a lot of dull details. Here also there are activities called **To Do Yourself.** They provide a way to see how life science works first hand. There is also a **Review** that will help you remember what you have learned. Both **To Do Yourself** and **Review** provide places where you may write answers in the book.

There are also reviews at the end of each unit. **Summing Up** sections in some units review everything you have studied in the book so far. Other units feature **Careers in Life Science** short descriptions of how people work using the ideas of life science. You can also find out what is needed to get into these careers.

Those are the parts of *Globe Life Science.* The whole book was put together with you in mind. Try it. You'll like it.

Mary C. Hicks
Bryan Bunch

LIVING
THINGS
IN
THEIR
ENVIRONMENT

What Are Living Things?

Exploring Science

It Walks, It Talks, It "Thinks"—Is it Alive? Rob is a "real-life" robot. It is not a character in a movie. It would be right at home in your living room. You would not think Rob was a living thing. Yet in some ways a robot does seem to be alive.

Just as you take in food for energy, Rob takes in electric energy. It uses the energy for its other actions.

The robot can move. It can "walk" forward, backward, and sideways. The robot can lift things, carry them, and put them down. It can even clean your rug.

The robot can "hear" and obey certain words you speak to it. It can talk back. It can "feel" things in its path. The robot moves away to keep from running into them. It can even "smell" a small fire and put it out.

Rob's brain is a computer. People, of course, build and run computers. So a robot does not really do anything on its own. Real living things run themselves. What else do living things do?

● Which seems more likely to be true?

A. In the future, people will invent more ways to run robots with computers.

B. Robots are only toys with no real use in the future.

A robot can do many things that a person does. Is it alive?

What Living Things Do

Look around you. What living things do you see? Anything that is alive is an **organism** (OR-guh-niz-um). Any animal, plant, or other living thing is an organism. You, too, are an organism.

Here are some things that living things can do. Nonliving things, like Rob the Robot, can also do many of these things. But Rob cannot do all of them. A living thing can.

What are some things that living things can do?

● MOVE. Living things can **move,** even if they stay in one place. The hydra (HY-druh) is an animal that usually stays in place by attaching its base to a twig or stone. It waves its arms to catch food. Some plants can move from place to place.

● GROW. Living things become larger in size, or **grow.** At birth, a red kangaroo is less than two centimeters long and weighs one gram. When

A hydra usually stays in one place. It moves by somersaulting.

Mimosa leaves are open during the day. They close at night, or when they are touched.

fully grown, it may be 210 centimeters long and weigh 90 kilograms.

● RESPOND. An organism's **environment** (en-VY-run-munt) is everything that is around it. Living things react, or **respond,** to changes in the environment. Touch the leaves of a mimosa tree and they close up. Living things also respond to changes from within themselves. What do you do when you feel hungry?

To Do Yourself

How Do Brine Shrimp React to Changes in Their Environment?

You will need:

Brine shrimp eggs, large wide-mouth jar, aged tap water, 6 teaspoons of table salt, hand lens, flashlight

1. Mix 6 teaspoons of salt in a liter of aged tap water, in the jar.
2. Add a teaspoon of brine shrimp eggs.
3. Let the jar with eggs sit for a day.
4. After 24 hours, observe the jar with a hand lens. Record your observations.
5. Shine a flashlight on the water for five minutes. Examine the shrimp with your hand lens. Describe what happens to the shrimp. Do they move toward or away from the light?

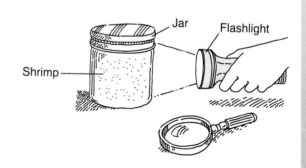

Questions

1. How long did it take for the shrimp eggs to hatch? _____
2. Which way did the brine shrimp move when you shone the light on them?

_____

● REPRODUCE. Living things can make more of their own kind, or **reproduce.** A pig can produce more pigs. The seeds of a corn plant become new corn plants. Yogurt gets its tangy taste from the work of tiny bacteria (bak-TEER-ee-uh). They reproduce by splitting in half.

● USE FOOD AND OXYGEN. Living things need energy to stay alive. **Food** supplies energy. Animals and other living organisms take in food. Plants and plant-like living things make their own food.

Most living things also need and use **oxygen** (OK-sih-jun) to help get energy from food. Oxygen is a part of the air you breathe. Other basic needs of living things are water and the right temperature (TEM-pur-uh-chur). The environment supplies all these needs: food, oxygen, water, and the right temperature.

● GET RID OF WASTES. Living things get rid of **wastes.** When you breathe, your body gives off the waste carbon dioxide (KAR-bun dy-OK-syd). Carbon dioxide is given off when energy is released from food.

All the things that organisms do to stay alive are its **life functions** (FUNGK-shuns). Moving, growing, and responding are life functions. So are reproducing, using food and oxygen, and getting rid of wastes. How, then, can you tell a living thing from a nonliving thing?

In some ways, nonliving things seem to have life functions. A hang glider moves in the wind. Blow air into a beach ball and it grows larger. Stretch and let go of a rubber band, and it reacts. A robot can make another robot. You cannot use any one life function to tell what is alive. Only a thing that is alive can carry on all the life functions.

Review

I. In each blank write the word that fits best. Choose from the words below.

**energy   environment   move   wastes   respond   functions   grow
organism   oxygen   reproduce   temperature   robot**

Any living thing is an _____ . Four things all living things

do are _____ , _____ ,

_____ , and _____ . Living things get

_____ from food. They use _____

from air. They get rid of _____ . The things an organism

does to stay alive are its life _____ . Everything around a

living thing is its _____ .

II. Write the word that matches each statement.

grow   respond   reproduce

A. _____ An earthworm moves away from light.

B. _____ A dog gives birth to puppies.

C. _____ A tree becomes taller.

III. You are an astronaut on another planet. You find an object that moves. How might you tell if it is an organism or not?

How Do Scientists Study Living Things?

Exploring Science

Living Things Come From Other Living Things. "Where did I come from?" asks the young child. "From us," say her parents. Today all scientists agree that living things come from other living things. A young fly, or frog, or mouse, like a young human, has parents like itself.

Long ago, people thought that some living things came from nonliving things. They believed that rotting meat produced maggots, which are young flies. They thought that mud could turn into frogs. Placing wheat on dirty shirts was supposed to produce mice.

Some scientists doubted such beliefs. They wanted proof. In the 1600s Francesco Redi (fran-CHES-kaw REH-di), of Italy, did an experiment (ik-SPER-uh-munt). He set out to test the belief about the origin of maggots. Redi put some rotting meat in an open jar. He watched it closely. He soon saw some flies near the meat. Three days later, maggots covered the meat.

After 19 days, the maggots stopped moving. Then they turned into small hard balls. Redi placed some of the balls in another jar that was empty. After eight more days, the balls broke open. Out came flies!

What happened was that the flies had laid eggs on the meat. The eggs then hatched into maggots.

Redi set up more jars of rotting meat. He sealed some of the jars shut. He left the others open. No maggots appeared in the sealed jars. As before, maggots soon appeared in the open jars. Redi had shown that baby flies (maggots) came only from flies' eggs.

Redi's work helped to change beliefs about where living things come from. Other scientists showed that frogs come from eggs laid by other frogs. They showed that all baby mice come from other mice. It just happens that mice like to eat wheat and to nest in dirty shirts!

After microscopes (MY-kruh-skohps) were invented, tiny living things called microbes (MY-krohbs) were discovered. Scientists no longer believed that animals could come from

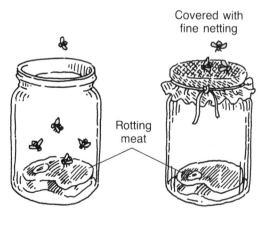

Redi's Experiment

Covered with fine netting

Rotting meat

Jar 1

Jar 2

Francesco Redi helped to prove that life comes from life.

nonliving matter. Yet some thought that microbes could. Late in the 1800s this idea was also shown to be wrong. Louis Pasteur (LOO-ee pah-STUR), of France, showed that microbes also have parents. Since then, no one has shown that any living thing comes from nonliving matter. All organisms have parents.

● Scientists have wondered where a certain kind of eel, which lives in a bay, comes from. The statement more likely to be true is:

A. Mud at the shore of the bay can turn into eels.
B. Eels lay eggs in a river, which hatch. The baby eels then swim into the bay.

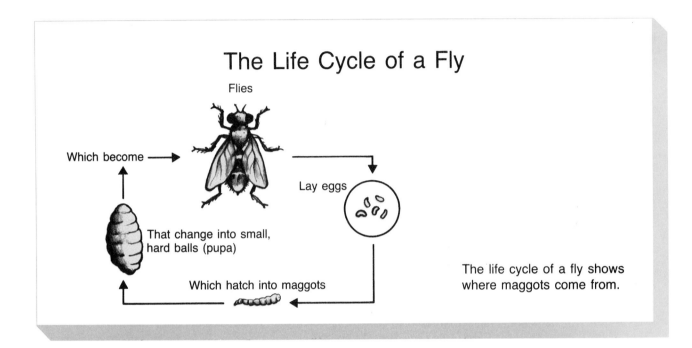

The Life Cycle of a Fly

Flies

Which become →

That change into small, hard balls (pupa)

Lay eggs

Which hatch into maggots

The life cycle of a fly shows where maggots come from.

The Ways of the Scientist

The study of living things is life science, or **biology.** Scientists who study biology are **biologists** (by-OL-uh-jists). Some biologists are **ecologists** (ih-KOL-uh-jists). They study **ecology** (ih-KOL-uh-jee), or the relationship of living things to their environment.

Like other scientists, biologists may work in laboratories (LAB-ruh-tohr-ees). Or they may work outside—in forests, in fields, or in the ocean. They may work anywhere in the **biosphere** (BY-uh-sfeer). The biosphere is the part of the earth in which life exists. A layer of soil, water, and air makes up the biosphere. Biologists sometimes also work in space, aboard spacecraft.

Scientists have many ways of working. Not all scientists work in just the same way. But there is a general pattern that they follow.

STATING A PROBLEM. Scientists are curious. They ask a lot of questions. For example, Redi wondered where maggots come from. His problem could be stated, "Where do maggots come from?"

OBSERVING. **Observing** is using one's senses. Observing can be seeing, hearing, touching, smelling, or tasting. All scientists use **observation.** When Redi saw maggots appear on rotting meat, he was observing.

In science, **measurement** is a way of observing. Counting is a kind of measuring. Redi was measuring when he counted the days between changes in his jars. Scientists also measure with tools. Their tools include scales, thermometers, and meter sticks. Using a microscope helped Pasteur study microbes.

COLLECTING FACTS. Scientists collect facts, or data, by observing. They also read reports of other scientists. This helps them build on the work of the other scientists.

MAKING HYPOTHESES. Scientists use the information they collect to make **hypotheses** (hy-POTH-ih-seez). A hypothesis is a guess or possible answer. Redi's hypothesis was that maggots come from flies.

TESTING HYPOTHESES. One way to test a hypothesis is to make new observations. Scientists also do **experiments** to test hypotheses. This is what Redi did.

CONCLUSION. The results of testing hypotheses are used to make **conclusions** (kun-KLOO-zhuns), or explanations. Redi concluded that maggots come from flies, not rotting meat. Pasteur concluded that microbes could grow only from other microbes. His conclusion was also based on experiment.

Scientists now accept that living things come only from other living things. Before this idea was tested, it was a hypothesis. After being tested many times, the idea became a **theory** (THEE-uh-ree). A theory may still be wrong. If new observations do not fit the theory, the theory must be changed.

To Do Yourself Does Mold Grow on Any Kind of Bread?

You will need:

2 slices of fresh packaged white bread
2 slices of fresh home-made white bread
4 plastic sandwich bags
  cellophane tape

1. Place the four slices of bread inside the plastic bags, one slice per bag.
2. Dampen each slice of bread with a few drops of water. Close the bags and seal with tape.
3. Label each bag. Tell the type of bread and the date.
4. Keep the bread in a dark, warm place.
5. Make a hypothesis as to which bread will become moldy first.
6. Observe your bread slices every day.
7. Collect your data and record your results in a notebook.
8. Try to make a theory about the two types of bread.

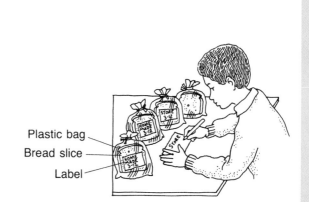

Plastic bag
Bread slice
Label

Questions

1. Which kind of bread became moldy first? _____

2. Where did the bread mold come from? _____

3. What is your theory about the two types of bread? _____

_____

_____

How a Scientist Works

| 1 State the problem | 2 Observe | 3 Collect facts | 4 Make a hypothesis | 5 Test the hypothesis | 6 Conclusion |

The most important steps in the way a scientist works are shown here.

Review

I. Fill each blank with the word that fits best. Choose from the words below.

biosphere   measuring   theory   biology   observing   biologists
hypothesis   ecology   guessing

Life science is _____ . Scientists who study biology are

_____ . The _____ is the part of the earth

in which life exists. Using one's senses is _____ . Counting

or using a tool like a meter stick is _____ . A possible

explanation is a _____ . A hypothesis that is tested and fits

all observations may become a _____ .

II. Show the order of events in developing a scientific theory. Place 1, 2, 3, or 4 in front of each item.

A. _____ testing hypotheses

B. _____ making hypotheses

C. _____ conclusion

D. _____ stating a problem

III. Write the word that matches each statement.

observation   measurement   hypothesis   facts

A. _____ A written report of Redi's experiment.

B. _____ A guess that maggots come from flies.

C. _____ Looking at microbes with a microscope.

D. _____ Counting the days it takes for maggots to appear.

What Is An Ecosystem?

Exploring Science

Wildlife in the City. When people built towns and cities in America, they drove a lot of the wildlife away. Lately, some wildlife is coming back. New York's Bronx has foxes. Owls and coyotes (ky-OH-tees) roam suburbs in California. Falcons nest on top of hotels in Atlantic City. Canada geese are seen in parks all around the country.

What kinds of wildlife live in your town or city? A few years ago, ecologists in New York City decided to find out. They counted the kinds of animals in Central Park. They found 269 kinds of birds, 3 kinds of turtles, and 2 kinds of frogs. There were 9 kinds of fish, 6 kinds of bats, and 3 kinds of woodchucks. They found many more.

Why do you think the animals are coming back to town? Ecologists say their environments in the wild have changed. Also, people are more aware of wildlife. They care more about animals than in the past. They make them feel welcome.

● Which seems more likely to be true?

A. The numbers and kinds of wildlife in towns and cities will stay the same.

B. As environments change, the wildlife both in cities and in the wild will change.

Populations, Communities, and Ecosystems

We share the earth with many other kinds, or **species** (SPEE-sheez), of living things. All the members of one species that live in an area make up a **population** (pop-yuh-LAY-shun). Do you know the population of people in your town or city? What other populations live there?

In a desert, the giant cactuses are one population. Kit foxes, sage, and lizards make up others. There are many more. A **community** (kuh-MYOO-nih-tee) is made up of populations. They live together and affect, or interact (in-tur-AKT) with, each other. Some species give shelter to others. In the desert, elf owls nest in the giant cactuses. In the heat of the day, coyotes rest in their shade.

One population may provide food for another. Cactuses are green plants that make their own food. Ground squirrels eat the seeds of cactuses. Coyotes eat the squirrels.

The desert is an example of an **ecosystem** (EK-oh-sis-tum). A living community and its nonliving environment make up an ecosystem. A lake, a rotting log, or the soil in a flowerpot can be an ecosystem.

An ecosystem can be small or large. A tidal pool on the beach is an ecosystem. So is the earth itself.

A desert ecosystem.

To Do Yourself Where Do Organisms Live on Your Block?

You will need:

Drawing paper, crayons or colored pencils

1. Make a map of your block or around your school building. Show the sidewalk, streets, buildings, playground or park, and vacant lots.
2. Show where each of the animals on the list below can find shelter, food, and water. Use a different color X for each animal.

dogs	squirrels	worms	roaches
cats	pigeons	rats	flies
mice	sparrows	ants	spiders

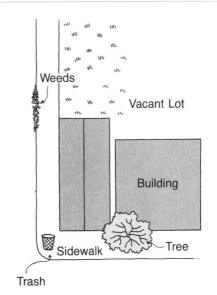

Questions

1. What other animals are there in your community? _____
2. Select a population on your block. Describe why it is important to your community. _____

Review

I. In each blank, write the word that fits best. Choose from the words below.

community   desert   living   population   ecosystem   nonliving

species   town

There are many kinds or _____ of living things. A

_____ is made up of all the organisms of one species in an

area. Populations that live together and interact make up a _____ .

All the organisms, or _____ things plus the

_____ environment make up an _____ .

II. Circle the word that makes each statement correct.

    A. All the grasshoppers in a meadow make up a *(population/ecosystem)*.
    B. The living and nonliving things in a river make up *(an ecosystem/a community)*.
    C. In a forest, all the organisms make up a *(community/population)*.

III. What needs of living things are met in a space station? Is the space station an ecosystem? Explain.

How Are Materials Cycled in Nature?

Exploring Science

Life in a Space Colony. It is the middle of the 21st century. A colony of 10,000 people dwell on the moon. Is this science fiction? Many things that are now real, such as television and rockets, were once fiction. In your lifetime, a space colony may also become real. What scientists know about organisms will help them design a space colony. You, and other living things, are always taking in air, water, and food. You are also always giving off water and carbon dioxide. The things that you take in and give off are used over and over again. They are **cycled.**

On the moon, the things you need to live on are not present. There is no air or water. The soil may not be good for growing food. You must take along what you need. A space colony would have all these things inside a huge bubble. There too the materials (muh-TEER-ee-uls) will be cycled—used over again.

● Wastes from living things in the space colony will probably be

A. shipped back to earth.
B. put to good use within the bubble.

Cycles of Materials

Materials in nature are used over and over again. They go through cycles. In a **cycle** (SY-kul), a material goes through steps that lead back to where it started.

The Water Cycle. On days when dark clouds form, it may rain. Where does the rain water go? It runs or flows into streams, rivers, lakes, and oceans. The water then evaporates (ih-VAP-uh-rayts)—it goes into the air as a gas, or vapor. In the air, the water vapor forms clouds. It then falls back to earth again as rain or snow. In the water cycle, water moves between air and earth and back again. Living things are also part of the water cycle. They take water in and give it off.

The Oxygen/Carbon-Dioxide Cycle. Take a deep breath. The air you breathe contains oxygen. You need it to release energy from the food you eat. As you use your food, carbon-dioxide gas forms. When you exhale, you breathe this carbon dioxide out.

The carbon dioxide is used by plants when they make food. As plants make food, they give off oxygen. When you inhale, you take in some of this oxygen. The cycle just described is called the oxygen/carbon-dioxide cycle.

The Nitrogen Cycle. The air you breathe is mostly nitrogen (NY-truh-jun), a basic element for life. Plants need it. Animals need it. But they need it in a different form. The nitrogen has to

be in a compound with oxygen. This compound is called a **nitrate** (NY-trayt).

By itself, nitrogen will not form a compound with oxygen. In the earth's soil, and in certain

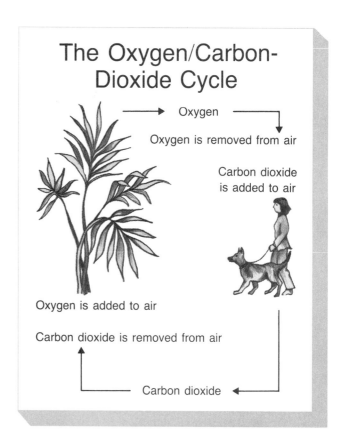

The Oxygen/Carbon-Dioxide Cycle

Oxygen

Oxygen is removed from air

Carbon dioxide is added to air

Oxygen is added to air

Carbon dioxide is removed from air

Carbon dioxide

The Nitrogen Cycle

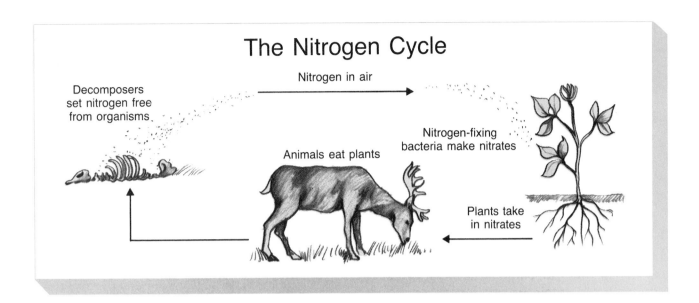

Decomposers set nitrogen free from organisms

Nitrogen in air

Nitrogen-fixing bacteria make nitrates

Animals eat plants

Plants take in nitrates

plant roots, though, there are bacteria that can do the job. They make nitrates.

Plants use the nitrates to make their **proteins** (PROH-teens). Animals eat the plant proteins and make their own proteins. When these plants and animals die, the nitrogen in them is put back into the air. This is known as the **nitrogen cycle.**

Review

I. In each blank write the word that fits best. Choose from the words below.

carbon dioxide   evaporates   bacteria   proteins   cycles   nitrates   oxygen   clouds   nitrogen

Water, carbon dioxide, oxygen, and nitrogen go through

_____ in nature. When water goes into the air as a gas it

_____ . People and animals add _____

to the air. Plants add _____ to the air. Plants use

_____ to make proteins. Nitrogen is made into nitrates by

_____ . Animal _____ are made from

plant proteins.

II. Write the letter of the cycle that matches each statement.

    A. water cycle   **B.** oxygen/carbon-dioxide cycle   **C.** nitrogen cycle

    1. _____ A tree takes in carbon dioxide.

    2. _____ A bean plant takes in nitrates.

    3. _____ A person gives off water in breathing.

III. What would happen if the cycles of materials in nature did not repeat themselves?

What Is a Food Chain?

Exploring Science

Plants That Eat Meat. Down in the swamp there are plants that eat meat. One is the Venus fly trap. Its outer leaves have "teeth." A fly crawls onto one of these leaves. It brushes against a trigger hair on the leaf. In less than a second, the leaf snaps shut. The "teeth" form a cage around the fly. The plant digests the fly.

The pitcher plant also eats meat. A sweet odor attracts an ant into the plant. When the ant tries to crawl out, pointed hairs block its way. It falls into a liquid, where the plant digests it.

Both these plants are green. They are unlike other green plants, which do not "eat" insects. What makes them different? Plants must take in nitrogen to make foods. The nitrogen usually comes from nitrates in the soil. Soil in the swamp is poor in nitrates. So the meat-eating plants get nitrogen from animal proteins. That is why these plants eat insects.

● Circle the correct word.

A kind of mushroom that feeds on a living tree also feeds on worms because the soil under the tree is (poor/rich) in nitrogen.

Links in the Chain

Green plants, and other food makers, use energy from sunlight to produce food. Food makers are **producers.**

Organisms that feed on other living things are **consumers.** Some animals eat only producers. These are **first-level** consumers. A rabbit that eats grass is a first-level consumer. Animals that eat first-level consumers are **second-level** consumers. A snake that eats the rabbit is a second-level consumer. A **third-level** consumer eats second-level consumers. A hawk that eats the snake is a third-level consumer.

The grass, rabbit, snake, and hawk are links in a **food chain.** At the start of any food chain is a producer. In a drawing of the chain, an arrow joins each organism to the one that eats it. The arrows show how energy flows along the chain. This chain is short. Many food chains are very long. An animal that eats other animals is called a **predator** (PRED-uh-tur). The animal a predator eats is its **prey.** In the food chain above, the hawk is a predator. Its prey is the snake. Which other organisms in the chain are predators? Which are their prey?

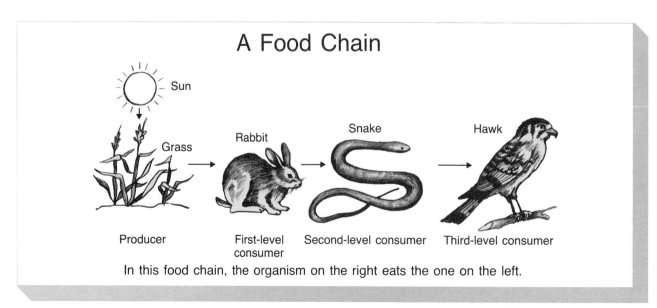

A Food Chain

Sun

Grass

Rabbit

Snake

Hawk

Producer

First-level consumer

Second-level consumer

Third-level consumer

In this food chain, the organism on the right eats the one on the left.

To Do Yourself   Where Do Producers Store Food That Consumers Eat?

You will need:

Iodine solution in a dropper bottle; samples of leaves, stems, roots, fruits, seeds, flowers

1. Place small pieces of each plant part on a paper towel. Crush any seeds.
2. Carefully drop iodine solution on each sample.
3. Observe each sample with a hand lens. The iodine will stain some things brown. Some parts, though, will turn blue-black. This color change shows where starch is stored.

Questions

1. Draw each plant part. Color where the starch is being stored.
2. If starch is the main food product of plants, which plant parts had the most food

stored in it? _____

Review

I. In each blank write the word that fits best. Choose from the words below.

food chain   predator   consumer   producer   prey   rabbit

A food maker is a _____ .

A _____ shows how energy passes from one organism to

another. An animal that eats another animal is both a _____

and a _____ . The food of a predator is its

_____ .

II. Match each entry in column **A** with the correct number in column **B**.

A	B
A. _____ mouse	1. producer
B. _____ corn	2. first-level consumer
C. _____ hawk	3. second-level consumer
D. _____ cat	4. third-level consumer

III. Draw a food chain with four links that includes both you and a mosquito.

What Is a Food Web?

Exploring Science

Fly Eats Toad—Toad Eats Fly. A spadefoot toad is about to start its life on land. In the mud nearby lives a maggot. This maggot is the larva (LAR-vuh) of a horsefly. Only the larva's head and jaws stick out of the mud. When the toad hops close to the larva, the larva attacks. The larva injects the toad with poison and sucks it dry.

The scientists who watched the fly eat the toad were amazed. They then observed not one, but hundreds of fly larvas eating toads. One scientist said, "This is unusual, because everyone knows that toads eat flies."

The scientists collected fly larvas and spadefoots from the mud. They took them to their laboratory, and observed the same events. Then they reported their findings.

● Which seems more likely to be true?

A. In a food chain, toads are always predators and flies are always prey.

B. In a food chain, a toad or a fly may be either predator or prey.

A young spadefoot toad (left) is being pulled into the mud by the larva of a horsefly. Right: A baby spadefoot, and the larva, or maggot, of the horsefly.

You Are What You Eat

Producers and consumers are part of food chains. A rabbit eats grass. A snake eats the rabbit. A hawk eats the snake. Here's another food chain: A frog eats a cricket. A fish eats the frog. A hawk eats the fish.

Most organisms are part of more than one food chain. The hawk, for example, eats the snake. It is part of one food chain. But the hawk also eats a fish. It is then part of another food chain. Two or more food chains can link to make up a **food web.** In a food web, food chains link together.

Consumers that eat only plant foods are **herbivores** (HUR-buh-vohrs). A deer is a herbivore. Consumers that eat only meat are **carnivores** (KAR-nuh-vohrs). A mountain lion is a carnivore. An **omnivore** (OM-nuh-vohr) eats both kinds of food. Which are you—omnivore, herbivore, or carnivore?

In a food chain, herbivores are first-level consumers. Carnivores are at the second level, or higher. So are omnivores.

Another kind of consumer is the **decomposer** (dee-kum-POH-zur). Decomposers break down, or decompose, wastes and dead organisms. **Scavengers** (SKAV-in-jurs) are one kind of decomposer. A vulture is a scavenger. It feeds upon dead animals that it finds. Tiny **decay bacteria** are another kind of decomposer. So are **fungi** (FUN-jy). These are nongreen plant-like organisms.

Decomposers of all kinds are important for the food web of a community. They return nitrogen and other materials to the soil.

A Food Web

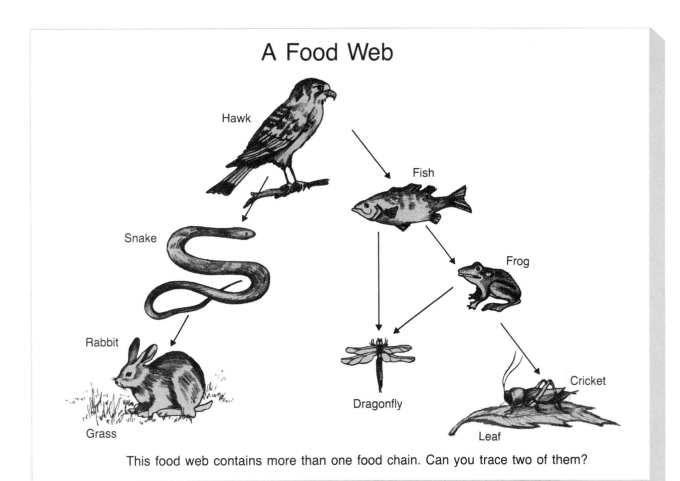

This food web contains more than one food chain. Can you trace two of them?

Review

I. In each blank write the word (or words) that fits best. Choose from the words below.

carnivore   **herbivore**   **food chain**   **food web**   **omnivore**   **decomposer**

Food chains link together in a _____ . A

_____ is a plant-eater. A _____ is a

meat-eater. An _____ eats both plants and meat.

II. If the statement is true, write **T**. If it is false, write **F**. Then correct the underlined word.

   A. _____ Fungi are nongreen and <u>animal-like</u>.

   B. _____ Scavengers are <u>decomposers</u>.

   C. _____ Decay bacteria return <u>oxygen</u> to the soil.

III. How can a person be both a first-level consumer and a second-level consumer? Explain.

What Are Food Pyramids?

Exploring Science

The Case of the Poisoned Fish. A strange disease had come to Minamata (mee-nah-MAH-tah), Japan, in the 1950s. First, the cats became sick and died. Next, children became ill. Some were paralyzed; some had signs of brain damage. At the end, 67 people died, and over 300 were disabled.

Scientists set out to find the cause. At the edge of Minamata's bay stood a factory. It gave off wastes containing the chemical element mercury. Mercury is a poison. The mercury wastes flowed into the bay.

In the bay lived plant-like algae (AL-jee). The algae took in only a little mercury. It was not enough to kill the algae. One fish, though, eats a large amount of algae. A little mercury in the algae becomes a lot of mercury in one fish. A cat or a child eats many fish. Enough mercury collected then for it to be poisonous to the cats and children. The deadly mercury had gone up the food chain.

● Which seems more likely to be true?

If children had eaten crabs from Minamata Bay instead of fish,

A. they would not have become sick.
B. they still might have become sick.

The Big Fish Eat the Little Fish

In Minamata Bay, the main food producers are algae. In an ocean, the main producers are also algae. They provide food for animals in the sea. We can write one food chain from the ocean like this:

algae → water fleas → minnows → bass
producer first-level second- third-
          consumer   level   level
                       consumer consumer

The water fleas eat large amounts of algae. Minnows eat lots of water fleas. Bass eat lots of minnows. A **food pyramid** (PIR-uh-mid) shows how much food each predator eats.

The same kind of thing happens on land.

plants → insects → mice → hawk
producer first-level second- third-
          consumer   level   level
                       consumer consumer

Insects eat large amounts of plants. Mice eat an even greater number of insects. Hawks eat lots of mice. The food pyramid shows how much food each organism eats.

At the bottom of the pyramid are the producers. Above them are the first-level consumers. Above them are the second-level consumers. At the top are third-level consumers.

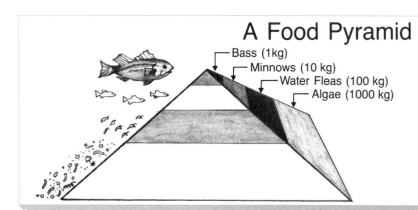

A Food Pyramid

Bass (1kg)
Minnows (10 kg)
Water Fleas (100 kg)
Algae (1000 kg)

In this food pyramid, a big fish eats a little fish.

To Do Yourself   Can There Be a Food Pyramid in a Terrarium?

You will need:

An empty glass tank, soil, clumps of moss and grass, rocks, beetles, earthworms, small frog, pieces of tree bark covered with fungi and algae, plastic wrap, water

1. Place 2½ to 5 centimeters of soil in the bottom of the tank.
2. Create an environment for your animals, using the grass, tree bark, algae and mosses. Water the terrarium until the soil is damp.
3. Release your living animals into the terrarium one at a time.
4. Cover your terrarium with plastic wrap. Keep it out of direct sunlight.

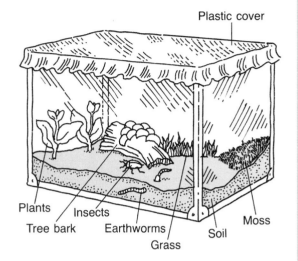

Questions

1. What does each animal in your terrarium eat? Does it eat any of the other animals or plants? _____
2. Which organism is at the top of the food pyramid? Which one is at the bottom?

   _____

3. Draw or describe the food chains or pyramid you observe. _____

Review

I. In each blank write the word that fits best. Choose from the words below.

pyramid   algae   bottom   top   energy   predators

In the ocean, _____ are producers. A food

_____ shows how much food each predator eats.

Producers are at the _____ of the pyramid. High-level

consumers are at the _____ of the pyramid.

II. Match column **B** to column **A**:

A. Organisms	B. Levels
a. _____ humans	1. bottom
b. _____ soy beans	2. middle
c. _____ pigs	3. top

III. Can energy be cycled the way materials are? Explain.

What Is a Succession?

Exploring Science

Life Comes Back to Mount St. Helens. Before May 18, 1980, a forest of fir trees covered Mount St. Helens, in Washington. Wildlife—elk, rabbits, gophers, birds, and insects—were everywhere. Then it happened: Mount St. Helens erupted. Shock waves felled the fir trees. Mudflows buried the rest of the plant life. The elk and the rabbits were no more. The mountain ecosystem was dead.

Or was it? A month later, scientist James McMahon flew into the blast zone. There he found ants, spiders, and beetles. Some gophers, who live underground, also survived. When the gophers surfaced, they had sand and soil on their fur. The soil contained roots and seeds of plants. Wind and rain were taking away ash that covered the soil. Soon new plants were growing from the roots and seeds.

● Which seems more likely to be true?

A. After a forest fire, things will begin to grow again on the burnt land.

B. After a flood washes away an ecosystem, nothing is likely to grow again on the land.

Changes Soon Take Place on Cleared Land

Land on which a forest once stood may be cleared. If left to nature, however, bare land will not stay that way. A series of changes called a **succession** (suk-SESH-un) will take place.

The first new plants that grow are weeds. They are the **pioneer** (py-uh-NEER) **plants.** Animals, such as insects, come too. Together the plants and animals make up a **pioneer community.**

The next year, shrubs begin to grow. The weeds and shrubs compete, and the shrubs win. Meanwhile, seeds of pine trees arrive. They sprout and grow well in the open, sunny field. They compete with and crowd out the shrubs. After 10 years, the pines are the most numerous, or **dominant** (DOM-uh-nunt), plants in the community. Animals such as chipmunks and wrens arrive. A pine forest has begun.

Mature pine trees shade the forest floor. There, seedlings of other arrivals, maples, compete with the seedlings of pines.

After 100 years, the maples have become the dominant plants. The young maples grow well in the shade of their parents. So the maples remain dominant. They are the **climax** (KLY-maks) **plants.** At the end of a succession, there is a **climax community.** No further changes take place. The community is stable.

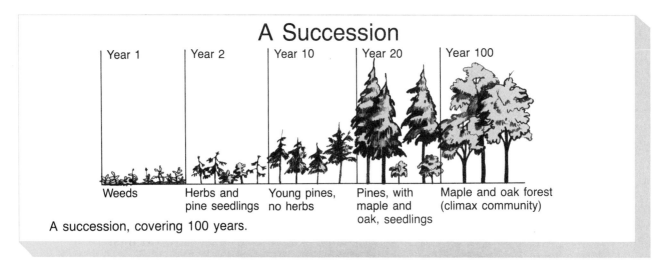

A succession, covering 100 years.

Year 1 — Weeds
Year 2 — Herbs and pine seedlings
Year 10 — Young pines, no herbs
Year 20 — Pines, with maple and oak, seedlings
Year 100 — Maple and oak forest (climax community)

To Do Yourself · Is There Succession in a Mini-Ecosystem?

You will need:

Dried grass, 2 small wide-mouthed jars, aged tap water, microscope, slides and cover slips, medicine dropper

1. Place grass in a jar, add water, and set in indirect light.
2. In the second jar, just add water.
3. Examine a drop of water from the first jar with the microscope. Look at water from the following areas: **a.** bottom, **b.** middle, **c.** surface.
4. Examine both jars every day for 2 weeks.
5. Draw sketches of life you observe.

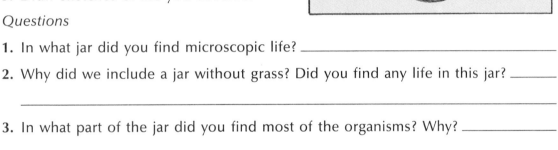

Water — Dried grass — Water

Questions

1. In what jar did you find microscopic life? _____

2. Why did we include a jar without grass? Did you find any life in this jar? _____
   _____

3. In what part of the jar did you find most of the organisms? Why? _____
   _____

Review

I. In each blank, write the word that fits best. Choose from the words below.

climax   dominant   succession   pioneer   community   shrubs

In a natural _____ , a series of changes takes place. On a

bare field, the _____ plants grow first. The most numerous

plants in a community are the _____ plants. At the end of a

succession, there is a _____ community.

II. Circle the word that makes each statement true.

   A. In a succession, a pine forest comes (*before*/*after*) a maple forest.
   B. When weeds and shrubs compete in a field, the shrubs (*win*/*lose*).
   C. The kind of community that is stable is a (*pioneer*/*climax*) community.

III. A pine forest can change the environment so that it is more favorable for a maple forest than for a pine forest. How does the pine forest do this?

What Is A Biome?

Exploring Science

A Trip to a Rain Forest. Imagine a trip into the Amazon rain forest. Dress lightly, for it is hot. If you want dry feet, wear boots. The soil is quite damp. So is the air. You are in the shade down here, but way above the sun shines brightly. This warm, moist, sunny habitat (HAB-ih-tat) is the most favorable of all for life on land.

Notice the lush growth of everything here. Trees are very tall. Vines thickly drape their trunks. In the tree tops are monkeys and parrots. The kinds of plants and animals here are amazing. Scientists believe that the world has 4½ million species of living things. Of these, 3 million live in the rain forests.

All the rich life of the rain forests could vanish. The increasing numbers of people means more forests must be cut down. The trees become timber and fuel. The land becomes farms and beef ranches. After a few years food crops for people and cattle do not grow well. While tropical forest plants are adapted (uh-DAPT-ud) for survival here, crops are not. The soil is poor. It must be used very wisely to keep the land from turning into desert.

Enough rain forest to cover the state of Ohio is destroyed each year. At this rate, the rain forests could all be gone by the year 2000. Can any part of the rain forests be saved? Some people think so, and they are trying.

In Brazil, the law says that 50 percent of all rain-forest land bought by developers must be left alone. Scientists called ecologists study the forest and help decide which parts to cut down. The other parts become reserves and parks. In other tropical countries, people are also trying to save their rain forests. In Chad, Africa, park rangers fight illegal fires set by poachers and ranchers. In Guatemala people are cooking with wood as a fuel. Their new stoves use half as much fuel as the old ones.

● Which of the following is more likely to be true?

A. By the year 2000, it may be impossible to visit a rain forest.

B. People will soon stop cutting down any trees in the rain forest.

The tropical rain forest is also known as a "jungle."

The tundra is cold and bleak most of the year.

Major Biomes of the World

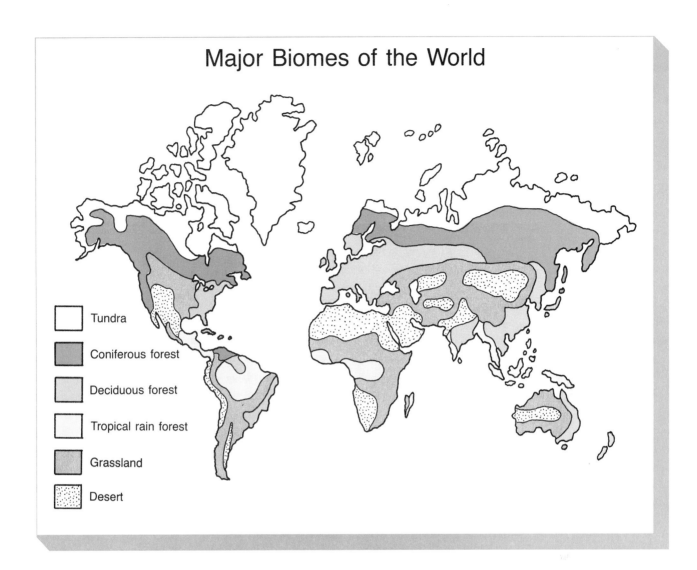

Tundra

Coniferous forest

Deciduous forest

Tropical rain forest

Grassland

Desert

Why Climate Is Important

The nonliving parts of the environment are not the same everywhere. The soil is rich in some places and poor in others. Some places have long summer days and short winter days. In other places, the days are the same length all year. Winter is long in some places and short in others. Still other environments have summer all year. It rains a lot in some areas, and not much in others.

Climate (KLY-mit) is the pattern of weather in a place over a long period of time. The main factors in climate are rainfall and temperature. A large area of the land that has the same climate is called a **biome** (BY-ohm). Only certain kinds of plants and animals live in each biome. Organisms in each biome are a **climax community**. Which organisms make up the climax community of a place depends upon the climate. You

would not find palm trees at the North Pole. Penguins do not roam the jungle.

The map shows where different biomes are found. Which kind of biome do you live in?

There are six major biomes. They are:

1. **Tundra** (TUN-druh)—This biome is near the arctic circle.

2. **Coniferous** (kuh-NIF-ur-us) **forest**—In North America, these forests are in Canada. Here, winters are long and cold.

3. **Deciduous** (duh-SIJ-oo-us) **forest**—Many trees have spectacular color in the fall.

4. **Grassland**—This region has a low total annual rainfall.

5. **Desert**—Here you will find the hottest temperatures on earth, with little or no rain.

6. **Tropical rain forest**—This biome has heavy rainfalls, and hot, humid air.

Major Biomes of the Earth

Biome	Soil	Climate	Climax Community	
			Climax Plants	*Some Animals*
Tundra	poor	little sun and rain or snow; winter long, cold	lichens (plant-like organisms) mosses low shrubs	arctic fox caribou mosquitoes
Coniferous* forest	poor	more sun and rain than tundra; winter shorter	pines firs spruces hemlocks	moose red squirrel woodpecker
Deciduous† forest	rich	more sun and rain than coniferous forest, moderate temperatures	maples birches oaks beeches	gray squirrel warblers bobcats chipmunk
Grassland	rich	different amounts of sun around world; less rain than any forests	grasses	bison grasshoppers prairie dogs
Desert	poor	much sun, very little rain; mild winter, hot summer	cactuses sages Joshua trees	kit fox rattlesnake lizards elf owls
Tropical rain forest	poor	much sun, much rain; warm all year	evergreens with broad leaves vines of many kinds	great variety, including: monkeys sloths toucans army ants

*coniferous trees are evergreen, with needlelike leaves
†deciduous trees are broad-leafed and shed leaves in the fall

Grasslands are common in flat regions with no mountains.

Coniferous forests are in cold regions. Here spruce and fir trees are most common.

In deserts, days are very hot and nights are very cold.

In North America, deciduous forests are located in the eastern part of the United States.

Review

I. In each blank, write the word (or words) that fits best. Choose from the words below.

climate   deciduous   desert   ocean   biome   grassland   tundra
coniferous   tropical rain   climax community

The pattern of weather in a place is its _____ . An area that

has the same climate is a _____ . The biome that has long

cold winters is the _____ . Trees that shed leaves in the fall

are climax plants in the _____ forest. It is warm and moist

all year round in the _____ forest. The biome with the least

rain is the _____ . Bison and prairie dogs live in the

_____ . Trees that are evergreen and have needlelike

leaves are climax plants in the _____ forest.

II. If the statement is true, write **T** in the blank. If it is false, write **F**. Then correct the underlined word.

A. _____ Cactuses are climax plants in the <u>grassland</u>.

B. _____ Mosses are climax plants in the <u>tundra</u>.

C. _____ Arctic foxes live in the <u>desert</u>.

D. _____ The soil in the deciduous forest is <u>poor</u>.

E. _____ Army ants live in the <u>tropical rain</u> forest biome.

III. If you climb a mountain, you may go from a coniferous forest into a tundra biome. Can you explain why?

What are Habitats and Niches?

Exploring Science

The Hare and the Lynx. Up in the Canadian tundra live the lynx and the snowshoe hare. As far back as 1750, records have been kept of their numbers. The graph shows their numbers between 1845 and 1945.

On the graph, the green line shows the numbers of hares. See how the size of the hare population rises and drops. The black line shows the numbers of lynx. The lynx hunt and eat the hares.

When the number of hares goes up, there is more food for the lynx. When the lynx have more food, they increase in numbers.

With more lynx to eat them, the number of hares goes down. Then the lynx begin to starve. Do you see why? Soon, there are fewer lynx. Then the pattern repeats itself. The predator appears to keep the numbers of its prey in check. The opposite also seems to be true. Do you see why?

● Which seems more likely to be true?
The human population has, so far, grown larger because

A. it has no major predators.
B. its food supply has become smaller.

Where Species Live

The place where a species lives is its **habitat**. Populations of both deer and wolves may live in a forest habitat. How each population fits into its habitat is its **niche** (nich). Deer eat plants and wolves eat animals. They eat different food. So the deer and wolf have different niches in the same forest habitat.

In any habitat, only one population can occupy each niche. In the forest, cardinals and indigo buntings both eat seeds. Yet they do not fill the same niche. The seeds the cardinal eats are large. Those the buntings eat are small.

Sometimes two populations try to fill the same niche. Each tries to get the same food. They compete. The species better fitted for the niche wins. It crowds the other one out.

There are limits to the size of any population. **Limiting factors** keep populations in check. Sunlight and soil are limiting factors for plants. Food and places for shelter put limits on animals. Water and temperature put limits on both plants and animals.

Another limiting factor is the predator. It is an animal that feeds on other living animals. A scavenger, which feeds on dead animals, is not a limiting factor. Can you explain why?

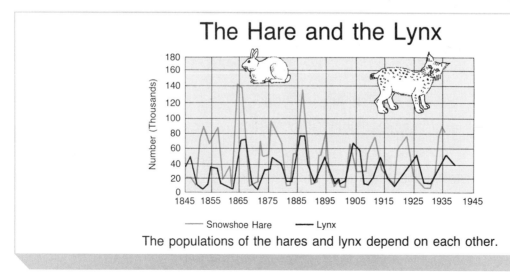

The populations of the hares and lynx depend on each other.

To Do Yourself What Is a Mealworm's Niche?

You will need:

Mealworms, a jar with a lid, a cereal such as corn flakes, hand lens, hammer and nail, apple

1. Punch a few air holes in the lid of the jar with the hammer and nail.
2. Place about 3 centimeters of cereal in the jar. You may treat your mealworms to a piece of apple if you wish.
3. Place your mealworms in the jar. Carefully observe one mealworm with your hand lens and draw it.
4. Close the lid and place the jar in a dark warm place.
5. Observe the mealworm environment every day and record your observations. Describe any changes in the mealworms that you observe.

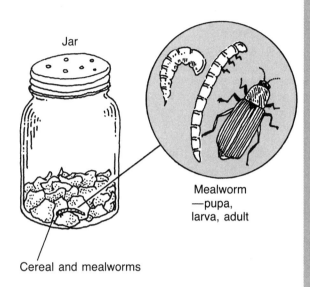

Jar

Mealworm —pupa, larva, adult

Cereal and mealworms

Questions

1. What do you think is good niche for a mealworm? Describe it. _____
2. How did the niche you made for the mealworms change? How did the mealworms change? _____

Review

I. In each blank, write the word that fits best. Use the words below.

predator   limiting   population   habitat   niche   tundra

An organism's _____ is where it lives. Its

_____ is how it fits into its habitat. Populations are kept

in check by _____ factors. An animal that feeds on other

living animals is a _____ .

II. Write **G** if the factor limits grass. Write **R** is the factor limits rabbits. Write **GR** if the factor limits both.

A. _____ soil   C. _____ water   E. _____ wolves

B. _____ food   D. _____ sunlight

III. In a certain ocean habitat, bass are predators and bullheads are scavengers. Are these two fishes in the same niche or different niches? Explain.

Can an Ecosystem Get Out-of-Balance?

Exploring Science

Foster Parents Help Save Whoopers. Huge flocks of whooping cranes once filled the skies. In the fall, the whoopers flew south to their winter home in Texas. In the spring, they flew north.

Then their numbers began to shrink. In 1941, only 15 were counted in Texas. Scientists wanted to help save the whoopers.

So they took two whoopers to a research center. In the wild, a whooper lays just two eggs in a season. In the center, scientists got each bird to lay as many as 11 eggs. They took each egg from the nest as soon as it was laid. Then the whooper would lay more.

Scientists then took the whooper eggs back to the wild. They placed the eggs in the nests of sandhill cranes. The sandhills raised the whoopers as their own. In this way, both scientists and sandhills helped the whooper population grow. By 1984, there were nearly 150 whoopers.

● If whoopers and other species are to be saved,

A. it is enough to help them produce more young.

B. their environments in the wild must also be saved.

To Do Yourself   Where Is the Most Pollution?

You will need:

Adhesive tape for wrapping packages, cardboard, stapler, scissors, ruler

1. Decide if you want to test the air indoors or outdoors. You may wish to test a place near a window or door.
2. To make the test-strips, cut several pieces of cardboard, 5 by 15 centimeters.
3. Cut a piece of adhesive wrapping tape 12 centimeters long. Staple it, sticky side up, to the cardboard strip. Make several of these.
4. Place your test-strips near windows or doors, where you would like to test for dust or soot.
5. Check your test-strips each day. Record your observations in a notebook.

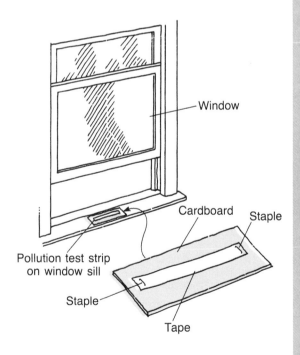

Window

Cardboard

Staple

Pollution test strip on window sill

Staple

Tape

Questions

1. How can you tell which areas have the most dirt, dust, and soot? _____

2. What kinds of pollution did you find? _____

3. What are some of the ways of reducing the amount of pollution in your home?

Endangered Species

In any ecosystem, changes happen all the time. The changes can work together to keep the ecosystem the same. Then the ecosystem is **balanced.** In a balanced ecosystem, the size of a population may go up, down, then up again. Over time, however, its average size does not change.

The balance of an ecosystem can be upset. The cause may be in nature, such as a storm, a forest fire, or a volcano. People also cause upsets. They turn forests into farms and towns. They build dams, dig mines, and drain wetlands.

Things that **pollute** (puh-LOOT) the environ-ment also cause upsets. Adding anything harm-ful to the environment pollutes it. Harmful gases from cars, power plants, and factories pollute the air.

Living things in danger of dying out are **en-dangered species.** Upsets in the balance of eco-systems have made it hard for these species to survive. Their habitats may have been de-stroyed. They may no longer be able to find enough food.

In the past, many species have died out or become **extinct.** Unless people help them, many endangered species may also become extinct.

The whooping crane, the giant panda, and the bald eagle are endangered species.

Review

I. In each blank write the word that fits best. Use the words below.

balanced   extinct   ecosystem   endangered   pollutes   species

In a _____ ecosystem, the average size of a population does not change. Adding harmful things to air, water, or land

_____ them. An _____ species is in danger of dying out. When a species dies out, it becomes

_____ .

II. Write **N** for each way nature can upset an ecosystem's balance. Write **P** for each way people can upset the balance.

A. _____ Oil spill   D. _____ Storm   G. _____ Building dam

B. _____ Gases from cars   E. _____ Trash   H. _____ Volcano

C. _____ Forest fire   F. _____ Digging Mine

III. How may people themselves become an endangered species?

Review What You Know

A. Use the clues below to complete the crossword.

Across

1. Study of living things
2. To get larger
5. Make more of its own kind
8. One way to observe
9. Animals do this to get energy
10. One of life's functions
11. Watery part of the biosphere

Down

1. All the earth's air, water, and land
3. Oxygen is a _____ .
4. Something an organism does to stay alive is a life _____
5. React to change in the environment
6. A step in the scientific method
7. What ecologists study

B. Write the word (or words) that best completes each statement.

1. Organisms that are producers include **a.** bacteria **b.** algae **c.** fungi

    1. _____

2. All the nonliving and living things in a desert make up **a.** a community **b.** an ecosystem **c.** a population

    2. _____

3. One way of observing in science is to make a **a.** hypothesis **b.** theory **c.** measurement

    3. _____

4. A bird that eats both seeds and insects is **a.** a carnivore **b.** an herbivore **c.** an omnivore

    4. _____

5. A gas given off by plants that animals use is **a.** oxygen **b.** nitrogen **c.** carbon dioxide

    5. _____

6. A second-level consumer eats **a.** first-level consumers **b.** third-level consumers **c.** producers

    6. _____

7. At the bottom of a food pyramid are the **a.** herbivores **b.** producers **c.** carnivores

    7. _____

8. At the start of a food chain are
 a. animals **b.** plants **c.** decomposers

8. _____

9. Kit foxes and rattlesnakes are animals
 in the **a.** tundra **b.** desert
 c. grassland

9. _____

10. In a succession, the first plants to
 grow are called **a.** dominant
 b. climax **c.** pioneer

10. _____

11. A vulture that eats only dead things
 is a **a.** predator **b.** scavenger
 c. producer

11. _____

12. Trees that shed leaves in the fall are
 the climax plants of forests called
 a. deciduous **b.** coniferous
 c. tropical

12. _____

13. A species of animal that has died out
 is **a.** endangered **b.** evaporated
 c. extinct

13. _____

14. Two animals that have different
 niches have different **a.** habitats
 b. food **c.** environments

14. _____

15. A corn plant taking in nitrates is part
 of the cycle of **a.** nitrogen
 b. water **c.** oxygen/carbon dioxide

15. _____

16. When limiting factors are at work in
 a population its growth **a.** slows
 down **b.** speeds up **c.** stays the
 same

16. _____

17. Two or more food chains make up
 a. an environment **b.** a food web
 c. a biome

17. _____

18. A large area of land that has the
 same climate is a **a.** habitat
 b. niche **c.** biome

18. _____

19. Over time, populations in a balanced
 ecosystem **a.** get larger **b.** get
 smaller **c.** stay the same

19. _____

20. A food web shows how the same
 organism can belong to more than
 one **a.** ecosystem **b.** biome
 c. food chain

20. _____

21. Redi showed that the parents of
 maggots are **a.** mice **b.** frogs
 c. flies

21. _____

22. Pasteur discovered that microbes
come from **a.** other microbes
b. nonliving matter **c.** rotting meat   22. _____

23. Among the decomposers are the
a. algae **b.** decay bacteria **c.** plants   23. _____

24. Trees with needle-like leaves are the
climax plants in a **a.** tundra
b. coniferous forest **c.** desert   24. _____

25. A factor that limits the number of a
species of animals is **a.** predators
b. sunlight **c.** scavengers   25. _____

C. Apply What You Know

1. Study the drawing of a food chain in Africa. Then use the words below to fill in
the blanks.

carnivore   energy   herbivore   producer   predator
third-level consumer   decomposer   first-level consumer
omnivore   second-level consumer   prey   scavenger

   a. Three terms that describe the zebra are (1) _____

   (2) _____ (3) _____

   b. Three terms that describe the lion are (4) _____

   (5) _____ (6) _____

   c. The grass is a (7) _____ because it makes food, using

   (8) _____ from the sun.

   When the lion in the drawing dies, its body is consumed by hyenas.

   d. Two terms that describe the hyena are (9) _____

   and (10) _____ .

2. Write the word (or words) that best completes each statement.
   a. The grass, zebras, lions, and hyenas are each members of different

   (1) communities (2) ecosystems (3) biomes (4) populations. _____
   b. If hunters are allowed to kill most of the lions in the area, the zebra
   population would probably (1) get larger, then smaller; (2) get smaller, then

   larger; (3) become extinct; (4) stay the same. _____

   Explain your answer. _____

   _____

   _____

   _____

   c. Laws have been made to protect the lions because (1) their food supply is
   almost gone; (2) they are extinct; (3) they are endangered; (4) nothing limits

   their numbers. _____

D. Find Out More

1. Visit a nearby ecosystem. It may be your school grounds, your backyard, a park, a vacant lot, a wooded area, or a field. Or it may be a mud puddle, a pond, a stream, a river, a tidal pool, or a lake. Make a list of the populations you observe. Describe the nonliving parts of the ecosystem. Draw one or more food chains that you observe.

2. In the library, find out how the world's human population has changed since the year 1 A.D. Draw a graph that shows its growth. Try to predict what the population will be in the year 2000.

UNIT 2

HOW LIVING THINGS ARE ORGANIZED

What Units Make Up Living Things?

Exploring Science

From 200 to 200,000 Times Life Size. It happened over 300 years ago, in Holland. Anton van Leeuwenhoek (AN-tun van LAY-vun-hook) had a new microscope that he had made. One day he looked through it at a drop of lake water. What he saw surprised him.

The water was alive with what Leeuwenhoek called "wee beasties." The microscope made the tiny organisms look 200 times larger than life size. Leeuwenhoek was one of the first to see living things that small. His work was a giant step ahead for life science.

Today, microscopes are much stronger. An electron microscope can make tiny organisms look 200,000 times life size. Pictures are made that show the organisms much bigger. The pictures add greatly to what we know about living things. Microscopes have come a long way in 300 years.

● Which statement is more likely to be true?

A. With the electron microscope, organisms smaller than "wee beasties" can be seen.

B. There are no organisms smaller than a "wee beastie."

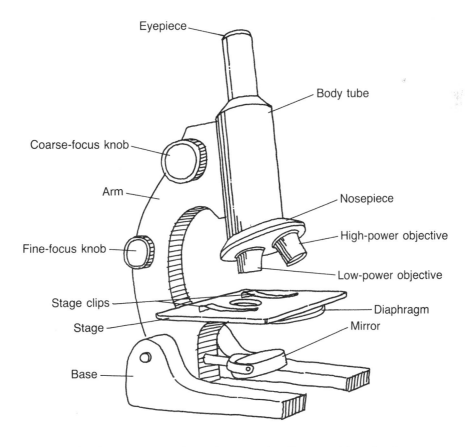

The Compound Microscope

Eyepiece

Body tube

Coarse-focus knob

Arm

Nosepiece

High-power objective

Fine-focus knob

Low-power objective

Stage clips

Diaphragm

Stage

Mirror

Base

A microscope, such as this one, is often used in school.

Microbes and Cells

Living things come in many sizes. Some, like whales and giant redwoods, are huge. Others, like mites, are very small. A hand lens makes a mite look larger. The lens is made of curved glass or plastic. Some hand lenses make small things look eight times larger than they are. That means their magnifying power is about eight times.

Microbes are living things too small to be seen with a hand lens. We use a microscope to see microbes. It has two or more lenses. Its magnifying power may be 100 times or more.

The microbes you see with a microscope may be animal-like **protozoans** (proh-tuh-ZOH-uns). Or they may be plant-like **algae.**

You know how Leeuwenhoek first saw microbes. A few years before that, the English scientist Robert Hooke had another "first." He also made microscopes. One day, while looking at a slice of cork, he noticed that it was made up of tiny boxes. He called these "cells." Later, it was found that living things are made up of tiny **cells.**

Hooke's cork cells were dead and empty. Only their walls were left. Living cells, though, are anything but empty. They are filled with living matter. There are living cells in a frog's blood. A bit of muscle in your stomach or heart is made up of living cells. So is a green leaf.

A cell has three main parts. These are somewhat like the parts of a plum. The **cell membrane**

Leeuwenhoek and his microbes.

(MEM-brayn) covers the cell, like the skin on a plum. At the plum's center is the pit. A cell's center is its **nucleus** (NOO-klee-us). Between the plum's skin and pit is the flesh. In a cell, the **cytoplasm** (SY-tuh-plaz-um) is between the cell membrane and the nucleus.

Many microbes are made up of just one cell. Bacteria are one-celled living things. So are the protozoans and many algae. Larger organisms are made up of many cells. That includes you, a tree, and an ant.

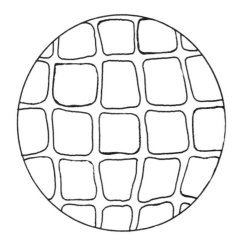

Cork cells seen through a microscope

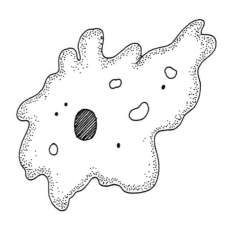

An ameba seen through a microscope.

To Do Yourself **What Are the Parts of an Animal Cell?**

You will need:

Microscope, slide, coverslip, iodine solution, toothpick, medicine dropper

1. Carefully use the toothpick to scrape the inside of your mouth. Then roll the tip of the toothpick on the center of the slide.
2. Place a drop of iodine over the cheek cells. Cover with a coverslip.
3. Examine the slide under low power and high power of the microscope. Draw what you see.

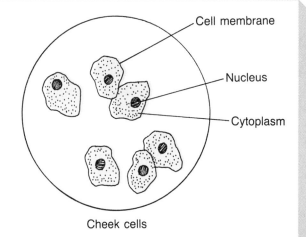

Cheek cells

Questions

1. What cell parts did you see in the cheek cells? _____

2. Why did you add iodine stain to the cells? _____

3. Describe the shape of the cells you saw. _____

Review

I. Fill each blank with the word that fits best. Choose from the words below.

cells   cytoplasm   nucleus   cell membrane   microbe

All living things are made up of tiny units called _____ .

The _____ is the cell's outside skin. In the center of a cell is

the _____ . Between the cell nucleus and cell membrane is

the _____ .

II. Circle the word that makes each statement true.

   A. The cells in (*cork/frog's blood*) have no cytoplasm.
   B. A hand lens may have a magnifying power of (*8/100*) times.
   C. Examples of one-celled living things are bacteria and (*ants/protozoans*).

III. Show how you find the answer to the following problem:

The top lens of a microscope magnifies 10 times, and the bottom lens 30 times. How many times larger will a cell look when seen through both lenses?

_____

_____

_____

What Are the Jobs of a Cell's Parts?

Exploring Science

Animal, Vegetable, or Mineral? You are a detective at the scene of a crime. You scrape up a speck of dried red stuff. Is it blood? Is it from a squashed cherry? Is it paint? What else could it be? This is like the game, "Animal, Vegetable, or Mineral." You need to take a closer look at what's in the speck.

Back at the police laboratory, the speck is placed in a special liquid. Under the microscope, cells may or may not be seen. If there are cells, are they blood (animal) cells? Or are they "vegetable" (plant) cells? How does a scientist tell the difference between a plant cell and an animal cell? Clue: Plant cells have one thing that animal cells don't have. You'll soon find out what it is.

The microscope is very useful in police work. It helps tell if a material was ever part of a living thing. The microscope helps tell if it came from an animal or a plant. It helps because living things are made up of cells.

● Under a microscope, cells might be seen in a thin slice of a toothpick made of

A. wood   **B.** silver   **C.** plastic

The Work of a Cell

When you look through a microscope, how can you tell whether the cells you see are "animal" or "vegetable"? One way is by the special parts of the cell. A plant cell has a **cell wall.** So do plant-like microbes, such as algae. Cells of animals have no cell walls. Neither do animal-like microbes, such as amebas (uh-MEE-buhs).

The cell wall is made of nonliving woody matter, called **cellulose** (SEL-yuh-lohs). It is what makes plant parts stiff.

Each part of a cell has a job to do. For a cell to do its work, it must take in food and oxygen. It must also give off wastes.

Plants have cells with green **chloroplasts** (KLOHR-uh-plasts). These cell parts contain **chlorophyll** (KLOHR-uh-fil), which gives them their green color. Chlorophyll is used to make food. Algae, which are also food-makers, have chlorophyll in their cells, too.

In the cytoplasm are bubble-like parts called **vacuoles** (VAK-yoo-ohls). A vacuole stores water and food until they are needed. It also stores wastes until the cell gets rid of them.

The nucleus, which is the center of the cell, controls what goes on in the cell. In the nucleus of each cell is an acid called **DNA.** DNA contains a code or pattern. One job of this code is to help define how living things look and act.

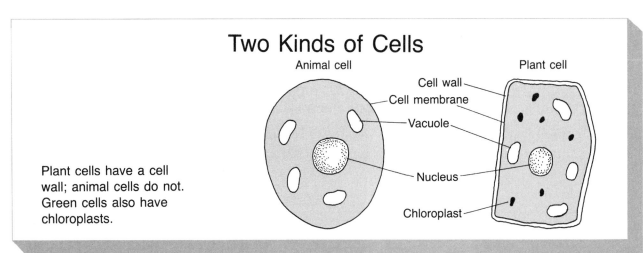

Two Kinds of Cells

Animal cell

Plant cell

Cell wall
Cell membrane
Vacuole
Nucleus
Chloroplast

Plant cells have a cell wall; animal cells do not. Green cells also have chloroplasts.

To Do Yourself   How Are Plant and Animal Cells Different?

You will need:

Microscope, slide, coverslip, medicine dropper, tweezers, iodine solution, *Elodea*, onion or lettuce leaf, your drawing of an animal cell

1. Use tweezers to tear off a very thin piece of the fleshy part of a lettuce leaf or onion.
2. Place the piece on a slide. Add a drop of water. Cover with a coverslip.
3. Observe the slide under low power, then high power, of the microscope. Draw what you see.
4. Add a drop of iodine solution under the coverslip. Repeat step 3.
5. Place a piece of *Elodea* on a slide. Repeat steps 2–4.

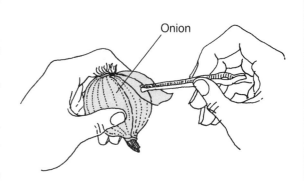
Onion

Questions

1. How were the two plant cells alike and different? _____

2. How were the plant cells like the animal cells? _____

3. How were the plant cells different from the animal cells? _____

Review

I. Fill each blank with the word (or words) that fit best. Choose from the words below.

DNA   cell wall   chlorophyll   nucleus   vacuoles

All plant cells have one part that animal cells do not have. That part is

the _____ . Green plants also have _____ , which they use to make food. Water, food, or wastes may be stored in

_____ . The code _____ decides how living things will look and act.

II. Write **A** for each part of an animal cell. Write **P** for each part of a plant cell. Write **A, P** if the part belongs to both plant and animal.

A. _____ cell wall   C. _____ chlorophyll   E. _____ vacuole

B. _____ chloroplast   D. _____ DNA   F. _____ cellulose

III. A human red blood cell loses its nucleus at one stage of its growth. A human brain cell always keeps its nucleus. Which cell do you think lives longer? Why?

How Do Cells Work Together?

Exploring Science

The One and the Many. Here's a puzzle. When its life began, it had just one cell. Soon there were many cells. When it is full grown, it will have 100 trillion cells. What is it? Answer: You.

You began life as one round cell. That one cell split into two. The two split again and again. By the time you were born, you already had billions of cells. When you are grown, you will have even more.

Here's a new puzzle. Now that you are almost grown, you have trillions of cells, but each one is different from the first one. Some are long and thin. Some are flat. Some have stripes across them. Some have no nucleus. How do you think one round cell could turn into so many different shapes?

Scientists think they know part of the answer to this puzzle. Your first cell carries directions for new cells to become special kinds of cells. Much of how this happens is, however, still a mystery.

● Circle the word (or words) that makes the statement true.

Cells of different shapes probably do work that is (*the same/different*).

Cells Working Together

Cells do everything that living things do. In a one-celled living thing, one cell does everything. An ameba, for example, has just one cell. What do you think that cell does? It takes in food. The cell uses oxygen to get energy from food. It gets rid of wastes. It responds to its environment. It grows and reproduces.

Many-celled organisms have several kinds of cells. Each kind is **specialized** (SPESH-uh-lyzed). That means it does a special job. For example,

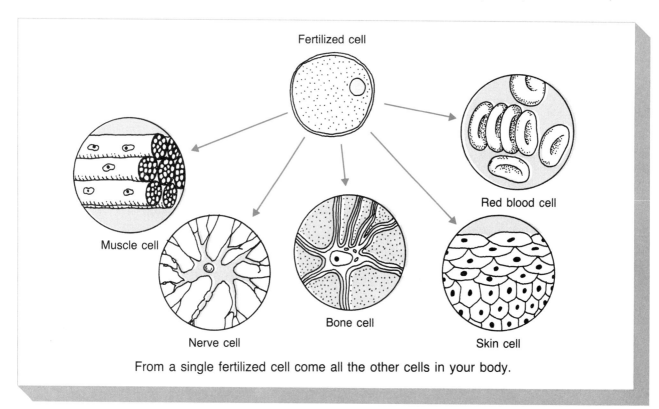

From a single fertilized cell come all the other cells in your body.

Fertilized cell

Muscle cell

Red blood cell

Nerve cell

Bone cell

Skin cell

the **covering cells** in your skin are flat. Their job is to protect what they cover.

Nerve cells in your arm are long and thin. Their shape fits them for their job. That job is to carry messages.

A group of cells that do a special job make up a **tissue** (TISH-oo). The cells in the tissue are all alike and do the same work. Many covering cells make up covering tissue. Many nerve cells make up nerve tissue.

Groups of tissue that do special jobs make up **organs.** Your hand and your eye are organs. The job of your eye is to see. One job of your hand is to put food in your mouth. What are some others?

A group of organs that work together make up a **system** (SIS-tum). For example, you have a nervous system. Your brain, nerves, eyes, and ears are some organs in your **nervous system.** This system controls your actions. In a complex **organism** several systems work together. You are a complex organism. Your nervous system works with other systems of your body, such as your skeletal system.

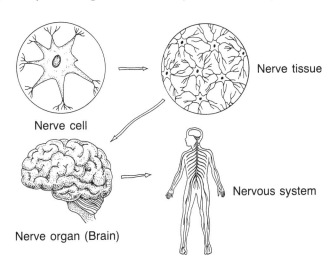

Nerve cell

Nerve tissue

Nerve organ (Brain)

Nervous system

Review

I. Fill each blank with the word that fits best. Choose from the words below.

organ   specialized   system   ameba   organism   tissue   cell

Cells that do special jobs are _____ . A group of cells that

are alike make up a _____ . In an _____
different tissues work together. Different organs make up

a _____ . Several systems work together in a complex

_____ .

II. Fill each blank in column A with the correct word from column B.

	A	B
A. _____	brain, nerves, and other organs	organ
B. _____	ear	organism
C. _____	whole human body	tissue
D. _____	group of nerve cells	system

III. What kinds of organisms have no tissues? Explain.

How Are Living Things Grouped?

Exploring Science

What's in a Name? "My father calls me William. My mother calls me Will. My sister calls me Willy. But the fellows call me Bill." Like the boy in the verse, do you have more than one name?

Many animals and plants have more than one name. Some people call a certain wild animal a mountain lion. Other people call it a cougar . . . or a puma . . . or a panther. In different places, this animal has different names.

Sometimes, different animals have the same name. In some places, a gopher has fur and digs burrows. In other places, it is a kind of turtle. "Gopher" also can mean a kind of snake.

People may even use the same name for both an animal and a plant. A sea urchin may be an animal in the sea. On land, the sea urchin is a shrub.

Scientists use a system of names that helps to end the confusion. The system was made up by Carolus Linnaeus (KAR-uh-lus lih-NEE-us). He lived in Sweden in the 1700s. The system of Linnaeus gives each kind of organism a scientific name. The system uses two Latin names. The name for a mountain lion is *Felis concolor*. A bobcat is *Felis rufus*. A house cat is *Felis domestica*. What do you think *Felis* means?

● Which name would a scientist probably give to Mickey Mouse?

A. *Mus musculus*   **B.** house mouse

Groups and Names of Organisms

The system of Linnaeus names organisms. It also is a way to classify organisms. When we classify things, we put them into groups. Biologists classify living things by their parts, or **structures** (STRUK-churs).

A group of organisms with all the same structures make up a **species** (SPEE-sheez). Species that are alike in many ways are grouped together in a **genus** (JEE-nus). *Felis* is a genus. It includes catlike animals.

A scientific name is made up of the genus and species. *Felis domestica* is the scientific name of a house cat. The first part of the name is the genus. This part of the name is always capitalized. The second part is the species.

Some catlike animals are not grouped in the genus *Felis*. They are placed in other genera. (**Genera** is the plural of genus). The cheetah is *Acinonyx jubatus*. Biologists place similar genera (JEN-ur-uh) in a larger group called a **family.** All catlike animals belong to the cat family.

Similar families are grouped into an **order.** The cat family is in the same order as the dog family. This is because cats and dogs are alike in many ways.

A group of similar orders forms a **class.** Birds form a class. So do snakes and lizards. Mammals are also a class. The mammal class contains many familiar animals. It contains cats, dogs, horses, mice, and even people.

Classes are put together in still larger groups called **phyla** (FY-luh). (**Phyla** is the plural of phylum.) Mammals and birds are in the same phylum. Insects are in another phylum. Earthworms are in still another phylum.

Mammals, insects, and worms are all animals. They are part of the animal kingdom. A **kingdom** is the largest grouping used by biologists. The two kingdoms you know best are the plant kingdom and the animal kingdom. Members of the plant kingdom make their own food. Members of the animal kingdom can't make food. They must eat food. Microbes and other simple living things belong to other kingdoms.

There are millions of kinds of living things on earth. Many are classified in the system of Linnaeus. Each of these living things has its own scientific name. This name is the same everywhere in the world. Your scientific name is *Homo sapiens*.

The Animal Kingdom

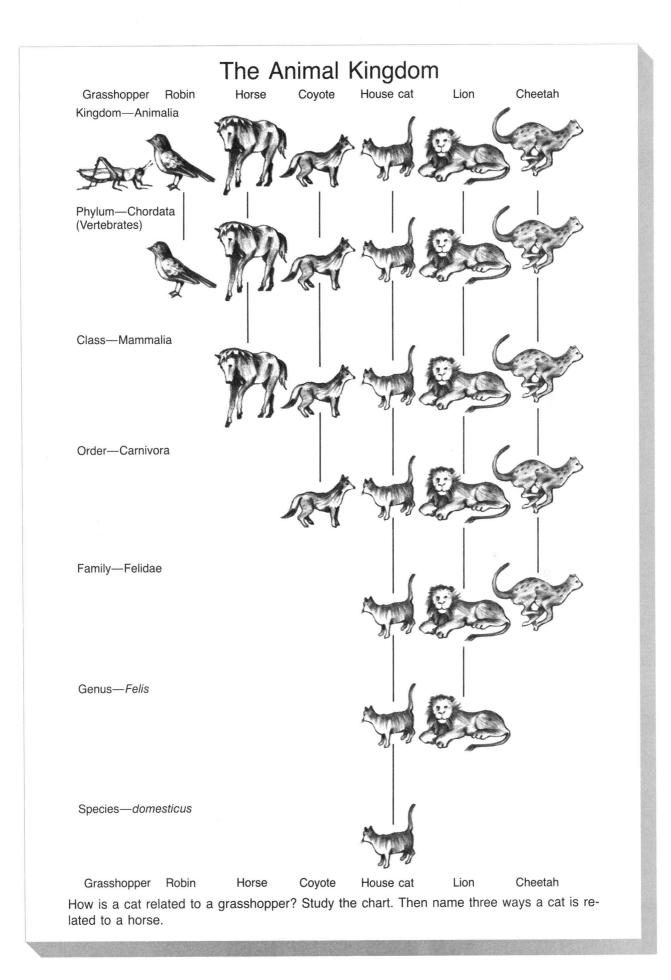

Grasshopper Robin   Horse   Coyote   House cat   Lion   Cheetah

Kingdom—Animalia

Phylum—Chordata
(Vertebrates)

Class—Mammalia

Order—Carnivora

Family—Felidae

Genus—*Felis*

Species—*domesticus*

Grasshopper   Robin   Horse   Coyote   House cat   Lion   Cheetah

How is a cat related to a grasshopper? Study the chart. Then name three ways a cat is re-lated to a horse.

To Do Yourself

How Can Ways Organisms Are Alike and Different Help to Group Them?

You will need:

Paper and pencil

1. Look at the list of animal pairs below:

   cat–lion   chicken–duck
   gorilla–chimpanzee   shark–whale
   fly–spider   rabbit–mouse
   snake–worm   squirrel–hamster
   mouse–rat

2. Choose the pairs of animals you are familiar with. List these in a chart like the one below. List things that are alike and things that are different for each pair of animals.

Animal Pairs	Alike	Different	
1. horse–zebra	hoofs on feet mane runs fast	zebra has stripes	horse has no stripes

Questions

1. What things about an animal would put it in a group with other animals? _____

2. What would put an animal in a different group? _____

Review

I. Fill each blank with the word that fits best. Choose from the words below.

classify   structures   species   genus   kingdom   phylum

Biologists group, or _____ , things by their structures.

Members of the same species have the same parts, or _____ .

There can be several _____ in each genus. A

_____ is the largest grouping of organisms.

II. Circle the word that makes each statement correct.

    A. A genus is larger than a (*kingdom/species*).
    B. In *Homo sapiens*, the genus name is (*Homo/sapiens*).
    C. An order is a (*smaller/larger*) group than a phylum.

III. Why should scientists use scientific names of organisms when they report on their research?

What Are the Simplest Living Things?

Exploring Science

The "Bad-Air" Disease. Over 2,000 years ago doctors wrote about a dread chills-and-fever disease. The victims first felt cold. After a few hours, they felt hot. They had headaches and sick stomachs. After a few more hours they felt better, but were weak and tired. They soon got sick again. The chills and fever returned over and over. In time, many of the victims died.

Most victims of the disease lived near swamps. People thought that swamp water poisoned the air. So they called the disease **malaria** (muh-LAIR-ee-uh), from two Italian words: *mal,* which means "bad," and *aria,* which means "air." Malaria was the "bad-air" disease.

Over the centuries, more people have died from malaria than from any other disease.

After the microscope came into use, scientists began to find that germs cause many diseases. They doubted that "bad air" was the true cause of malaria.

In 1878 Charles Laveran (lah-vuh-RAN), a French doctor in Algiers, looked for germs in the blood of malaria victims. He observed long, thin, and very tiny organisms. They were protozoans—one-celled animal-like microbes. Could these microbes be the cause of malaria? If so, then how did they get into the body? And if swamp air is not really "bad," why did people living near swamps get malaria?

The work of Ronald Ross, a British doctor in India, helped answer these questions. Ross showed that certain mosquitoes that breed in swamps carry the malaria germs. The germs breed inside the stomachs of the mosquitoes. A person gets malaria by being bitten by a mosquito whose stomach is full of the germs.

● Draining swamps is one way of fighting malaria. It helps because it gets rid of (still water/ the breeding ground of mosquitoes).

Certain mosquitoes that grow in swamps may carry malaria germs.

Kingdoms of Simple Living Things

Did you know that there are thousands of different kinds of simple living things? Scientists classify these groups into three kingdoms. These are the monerans (moh-NEH-rans), the protists (PROH-tists), and the fungi (FUN-jy).

MONERANS. **Monerans** are microbes with just one cell. Their cells do not have a definite nucleus. Some monerans live together in chains or colonies.

Monerans include bacteria and blue-green algae. **Bacteria,** the smallest living things, are found in the air, soil, water, and in plants and animals. **Blue-green algae** live in salt water and fresh water.

PROTISTS. **Protists** may have just one cell, or they may live in colonies. Their cells have a nucleus.

Protists include **protozoans.** They are like animals in some ways. They move about and catch food. Some protozoans are **parasites** (PAR-uh-syts) and live off of other living things.

Protists also include several kinds of algae. They are like plants because they have cell walls and can make their own food.

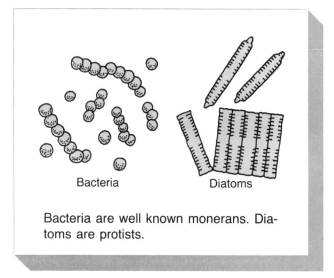

Bacteria are well known monerans. Diatoms are protists.

Many **green algae** live in fresh water. They also grow on damp soil and on tree trunks. **Diatoms** (DY-uh-tums), the **golden algae,** are the most beautiful of all algae. Their cells have two glassy shells. The largest algae are a kind of **brown algae,** seaweed.

FUNGI. Most **fungi** are many-celled. Like

Some mushrooms, such as this one, are poisonous.

plants, they have cell walls, but they do not make their own food. They can live on dead matter or on living things.

The best known fungi are the mushrooms. Many of them can be eaten. Some are very poisonous.

Fungi also include the **yeasts** (YEESTS), used in making bread. Bread mold is a fungus. So is a mold used to make **penicillin** (pen-ih-SIL-in).

VIRUSES. Have you ever felt ill and been told you have a **virus** (VY-rus)? Viruses cause many diseases of plants and animals. These diseases include colds, flu, measles, and chicken pox. Viruses are microbes, but scientists cannot classify them. They do not fit into any kingdom. Scientists can't decide whether viruses are even alive.

Viruses are very tiny. Most are smaller than the smallest bacteria. Viruses are not made up of whole cells. The center of a virus has only a part of a cell nucleus. A virus has no cytoplasm. It does not grow or move like a living thing. Yet when a virus is inside a living cell, it can reproduce itself. In this way, viruses are like living things. In other ways, they are not like living things.

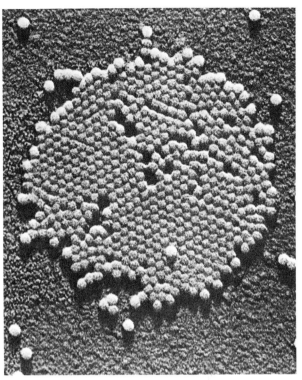
The virus that causes polio is very tiny.

Review

I. Write the number of the item in list **B** that best fits each item in list **A**.

A	**B**
A. _____ viruses	1. have no definite nucleus
B. _____ algae	2. have no cells
C. _____ monerans	3. live on dead matter
D. _____ fungi	4. make own food
E. _____ protists	5. include protozoans

II. For each organism, write **M** if it is a moneran. Write **P** if it is a protist. Write **F** if it is a fungus.

A. _____ bacteria   D. _____ blue-green algae   G. _____ diatoms

B. _____ mushroom   E. _____ green algae   H. _____ malaria parasite

C. _____ bread mold   F. _____ seaweed   I. _____ yeast

III. All algae are plant-like and live in water. Why are some grouped as monerans and others as protists?

_____

_____

What Are the Main Groups of Plants?

Exploring Science

A Fruit-Salad Tree: Fact or Fake? Picture in your mind a sort of fruit-salad tree. Most of its branches have peaches. But one branch has apricots. Another branch has plums. Fact or fake? Strange as it may seem, such a tree really can be grown.

The fruit grower starts with a young peach tree. Two of its branches are cut off. A twig from an apricot tree is joined, or **grafted,** onto one cut. A twig from a plum tree is grafted onto the other cut. Each twig grows into a branch that bears its own kind of fruit.

In the early part of this century, Luther Burbank was the "plant wizard" of California. As a boy, Burbank lived on a farm, where he learned to love plants. He also learned about grafting, used on his family farm to grow apples. Breeding better kinds of plants became Burbank's life work. He developed hundreds of new fruits and other plants.

Grafting was an important part of Burbank's work. Suppose a new type of fruit had to be grown in large numbers. Often, it could only be reproduced by grafting onto another tree, called the stock. Sometimes, but not always, a graft would "take." When a graft takes, the stock accepts the graft as part of itself.

Plum and apricot grafts take on a peach stock. But a pear graft does not take on an apple stock. Why? Here's a clue. Plums, apricots, and

Luther Burbank created many new kinds of plants by grafting.

peaches all belong to the same group, or genus, of plants.

Pears and apples are not grouped into the same genus. Usually, grafts are more likely to take between closely related plants. Knowing how plants are grouped helps to know if grafts will take.

● Lemons and oranges both belong to the genus *Citrus.* Growing an orange graft on a lemon stock is probably (*possible/impossible*).

The Plant Kingdom

There are two broad groups of plants. Each group is called a **phylum.** The grouping depends on how a plant takes up water.

All plants need water. Some plants have veins, which are tubes that carry water. These plants belong to the phylum of **vascular** (VAS-kyuh-lur) **plants.** Ferns, grasses, shrubs, and trees are vascular plants. All have true leaves, stems, and roots.

Plants with no veins to carry water belong to

the phylum of **nonvascular** (non-VAS-kyuh-lur) **plants.** These are the mosses and liverworts (LIV-ur-wurts). These plants have leaf-like, root-like, and stem-like parts. But because these parts have no veins, they are not true leaves, stems, or roots.

You can see many kinds of mosses in North American woods today. Mosses grow where it is damp and on the shady parts of trees, close to the ground. Liverworts also grow where it is

The ponderosa pine is a conifer that grows in western North America.

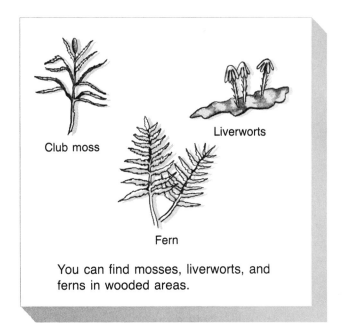

Club moss

Liverworts

Fern

You can find mosses, liverworts, and ferns in wooded areas.

The red oak of North America is a flower and seed-bearing tree.

dark and moist. They have leaf-like parts that look like livers. You can see them flat on the ground, on rocks, or on trees.

There are three main classes of vascular plants. Ferns make up one class. Another class are the cone-bearing plants, or **conifers** (KOH-nuh-furs). A pine tree is a conifer. So is a red-wood. The third class of vascular plants are the **flowering plants.** Both the rose and the red oak are flowering plants.

Review

I. Fill each blank with the word that fits best. Choose from the words below.

nonvascular   vascular   veins   grafts

Tubes that carry water in a plant are _____ . Plants that

have no veins are _____ . Plants with veins are

_____ .

II. Write the letter of the group to which each plant belongs. Use the pictures and captions in this lesson to help find the answers.

A. **a.** Vascular plants   **b.** Nonvascular plants

   (1) _____ grass **(2)** _____ moss **(3)** _____ fern **(4)** _____ liverwort

B. **a.** Cone-bearing plant **b.** Flowering plant **c.** Fern

   (1) _____ pine **(2)** _____ Boston fern **(3)** _____ red oak

   (4) _____ cedar **(5)** _____ rose

III. Why do you think mosses and liverworts never grow tall?

What Are the Main Groups of Animals?

Exploring Science

The Beast That Wears a Girdle. The odd-looking little "beast" has spines around its head. It can pull its tube-like mouth in and out. As a baby, it swims with its toes. As an adult, it has no toes. Thick plates of skin go around its middle. The plates make a kind of girdle. The animal is microscopic, and lives in the sea. Until a few years back, this "beast" was never seen. The scientists who found it named it *Loricifera*. That means "girdle wearer." When the animals grow, they molt. That means they shed their skin, girdle and all. "They just change corsets when they need a bigger size," said one of the scientists.

Scientists find and report 6,000 new species a year. Why is this one special? It does not fit into any known phylum. (As you know, a phylum is a major group in a kingdom.) This little girdle wearer goes into a new phylum by itself. Only once before in this century has a new phylum been added to the animal kingdom. There are now about 30 phyla of animals in all.

● Which statement is more likely to be true?

A. No new phyla of animals will be found in the future.

B. Some of the new species found in the future may be placed in new phyla.

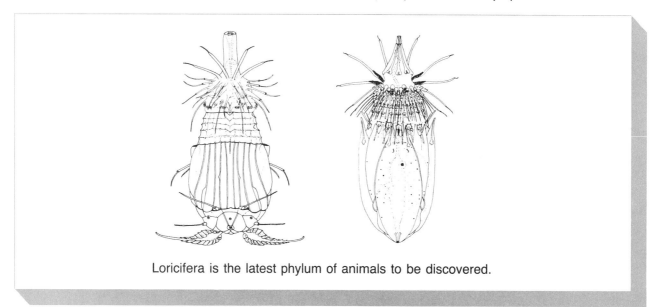

Loricifera is the latest phylum of animals to be discovered.

The Animal Kingdom

If you have a pet cat or dog, rub its back. You can feel its backbone. A backbone is made up of many small bones. Each bone is a **vertebra** (VUR-tuh-bruh). Animals with backbones are **vertebrates** (VUR-tuh-bruhts). Do you think you are a vertebrate? How can you tell? What kind of pet do you have? Is it a vertebrate?

Most phyla of animals have no backbones. These are **invertebrates** (in-VUR-tuh-bruhts).

The girdle wearer is an invertebrate. The invertebrates you know best are insects and worms. Some others may surprise you. You may have thought they were not even animals!

The tables below and on the next pages list groups of animals. You will find phyla and classes. You will also find several orders of the class of mammals. Can you find yourself in one of those orders?

Table 1 Phyla of Some Animals

Phylum	Description	Examples	
Sponges (Pore Bearers)	Live on objects in water; take food from water that flows in tiny pores and out of the large holes.	bath sponge	
Cup Animals (Hollow Insides)	Live attached or free in water; arms (tentacles) catch food; one opening for food and wastes.	jellyfish	
Flatworms	Live free or on other organisms; one opening for food and wastes.	planarian	
Roundworms	Live free or on other organisms; food passes in mouth and wastes pass out at other end (anus).	nematode	
Segmented Worms	Body in sections (or segments).	earthworm	
Mollusks (Soft Bodied)	Soft bodies, many with shells, organs, and systems.	clam	Credit: Gordon S. Smith/Photo Researchers, Inc.
Spiny Skinned Animals	Tube feet and spines; one opening for food and wastes.	starfish	
Joint-Legged Animals (Arthropods)	Hard outside covering; jointed legs.	grasshopper, crab	Credit: Tack Dermid/Photo Researchers, Inc.

(continues next page)

Table 1 (continued)

Phylum	Description	Examples	
Vertebrates	Animals with backbones	human, cat, dog	

Table 2   Classes of Vertebrates

Class	Description	Examples	
Fishes	Scales on body, live in water; most lay eggs.	trout guppy	
Amphibians	Young live in water; adults live on land; smooth skin, lay eggs.	frog salamander	
Reptiles	Scales on body; live on land (air-breathing); most lay eggs.	snake lizard turtle crocodile	

Credit: Gordon S. Smith/Photo Researchers, Inc.

Class	Description	Examples	
Birds	Feathers on body; live on land (air-breathing); lay eggs; usually have wings.	parakeet eagle robin	
Mammals	Hair on body; produce milk for young.	rabbit whale gorilla	

Table 3 Some Orders of Mammals

Order	Description	Examples	
Egg Layers	Lay eggs	platypus	
Pouched Mammals	Carry young in pouch.	opossum kangaroo	
Flying Mammals	Web of skin between toes.	bat	
Toothless Mammals	No teeth in front, armor plated body.	sloth armadillo	
Rodents	Teeth in front shaped like chisels.	squirrel chipmunk	

(continues next page)

Table 3 (continued)

Order	Description	Examples	
Sea Mammals	Live in ocean. Flippers.	whale	
Trunk-Nosed Mammals	Trunk noses and tusks.	elephant	
Hoofed Mammals	Hoof as toenail.	cow	
Carnivores	Meat-eaters.	dog, cat	
Primates	"First animals"; walk on hind legs.	gorilla human	

To Do Yourself　How Can You Group Vertebrate Animals?

You will need:

Pencil and paper

1. Make five columns on your paper. Head these columns Bird, Fish, Reptile, Amphibian, and Mammal.

2. Then make a list of animals that you are familiar with. Start with the following list: Frog, eagle, camel, penguin, dolphin, snake, pig, turkey, guppy, ape, deer.

3. Use the Key to Vertebrate Classes. Ask yourself the questions in the key about each animal. Write the name of the animal in the correct column.

Key To Vertebrate Classes

A. Does the animal have feathers?
   1. If YES, it is a BIRD.　**2.** If NO, go to B.

B. Does the animal have fins?
   1. If YES, it is a FISH.　**2.** If NO, go to C.

C. Does the animal have hair or fur?
   1. If YES, it is a MAMMAL.　**2.** If NO, go to D.

D. Does the animal have scales?
   1. If YES, it is a REPTILE.　**2.** If NO, it is an AMPHIBIAN.

Review

I. Fill in each blank with the word that fits best. Choose from the words below.

vertebra　**vertebrate**　*Loricifera*　**invertebrate**　**mammal**

Each bone in a backbone is a _____ . An animal without

a backbone is an _____ . An animal with a backbone is

a _____ .

II. Write the letter of the group to which each animal belongs.

A. **a.** vertebrates　**b.** invertebrates

   (1) _____ bird　**(2)** _____ spider　**(3)** _____ snake　**(4)** _____ flatworm

   (5) _____ sponge

B. **a.** mammal　**b.** mollusk　**c.** crustacean　**d.** cup animal　**e.** fish

   (1) _____ clam　**(2)** _____ crab　**(3)** _____ whale　**(4)** _____ trout

   (5) _____ jellyfish

C. **a.** amphibian　**b.** segmented worm　**c.** primate　**d.** rodent　**e.** joint legged animal

   (1) _____ earthworm　**(2)** _____ gorilla　**(3)** _____ rat

   (4) _____ centipede　**(5)** _____ frog

Review What You Know

A. Unscramble the groups of letters to make science words. Write the words in the blanks.

1. Y T C O P L M A S (part of cell between the nucleus and the cell membrane)

   _____

2. C E N L S U U (center of control in a cell) _____

3. R H O O P T A S C L L (green part found in plant cells but not in animal

   cells) _____

4. G N O A R (group of tissues that does a special job) _____

5. I R V S U (microbe that has no cytoplasm) _____

6. A V R S C L U C A (plants that have water tubes) _____

B. Write the ending that best completes each statement.

1. _____ Compared to a microscope, a hand lens has a
   magnifying power that is **a.** larger **b.** smaller **c.** the same.

2. _____ Microbes that have chlorophyll include
   a. bacteria **b.** algae **c.** viruses

3. _____ A cell's DNA is found in its **a.** vacuole **b.** cell
   membrane **c.** nucleus

4. _____ A tissue is made up of a group of **a.** cells
   b. organs **c.** systems

5. _____ In *Felis leo,* the name for a lion, *leo* is the
   a. phylum **b.** genus **c.** species

6. _____ Fungi are a kingdom of organisms that includes
   a. bread mold **b.** malaria germs **c.** green algae

7. _____ Plants that are nonvascular include **a.** conifers
   b. mosses **c.** roses

8. _____ Among the vertebrate animals are **a.** crabs
   b. earthworms **c.** dogs

9. _____ The "skin" of a blood cell is its **a.** cell
   membrane **b.** cell wall **c.** cytoplasm

10. _____ A system is made up of a group of
    a. organisms **b.** organs **c.** phyla

11. _____ A part in both plant and animal cells that stores
    water is the **a.** cell wall **b.** vacuole **c.** chloroplast

12. _____ An animal without a backbone is **a.** a vertebra
    b. a vertebrate **c.** an invertebrate

13. _____ The stiff woody matter in a cell wall is
   a. cellulose   **b.** DNA   **c.** chlorophyll

14. _____ In *Homo sapiens,* the name for a human, *Homo*
   is the   **a.** class   **b.** family   **c.** genus

15. _____ The largest group into which living things are
   classified is a   **a.** kingdom   **b.** species   **c.** phylum

C. Apply what you know

   1. Study the drawings below of different kinds of living things. Then answer
   the questions on the next page.

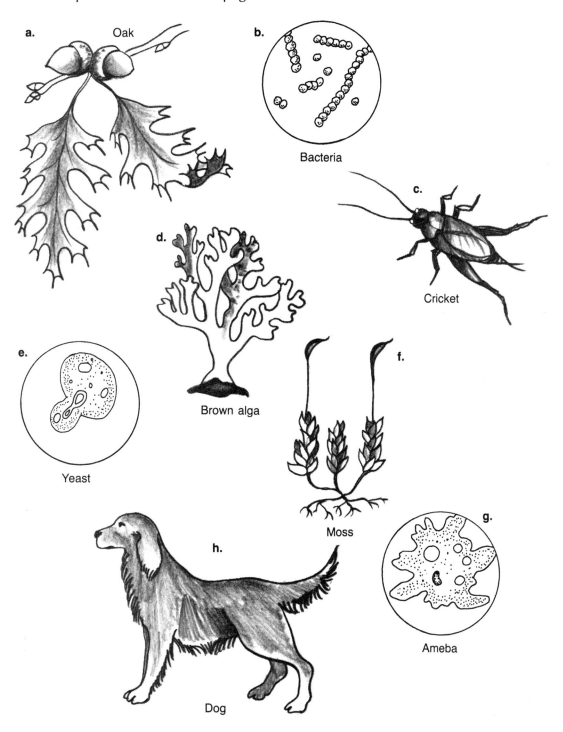

a.   Oak

b.   Bacteria

c.   Cricket

d.   Brown alga

e.   Yeast

f.   Moss

g.   Ameba

h.   Dog

Write the kingdom to which each organism in the drawing belongs. Use these kingdoms:

monerans   protists   fungi   plants   animals

a. _____   e. _____

b. _____   f. _____

c. _____   g. _____

d. _____   h. _____

2. Which drawing shows a vertebrate? _____ An

invertebrate? _____ A vascular plant?

_____ A nonvascular plant? _____

3. Study the drawings of cells below. Write labels for each numbered part. Use these labels:

cytoplasm   cell wall   cell membrane   nucleus   chloroplast

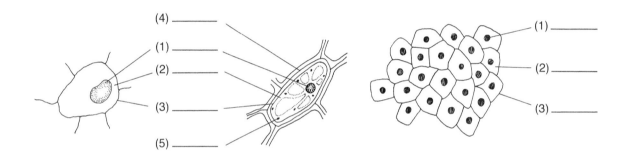

4. Which drawing shows a plant cell? _____ An animal cell?

_____ A tissue? _____

D. Find Out More

1. Make a model of a cell. Place 1 packet of plain gelatin in a 2-cup heat proof measuring cup. Fill to the 1-cup mark with boiling water. Stir to dissolve the gelatin. Fill to the 1½-cup mark with cold water. Add a teaspoon of cologne. Stir to mix. Pour the gelatin mixture into a small (sandwich-size) plastic bag. Place a marble in the bag. Close tightly with a bag-tie or string. Let stand overnight. What does the plastic stand for? The gelatin? The marble?

    Place the bag into a jar. Add enough warm water to cover the bottom half of the bag. Let stand a few hours. Take the cell model out of the dish. Smell the water. Explain what you observe.

2. Make a collection of examples of living things from some or all of the five kingdoms. Try to find out the names of each one and make a labeled display.

Careers in Life Science

Plants in the Human World. Wherever there are people, there are plants. It takes many people, doing many special jobs, to provide the outdoor settings—trees, flowers, lawns, and shrubs—of places where people live, work, and play. All these plants must be arranged, grown, and cared for.

Gardeners and Landscape Maintenance Contractors. To be a gardener, you should like working outdoors. Do you have a "green thumb?" That's a help, too. You can learn gardening through on-the-job training. Gardeners plant seeds, do grafting, and care for the plants they grow.

After a year or so of technical school, you can start a career as a landscape maintenance contractor. This job carries more responsibility than that of a gardener. You can become your own boss and run your own business. Landscape maintenance contractors are called in by landscape architects to carry out their plans.

Landscape Architects. A landscape architect plans and designs outdoor settings of all kinds. There are parks, gardens, golf courses, and sports fields and arenas. There are the grounds of hotels, schools, resorts, hospitals, factories, office buildings, and housing developments. There are parkways, freeways, and airports. (Can you think of other places where people build, or move the land, and thus need the services of landscaping?)

A landscape maintenance contractor cares for trees, shrubs, and lawns.

A landscape architect combines art, engineering, and science. Talent in these areas—and in math—is needed. So is college training for four or more years. After graduation, the person must gain work experience for a period. Then, in many states, he or she may become licensed as a full-fledged landscape architect.

From gardener to landscape architect, everyone in the field of landscaping helps make our world more beautiful and easier to live in.

A gardener works both indoors and outdoors.

Landscape architects often make scale models of their projects.

UNIT

3

FOOD
FOR
LIFE

What Chemicals Make Up Living Things?

Exploring Science

Life in the Soup. There's an old movie you may have seen about Dr. Frankenstein. He is working in a lab full of flasks, test tubes, and wires. Dr. Frankenstein has "created" a monster that lies on the table. The monster is not alive. Suddenly the doctor throws a switch. Through the flashes of "lightning" and smoke, you see the monster rising. It has come to life!

Scientists have often wondered if life did come from nonliving matter. They have done many experiments to try to find out. Like the doctor in the movie, these scientists have used flasks, test tubes, and wires. The scientists experiment with chemicals that make up living things.

Sparks fly through the top flask, which is filled with gases. Water boils in the bottom flask. After a while, the water is tested. The water has changed! It is now a kind of chemical "soup."

The "soup" contains some different chemicals. Scientists call these chemicals the "chemicals of life." These chemicals form the building blocks of living things.

Did the first living things come from a "soup" like this one? Some scientists think so. That "soup" was the early warm sea. There, the chemicals of life may have been put together. No one knows how. But experiments still go on to try to find out.

● Scientists think that the chemicals of life were made from

A. living chemicals   **B.** nonliving chemicals
C. the earth's sea as it is today.

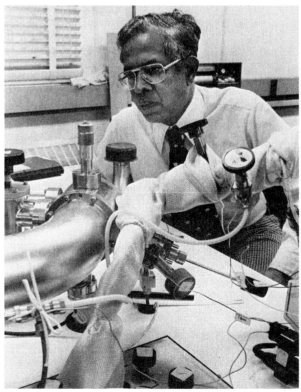

Dr. Cyril Ponnamperuma has pioneered research into life's origins.

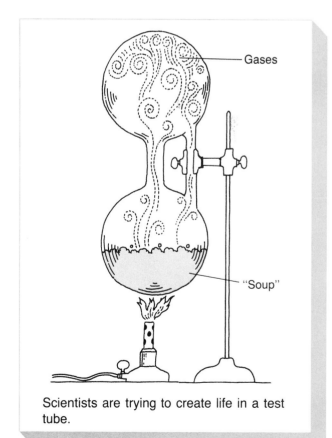

Gases

"Soup"

Scientists are trying to create life in a test tube.

The Chemicals of Life

What do you think was in the "soup?" What are these chemicals of life? What chemicals are in your body? A chemist would say that your body is made up of **matter.**

Matter includes all material things, living or nonliving. Matter can be a solid, a liquid, or a gas.

All matter is made up of **elements.** There are about 100 different elements on earth. Oxygen and hydrogen are elements. They are gases that you can't see, taste, or smell. These elements are part of the chemicals of life.

Carbon is another element. The black substance on a burnt marshmallow is carbon. The soot from a candle or a match flame is carbon. Carbon, like oxygen and hydrogen, is an element found in all living things.

Elements can join together and form totally new **compounds.** These compounds are not like the elements from which they are made.

Water is a compound; it is one of the chemicals of life. It is made up of the elements hydrogen and oxygen. When hydrogen gas and oxygen gas combine in a special way, water forms. Would you have guessed that water makes up over three-fourths of your body? If you know how much you weigh, you can figure about how much water is in your body.

Scientists use a shorthand way of writing the names of elements and compounds. Each element has a **symbol.** C is the symbol for carbon. H is the symbol for hydrogen. O is the symbol for oxygen.

A **formula** is the way you write the symbols for a compound. In the formula for water, H_2O, there is twice as much hydrogen as there is oxygen. The small number 2 in the formula tells you this. The formula for carbon dioxide is CO_2. Can you tell what this formula means?

Carbon Can Be Found in Many Things

Burnt marshmallow

Candle flame

Pencil

Elements That Make up Living Things

Element	Symbol	Percentage
Oxygen	O	76.0%
Carbon	C	10.5%
Hydrogen	H	10.0%
Nitrogen	N	2.5%
Phosphorus	P	0.3%
Potassium	K	0.3%
Sulfur	S	0.2%
Chlorine	Cl	0.1%
Sodium	Na	0.04%
Calcium	Ca	0.02%
Magnesium	Mg	0.02%
Iron	Fe	0.01%

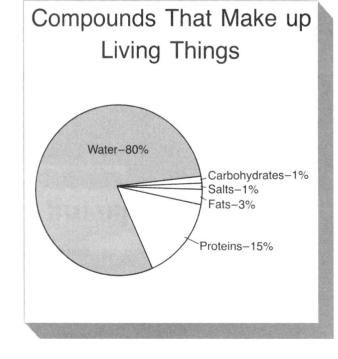

Compounds That Make up Living Things

Water—80%

Carbohydrates—1%
Salts—1%
Fats—3%

Proteins—15%

To Do Yourself   What Chemicals Are in Sugar?

You will need:

Old metal spoon, ¼ spoonful of sugar, pot holder, heat source

1. Hold a spoonful of sugar over a flame. Do this under an adult's supervision. **Caution:** Use a pot holder to hold the spoon, as the metal gets very hot.
2. Observe and record what happens to the sugar.

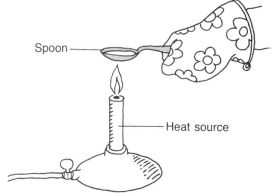

Spoon

Heat source

Questions

1. What happened to the sugar first? _____

2. What were your next observations as you heated the sugar? _____

3. What is the black material? _____

Review

I. Choose from this list the word that fits best.

elements   compounds   symbols   water   scientist   matter   formula

All matter is made up of _____ . Elements often join

together to form _____ . Scientists use

_____ to write the names of elements. They use

_____ to write the names of compounds. One of the

"chemicals of life" is _____ .

II. Use the graph and table to answer the following questions.

   A. The element that makes up most of the body is
      (1) oxygen   (2) carbon   (3) hydrogen
   B. The compound that makes up most of the body is
      (1) carbohydrate   (2) fat   (3) water

III. A scientist writes H_2O. Explain in a few sentences what this means. Include the words *element, compound, symbol,* and *formula* in your answer.

_____

_____

_____

How Do Green Cells Make Food?

Exploring Science

Farming the Sea. Did you know that one kind of algae is used in ice cream? Other algae are dried and eaten. Some can be ground up into flour. And some algae can be used to make a fuel gas to burn. Some day you may use this gas to heat your house.

Algae are plant-like organisms that live and grow in ponds, lakes, and streams. Algae are the green organisms you see growing in a fish tank. Fish eat algae. Many other sea animals do too. Algae, as you have just read, are even eaten by people as food.

Algae cover the corals in a tank at the Smithsonian Museum in Washington, D.C. You can get a close-up view. So can scientists. They study the life of the algae and the rest of a coral reef community. It is the first such community ever set up away from the sea. What kinds of things are scientists finding out?

Scientist Susan Brawley has studied the way algae grow. She watched fish eat the tops of algae. Then she observed how long it takes for the algae to grow back. They grew back very fast. Huge amounts of algae can be grown quickly.

Scientists are studying algae to find a fast way to grow certain kinds of food. Some scientists have been "farming" algae. They have been growing algae in a special way in the sea.

● Explain why scientists might want to take algae along with them as a food source on a trip into space.

The coral-reef tank at The Smithsonian Institution.

How Green Cells Make Food

Algae can make their own food. So can plants and other green organisms. How can they do this? To find out, you must look inside the cells of green organisms.

A cell of a green organism is different from the cell of an animal. A green cell has a green compound, called **chlorophyll** (KLOHR-uh-fil), inside it. Chlorophyll makes it possible for cells to make food. Structures called **chloroplasts** (KLOHR-uh-plasts) contain the chlorophyll.

A green cell needs more than chlorophyll to make food. It also needs two materials. One material is carbon dioxide from the air. Another material is water.

Chlorophyll traps light from the sun. It uses light energy to change carbon dioxide and water into food. The light energy is changed into energy that is stored in a simple sugar. This is the food that the green cell makes.

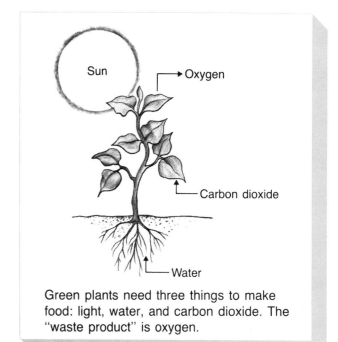

Green plants need three things to make food: light, water, and carbon dioxide. The "waste product" is oxygen.

To Do Yourself How Can You Find the Green in a Leaf?

You will need:

Spinach leaf, saucepan, electric hot plate, water, test tube, nail-polish remover, cork for test tube, test-tube rack

1. Tear a spinach leaf into small bits.
2. Boil the bits in a pan of water for a few minutes.
3. Place some boiled leaf bits in the test tube.
4. Fill the tube one-fourth full of nail-polish remover. **Caution:** Do not breathe the liquid or use it near a flame.
5. Cork the tube and shake it every so often.
6. After 5 minutes, pour off the liquid.
7. Record your observations of the leaf and liquid.

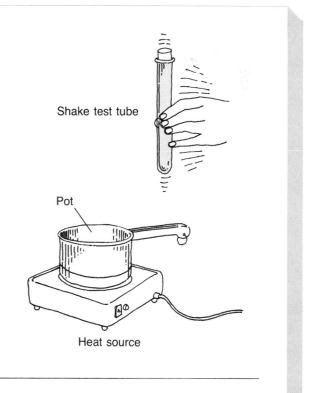

Questions

1. What color is the liquid? _____
2. What caused the change? _____
3. What color is the leaf? _____

Changing carbon dioxide and water into sugar in the presence of sunlight is called **photosynthesis** (foh-tuh-SIN-thih-sus). *Photo* means "light." In photosynthesis, the light is from the sun. *Synthesis* means "putting together." In photosynthesis, carbon dioxide and water are put together by light.

We can show this process by using an **equation** (ih-KWAY-zhun). The first equation below uses words to tell the story. The second uses symbols. See if you can follow both equations. The arrows in the equations mean "makes" or "gives." Notice the numbers in front of the formula for some compounds. These numbers tell how much of each compound is used.

Carbon dioxide + Water + Light energy $\xrightarrow[\text{chlorophyll}]{\text{with}}$ Sugar (with stored energy) + Oxygen

$6\,CO_2 + 6\,H_2O +$ Light energy $\xrightarrow[\text{chlorophyll}]{\text{with}}$ $C_6H_{12}O_6 + 6\,O_2$

Review

I. Choose from this list the word that fits best.

**energy   chlorophyll   photosynthesis   chloroplasts   oxygen   sugar
light   carbon dioxide**

The green substance in a plant cell is _____ . A food that a

plant makes is _____ . The plant makes food by the

process of _____ . To make food, a plant needs carbon

dioxide, water, and _____ . Chlorophyll in a green

organism can be found in _____ . Animals eat green plants

and other green organisms to get _____ .

II. Choose the answer that best completes each sentence. Write the letter of the answer in the blank.

A. Chlorophyll uses light energy to change carbon dioxide and water into

(a) nitrogen (b) food (c) chloroplasts _____

B. Plants and other green organisms store energy

in (a) sunlight (b) sugar (c) carbon dioxide _____

III. Explain why some animals need to eat green plants.

_____

_____

_____

How Do Living Things Get Energy?

Exploring Science

Food for the Long Run. The marathon race is about to begin. The starter's gun fires, and they're off!

When you get ready for a race, you need to eat the right food. But not everyone has the same idea of what food is right.

George has heard that sugar gives you quick energy. He eats candy on the day of the race. Joyce thinks a lot of meat makes muscles strong. She eats a steak dinner the night before the race. José believes **vitamin** (VY-tuh-min) pills give you energy. He takes a handful of these before the race.

George, Joyce, and José all have ideas that people have believed to be true for a long time.

But Maria has a new idea. She has read about some new work of food scientists. They wrote that eating a lot of starch can help runners endure longer. So Maria has a meal of pasta and bread the night before the race. Both of these foods are rich in starch.

After running for two hours, George, Joyce, and José suddenly become very tired. In runner's talk, they "hit the wall." They all drop out of the race. But Maria keeps on going. She has enough energy to last more than two hours.

● You are going on a bicycle trip that will last several hours. The best food to eat before the trip is probably (*bread*/*candy*).

Jean Benoit wins the gold medal in the first women's marathon, the 1984 Olympics.

Getting Energy from Food

You need energy for living—for play, for exercise, and even for thinking. Where do you get all this energy?

Living things get energy from **fuels** (FYOO-uls). These fuels are foods, such as sugar. To get energy, the sugar is "burned."

When fuels burn, they combine with oxygen. Wood is a fuel. When wood burns, it combines with oxygen. Some of the energy it gives off is light. Some of the energy is heat energy.

In your cells, sugar is the fuel. When sugar "burns," it combines with oxygen. There is no flame in this type of burning. You use some of the energy given off in your cells for living. And some of this energy is heat energy. Your body's warmth comes from "burning" sugar.

Where does this sugar come from? It comes from the food you eat. Your body breaks down the food into parts that the cells can use. The food is then transported to your cells. In the cells the food is "burned."

During this "burning," carbon dioxide and water are formed. The energy that was stored in the sugar is given off. This kind of "burning" is called **respiration** (res-puh-RAY-shun).

One way to understand respiration is to put it in the form of an equation:

$$\text{Sugar} + \text{Oxygen} \rightarrow \text{Carbon dioxide} + \text{Water} + \text{Energy}$$
$$C_6H_{12}O_6 + 6\,O_2 \rightarrow 6\,CO_2 + 6\,H_2O + \text{Energy}$$

Do you see how respiration is the opposite of photosynthesis? Photosynthesis uses energy to make sugar and oxygen. Respiration joins sugar with oxygen to give off energy.

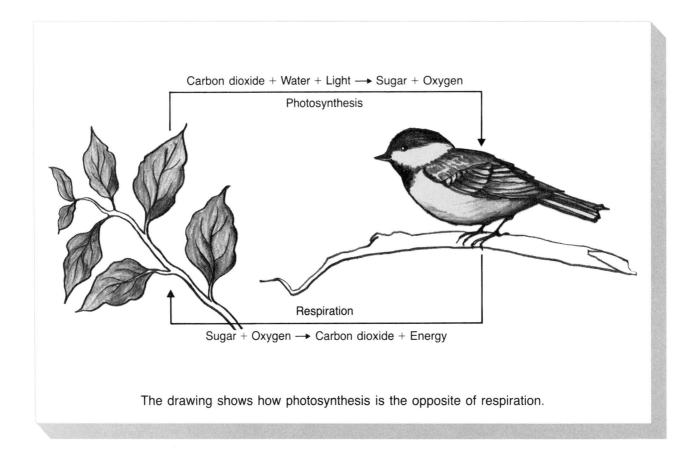

Carbon dioxide + Water + Light ⟶ Sugar + Oxygen

Photosynthesis

Respiration

Sugar + Oxygen ⟶ Carbon dioxide + Energy

The drawing shows how photosynthesis is the opposite of respiration.

To Do Yourself Does Energy Make Heat?

You will need:

A thermometer

1. Tuck a thermometer under your armpit. Keep it there for two minutes. Record the temperature.
2. Run 50 steps in place.
3. Again take and record your temperature.
4. Do 10 jumping jacks.
5. Take and record your temperature.
6. Repeat the exercise and check the temperature at least three times. Record your temperature.

Questions

1. What kind of temperature change did you observe? _____

2. What caused the temperature to change? _____

Review

I. Choose from the answer list the word or words that fit best.

chlorophyll **respiration** **carbon dioxide** **photosynthesis** **oxygen**
energy **cells** **food**

The energy we need to move, play, and stay alive comes from

_____ . In the body, foods are moved to

_____ , where they are broken down. There the food is

"burned" to give off _____ . This process is called

_____ . When this food is burned in the cells,

_____ and water are given off with the energy. This

process is just the opposite of the process of _____ that
happens in plants.

II. Explain how photosynthesis is different from respiration. Explain which applies to plants and which applies to animals.

What Are The Parts of Plants?

Exploring Science

The Plant and the Mouse. In the 1700s, everyone knew that animals need air to live. But no one knew why. Joseph Priestley, of England, wanted to find out. He also thought that plants change the air in some way that is useful to animals.

To test his ideas, Priestley placed a lively mouse in a covered jar of air. The mouse soon became drowsy and seemed to go to sleep. The mouse had used up the part of the air—which we now know to be oxygen—that it needed.

Next, Priestley kept a mint plant under a jar in a sunny spot for a few days. Then he placed a mouse in the jar with the plant. The mouse stayed lively much longer than before. Why?

As the plant made food, it gave off oxygen. So the air around the plant had extra oxygen in it, which helped the mouse stay lively longer.

The leaf is the part of a plant that makes food. It is also the part of the plant that gives off oxygen. But a leaf by itself usually dies. It depends on the other parts of a plant to "keep going."

● Suppose Priestley had kept the jar with the plant in the dark. What would happen to a mouse put in the jar? Explain.

Priestley's Experiment

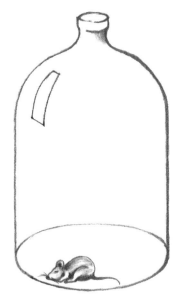
Sleepy mouse

Mint plant

Lively mouse

Parts of Plants, the Food-Makers

The main parts of seed plants are leaves, stems, and roots. Each of these parts has special jobs to do. But one job that all of these plant parts do is to store food.

Leaves. The main job of the leaf is to make food. Most of the chlorophyll in a plant is in the cells of the leaf. Here, in the leaves, green cells make food by photosynthesis. Some leaves also store a lot of food. Many vegetables, such as lettuce, cabbage, and brussels sprouts, store food in their leaves.

Stems. A plant's stem holds up its leaves to the sun so they can make food. It also connects the leaves with the roots. Some seed plants have a **nonwoody** (non-WOOD-ee) stem. Most of a nonwoody stem is made up of soft **pith** (PITH) tissue. The job of pith is to store food. We get table sugar from the pith of the plant, sugar cane.

A ring of tissue in the stem moves food and water to the other parts of the plant. There are two kinds of tissue. **Xylem** (ZY-lum) moves water and minerals up through the stem. **Phloem** (FLOH-em) moves food down through the stem.

Trees have **woody** (WOOD-ee) stems. Between the xylem and phloem layers of a woody stem is a layer called the **cambium.** (KAM-bee-um) The cambium is a growth tissue. As it grows, the cambium makes new xylem and phloem. Old xylem becomes wood.

You can see this if you look at the cross-section of a tree. The new wood made each year looks like rings. The light part of a ring is made in the spring. The dark part is made in the summer. By counting the rings in the stem, you can tell the age of the tree.

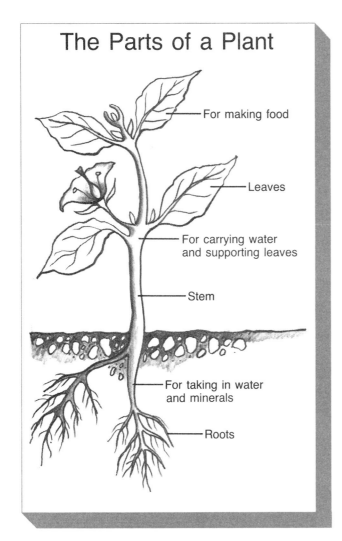

The Parts of a Plant

- For making food
- Leaves
- For carrying water and supporting leaves
- Stem
- For taking in water and minerals
- Roots

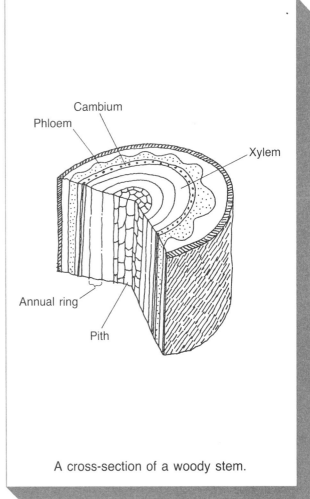

Phloem — Cambium — Xylem — Annual ring — Pith

A cross-section of a woody stem.

Roots. Roots anchor the plant to the ground. Both the xylem and phloem are at the center of each root. Water and minerals move from the soil into the **root hairs** of the root. The root hairs are root cells with thin parts that stick out into the soil. In the outer parts of a root, food can be stored.

Some plants have one large root that stores a lot of food. Carrots and beets are among these plants. Their roots can grow very long and take in water from deep in the ground.

Other plants have thread-like roots that branch a lot. These plants include grasses, strawberries, and pansies. Their roots spread out and take in water over a wide area.

The roots of some plants grow in the air. These include orchids and mistletoe. They grow where the air is moist.

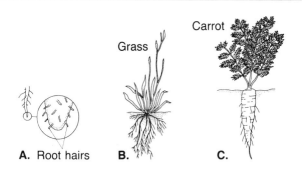

A. Root hairs   **B.**   **C.**

A. An enlarged view of the root shows the root hairs.
B. Grass roots spread out in tangles.
C. Carrot plant grows a taproot.

To Do Yourself   Do Foods From Plants Contain Sugar and Starch?

You will need:

Sugar-test tablets; test tubes or jars; water; food samples such as raisins, corn, banana, butter, apple, egg white

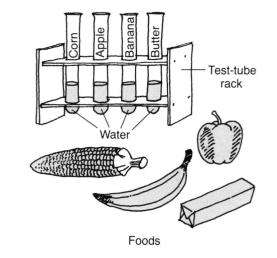

1. Crush a food sample and place it in a test tube or jar. Add some water and label.
2. Add a sugar-test tablet to the test tube.
3. Observe the color that forms. A green, yellow, or red color shows that sugar is present.
4. Record your observations in a table.
5. Test each food sample for sugar.

Questions

1. Which foods contain sugar? _____

2. Where does the sugar in the food come from? _____

Review

I. Choose from the answer list the word or words that fit best.

**cambium   nonwoody   woody   pith   phloem   xylem   leaves
stems   root hairs**

A plant tissue that moves food is _____ . A plant tissue that

moves water and minerals is _____ . Soft plant stems are

_____ . In a stem, food is stored in the

_____ . Trees have _____ stems.

Growth tissue of _____ makes new wood in a tree. Water

and minerals enter a plant through _____ .

II. Write the number of the plant part next to the job that it does. Answers can
be used more than once.

A. _____ becomes wood

B. _____ anchors plant

C. _____ holds up leaves

D. _____ makes food

E. _____ moves food down through the stem

1. phloem

2. xylem

3. leaf

4. stem

5. root

III. The veins of a leaf have both xylem and phloem tissue. What are the jobs of
the veins? Explain your answer.

IV. Write the names of the tree parts on the blanks.

What Are Some Useful Things in Foods?

Exploring Science

Space Ship Menu. What do astronauts (AS-truh-nawts) get to eat? Here are menus for one day on a Space Shuttle trip:

Breakfast	Lunch	Dinner
peaches	ham	mushroom soup
sausage	bread	turkey
scrambled eggs	cheese spread	mixed vegetables
	broccoli	strawberries
orange drink		
	cookies	vanilla pudding
cocoa		
	tea with lemon	fruit punch

Planning such meals in space takes a lot of scientific (sy-un-TIF-ik) know-how. The total weight of a spacecraft must be as small as possible. Scientists had to find ways to save weight. A large part of most foods is water. Drying the foods makes them lighter. It also helps keep them from spoiling. But before the foods can be eaten, the water must be put back. If water for this purpose is carried along, no weight is saved. The scientists looked for a way to use water from another source, and they found it.

Fuel cells make electricity (ih-lek-TRIS-ih-tee) for the spacecraft. A fuel cell combines hydrogen and oxygen gas. Water forms as a byproduct. The scientists invented ways for the astronauts to use this water. One of its uses is to put the water back into their dried foods.

Each dish in a space meal is in a can or a pouch. To get a meal ready, astronauts add water. They then heat or chill each dish. A meal on its tray may look strange. It still seems to taste fine, from the look on the face of an astronaut who eats it.

● Water for washing on a spacecraft is probably

A. carried in a tank.
B. collected from the fuel cells.

An astronaut enjoys one of the Space Shuttle's meal.

Useful materials in foods

The materials in foods that you and the astronauts eat are called **nutrients.** (NOO-tree-unts). The nutrients are grouped into six types. They are carbohydrates (kar-boh-HY-drayts), fats, proteins, vitamins, minerals (MIN-ur-uls), and water. Most foods contain several nutrients. Some foods are rich in one or two nutrients.

Carbohydrates. There are two main kinds of **carbohydrates.** Sugars are **simple carbohydrates.** Sweet foods are rich in sugars. Some of these include honey, ice cream, cake, fruits, candy, cookies, and pie.

Starches are one group of **complex carbohydrates.** Pasta, bread, potatoes, cereals, rice, and beans are some foods rich in starch.

Both sugars and starches give energy to your body. Your body can change extra sugars or starches into fat. Stored fat helps keep your body warm. Fat also cushions certain organs.

Another kind of complex carbohydrate is **fiber** (FY-bur). The body cannot get energy from fiber. But your body needs fiber for healthy **digestion** (dih-JES-chun) of foods. Whole grains, **vegetables** (VEJ-tuh-buls), and fruits are rich sources of fiber.

Fats. Fats are foods that supply fuel for energy in the body. One group of fats are solids. They are found in animal foods like meat, milk, and eggs. Animal fats contain **cholesterol** (kuh-LES-tuh-rohl). Some cholesterol is needed for a healthy body. Too much cholesterol, however, may help cause certain diseases.

Another group of fats are the **oils.** Oils are found in plant foods, like nuts, seeds, and grains. Salad oils and cooking oils are plant fats. Plant fats contain no cholesterol. Everyone needs some plant fats for a healthy body.

Proteins. Proteins build and heal tissues. You, and other living things, need proteins for growth and repair. Your body can also get energy from proteins. You get proteins from both plants and animals.

All proteins are made up of building blocks called **amino acids** (uh-MEE-noh AS-ids). There are 20 kinds of amino acids. Your body can make all but eight of them. Those eight must come from your food.

Vitamins, Minerals, and Water. Vitamins and **minerals** help control how your body works. To

This meal contains proteins, carbohydrates, fats, vitamins, water, and minerals.

stay in good health, you need many kinds of vitamins and minerals. Vegetables, fruits, milk, meats, and whole grains are rich in vitamins and minerals.

Water is part of every cell. Water helps move food, wastes, and other materials throughout your body. All foods have some water. You also need to drink some water each day.

To Do Yourself   **What Foods Contain Protein?**

You will need:

Biuret solution; medicine dropper; water; test tubes or jars; food samples such as peanuts, powdered milk, maple syrup, hamburger, egg white, cheese, gelatin

1. Choose a food sample and crush it. Place it in the test tube.
2. Add several drops of water. Add several drops of Biuret solution.
3. Record any color changes. A purple color shows that protein is present. Record your observations in a table.
4. Test each food sample for protein.

Questions

1. What are some foods that contain protein? _____

2. How could you find out if the food also contained starch or sugar? _____

_____

Food sample

BIURET SOLUTION

Review

I. What is meant by a nutrient? List the main groups of nutrients.

_____

_____

II. Match the answers in **B** with the statements in **A**. Some statements have two answers. One has three answers. Write the numbers of the answers in the blank.

	A		**B**
A. _____	needed to heal a broken bone	1.	water
B. _____	control how your body works	2.	fats
C. _____	can be used for energy	3.	proteins
D. _____	cushion organs and keep body warm	4.	carbohydrates
E. _____	transports materials	5.	minerals
F. _____	can be changed to fat	6.	vitamins

III. A fad diet that consists only of rice and seaweed can make people become sick or die. Explain why.

Why Do You Need Vitamins and Minerals?

Exploring Science

The Story of Vitamin A. During World War I, many children in Denmark came down with a terrible eye disease. At first, their eyes became dry. Then their eyelids became swollen and red. Finally, they went blind.

Dr. C. E. Bloch set out to find a cure for this disease. In his search, he read about the work of Dr. E. V. McCollum, an American scientist. McCollum fed rats what scientists then thought was a good diet. Yet the rats stopped growing and got sick. Like the Danish children, the rats came down with the eye disease. Then McCollum added milkfat to the diet of the rats. Soon their eye disease was cured.

What special substance was in the milkfat that cured the eye disease? After months of research, McCollum found out. The special thing was Vitamin A.

Dr. Bloch knew that Danish children did not have enough milkfat in their diets. Because of the war, the children ate no butter and drank only skim milk. This caused the children to get sick. Bloch added whole milk and butter to the diets of the sick children. The children got well.

Today, in America, vitamin A is added to all skim milk. It is also added to low-fat milk. We have other foods that are also rich in vitamin A. It should be easy to get enough vitamin A from eating the proper foods. Yet many people still get too little vitamin A. These people may have dry hair or skin.

Too little vitamin A also causes night blindness.

Too much vitamin A, though, can make you sick. Signs of too much vitamin A are a sick stomach, loss of hair, and a skin rash.

● In his later work, McCollum studied the diets of cattle. He observed that cattle fed only on grain can become blind. Cattle fed on both grain and green leaves stayed healthy. McCollum concluded that

A. grain is rich in vitamin A.

B. green leaves are rich in vitamin A.

Vitamins and Minerals for Health

What are vitamins and minerals? **Vitamins** and **minerals** are nutrients you need for health. Foods have small amounts of these nutrients in them. Yet these small amounts have big effects. A lack, or **deficiency** (dih-FISH-un-see), of one of these nutrients can cause a disease. Night blindness is one example of a **deficiency disease.** It results from too little vitamin A.

Too much, or an **overdose** (OH-vur-dohs), of some vitamins and minerals can also cause illness. Overdoses come from taking large amounts of vitamins or minerals in the form of pills.

Eating the right foods is the best way to get enough vitamins and minerals. Table 1 and Table 2 list many foods that are rich in vitamins and minerals. Getting enough of certain vitamins and minerals prevents deficiency diseases. The names and signs of these diseases are listed in the tables. The tables also give some other important facts about certain vitamins and minerals.

Notice that many foods are rich in more than one nutrient. Whole-grain breads are an example. They give you a group of vitamins called the B vitamins. **Niacin** (NY-uh-sin) is one of these B vitamins, along with B_1 and B_2. Whole-grain breads also give you vitamins E and K. Why are these vitamins needed in your body?

Can you find five vitamins and minerals that are found in milk? Eggs are also rich in several different vitamins. What are they? Why are these vitamins needed in your body? What are some signs of a deficiency of these vitamins?

Table 1   Important Vitamins

Vitamin	Some Good Sources	Uses in Body	Deficiency Disease and Its Signs	Other Signs of Deficiency	Signs of Overdose
A	milk; butter; margarine; eggs; yellow, orange, and dark-green vegetables and fruits; liver	healthy skin and eyes; good ability to see at night; healthy bones and teeth	night blindness (poor ability to see in dim light)	rough, dry skin; dry hair; eye infections	skin rash; hair loss; nausea
B_1 (thiamin)	pork; whole-grain bread, cereals, and pasta; lima beans; peas; oatmeal	healthy nerves, skin, and eyes; helps body get energy from carbohydrates	beriberi (weakness, leg cramps, mental confusion)	tiredness	none known
B_2 (riboflavin)	milk; meat; dark-green vegetables; eggs; whole-grain cereals, pasta, and bread; dried beans and peas; liver	healthy nerves, skin and eyes; helps body get energy from carbohydrates, fats, and proteins	skin disorders (especially at nose and mouth)	eyes sensitive to light; poor growth; oily, scaly skin	none known
niacin (a B vitamin)	chicken; eggs; tuna; beef; whole-grain cereals, pasta, and bread; nuts; dried peas and beans; liver	works with other B vitamins to get energy from other nutrients in the cells	pellagra (skin disorders; diarrhea; mental confusion; swollen mouth)	depression	ulcer in intestine; high blood sugar
C (ascorbic acid)	oranges, lemons, grapefruit, limes; tomatoes; melon; strawberries; potatoes; dark-green vegetables	healthy bones, teeth, and blood vessels; clear skin	scurvy (bleeding gums; loose teeth; dry, rough skin; weakness)	bruise easily; sore gums	kidney and bladder stones; body comes to depend on high dose to prevent scurvy
D	milk (fortified); liver; tuna; salmon; egg yolk; cod-liver oil	healthy bones, teeth; helps body take in calcium	rickets (bowed legs, poor growth of bones and teeth)	soft bones; muscle disorders	too much calcium in body; weak bones; nausea; kidney stones; deafness

Table 1 (continued)

Vitamin	Some Good Sources	Uses in Body	Deficiency Disease and Its Signs	Other Signs of Deficiency	Signs of Overdose
E	vegetable oils; margarine; wheat germ; whole-grain cereals and bread; green, leafy vegetables; dried beans; liver	healthy blood and muscles; protects other nutrients	signs of deficiency not seen in humans	none known	none known
K	cabbage; cauliflower; peas; potatoes; whole-grain cereals and bread; green, leafy vegetables	normal blood clotting	poor blood clotting	soft bones	turns skin yellow in babies

Table 2 Important Minerals

Mineral	Some Good Sources	Uses in Body	Signs of Deficiency	Signs of Overdose
Calcium	milk, yogurt, and hard cheeses; sardines and salmon eaten with bones; green, leafy vegetables	healthy bones and teeth; helps blood clot; healthy muscles	soft bones, leading to breakage; poor teeth	sleepiness; tiredness
Iron	liver, eggs, fish, beef, poultry; leafy, green vegetables; raisins; apricots	healthy red blood cells and muscles	anemia (paleness, weakness, tiredness); brittle fingernails	damage to liver and heart
Iodine	iodized salt; seafood; seaweed	healthy thyroid gland; helps body get energy from nutrients	goiter (enlargement of thyroid gland in neck)	none known
Potassium	bananas, oranges, dried fruits; meat; potatoes; peanut butter	healthy muscles and nerves; regulates water in cells	loss of too much water from cells; problems with heart and (maybe) with high-blood pressure	none known
Sodium	salt; milk; celery; beets	healthy muscles and nerves	none known	none known

To Do Yourself   What Foods Contain the Mineral Iron?

You will need:

Several small jars, water, ½ liter of strong tea, samples of juice such as apple, pineapple, orange, cranberry, grapefruit

1. Fill each jar one-fourth full of juice sample and label it.
2. Add tea until the jars are half full.
3. Observe and record any changes. Juices that contain iron will combine with the tea and form solid particles.

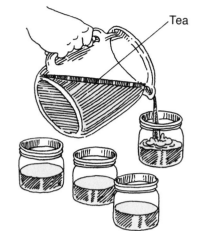
Tea

Questions

1. What is a test for iron in food? _____

2. What are some foods that contain iron? _____

Review

I. Choose from the answer list the word or words that fit best.

deficiency   vitamins   deficiency disease   minerals   overdose   foods

Foods have small amounts of _____ and

_____ in them. A lack of one of these nutrients can cause

a _____ _____ . Taking too much of a

vitamin is called an _____ . B_1 and B_2 are examples of

_____ .

II. Use the tables to help you find the cure for each deficiency disease. Write the answers in the blanks.

A. _____ pellagra   1. iron
B. _____ goiter   2. vitamin B_1
C. _____ rickets   3. niacin
D. _____ scurvy   4. vitamin C
E. _____ night blindness   5. vitamin D
F. _____ anemia   6. iodine
G. _____ beriberi   7. vitamin A

III. Goiter, caused by a lack of iodine in the diet, was once a common disease in places far from the sea.

A. Why do you think that was so?
B. Why do you think this is not so now?

What Are Calories?

Exploring Science

The Winter Sleep of Griz, the Bear. People once thought that there were no more grizzly bears in Colorado. One day when Marty Stouffer, a naturalist (NACH-ur-uh-list), was in the Colorado wilds he was surprised to see a male grizzly bear. There was not another bear around.

Stouffer had a plan. He went to the zoo and arranged to adopt a female grizzly cub. He named her Griz, and raised her the way her mother would have.

Stouffer knew that bears sleep all winter. He saw that during the fall, Griz began to overeat.

She became very fat. The first winter, she slept, and while sleeping she began to get thin again. In the spring when she came out of her den, she was healthy and "hungry as a bear."

The next year, after her second "big sleep," Griz met the male grizzly. Stouffer hoped that in another year, Griz would have her own cubs. Once again, Colorado would have grizzlies.

● The energy a bear needs during the spring and summer comes from food that is

A. eaten daily   **B.** stored from the winter

Baby Griz shortly after being adopted by Marty Stouffer.

Calories and Energy

How could Griz live all winter long without eating? During the fall, Griz ate more food than she used up. This was stored in her body as fat. In the winter, she "burned" that food and used up the **calories** (KAL-uh-rees).

Just what is a calorie? You see the word on almost every food label. A bread wrapper says, "One slice equals 70 calories." You may have heard that calories are "fattening." To lose weight, people say you have to cut down on calories. So what are they?

Food gives you energy to live. A **calorie** is a measure of food energy. When your body "burns" one gram of sugar, starch, or protein you get four calories of energy. One gram of fat gives nine calories of energy.

Any food that contains sugar, starch, protein, or fat provides calories. "Burning" food provides calories. Table 1 shows the number of calories in some foods.

What do calories have to do with weight? If your input of calories equals your output, your weight stays the same.

If your input of calories is more than your output, you will gain weight. It is normal to gain weight as long as you are still growing. People who gain more weight than they need for growth get fat.

If your output of calories is more than your input, you will lose weight. Like the bear, you will be "burning" stored food.

Table 1   Calories in Some Foods

Food	Amount	Calories
Apple	1 medium	75
Bread	average slice	70
Cornflakes	1 cup	80
Egg	1 (boiled)	75
Green peas	½ cup	55
Hamburger	1 medium size	250
Hamburger roll	1 average	110
Margarine	1 teaspoon	35
Milk (whole)	1 cup	150
Orange juice	½ cup	55
Swiss cheese	average slice	100
Tomato	1 medium	30

Table 2   Calories Used in Some Activities*

Activity	Calories per hour	Activity	Calories per hour
Sitting quietly	20	Bicycling (moderate speed)	110
Standing	20	Dancing	170
Eating	20	Playing ping-pong	200
Typing rapidly	50	Violin playing	330
Dishwashing	50	Running	330
Walking	90	Bicycling (racing)	340
Carpentry, heavy	100	Swimming	360

*For a 46-kg (100-lb) person. If you weigh less, you use fewer calories per hour. If you weigh more, you use more calories.

A nutritionist and a food chemist measure the calories consumed by a white rat.

Review

I. Choose from the answer list the word that fits best. You can use words more than once.

fat   starch   protein   weight   winter   calories   sugar   energy
burning

Food energy is measured in _____ . One gram of

_____ , _____ , or

_____ provides four calories of _____ .

One gram of _____ provides nine calories of

_____ . If your input equals your output, your

_____ stays the same. If your input of calories is more

than your output you will gain _____ .

II. Use Table 1 to help you answer the following questions.

    A. Find the total number of calories in a breakfast that consists of: ½ cup orange juice, 1 cup cornflakes, ½ cup milk, 1 egg, 1 slice of toast, and 2 teaspoons of margarine. _____

    B. How many calories are in lunch that consists of the following: hamburger on a roll, ½ tomato sliced, 1 apple, 1 cup milk? _____

III. Circle the word that makes each statement true.

    A. A person whose calorie intake each day is 2500 and whose calorie output is 2000 will (*gain/lose*) weight.

    B. A person whose calorie output each day is 2600 and whose calorie input is 2100 will (*gain/lose*) weight.

IV. For a 46-kilogram (100-pound) person to "burn up" a 300-calorie snack, about how long must that person run (at 9 miles/hour)?

How Can You Balance Your Diet?

Exploring Science

The Diet That Killed. A diet called the liquid-protein diet was once popular. It was supposed to help people lose weight easily.

What was the liquid-protein diet? It was a powder that came in a can. The label said that the powder had all the needed amino acids in it. When mixed with water, the powder became "liquid protein." Vitamins and minerals were also to be taken.

The liquid-protein diet provided 420 calories a day. Many people on the diet lost weight. One person dropped from 107 to 60 kilograms. Then the person died. At least 60 other people also died after using the diet. A government agency finally declared the diet a health risk. Scientists also found that the diet could cause people to develop serious heart trouble. It seems clear that a person can't stay healthy on protein, water, vitamins, and minerals.

● What nutrients do you need for health that the liquid-protein diet did not include?

A Balanced Diet

To have a healthy body, you need to eat a balanced diet (BAL-unst Dy-it). A **balanced diet** supplies all the nutrients you need. It should taste good also.

The study of how the body uses food is called **nutrition** (noo-TRISH-un). **Nutritionists** (noo-TRISH-uh-nists) are scientists who study how the body uses food. They have placed all foods into **four food groups.** To have a balanced diet you need to eat certain combinations of foods from the four-food groups. The groups are:

1. Milk group—4 servings or more a day
2. Fruit-and-vegetable group—4 servings or more a day
3. Meat group—2 servings or more a day
4. Grain group—4 servings or more a day

A balanced diet includes water. You need about two liters (LEE-turs) of water a day.

Do you need to gain weight? Follow the four food groups plan, but add extra servings. Do you need to lose weight? First, check with your

Table 1   The Four Food Groups

Food Group	Amount Needed	Foods	Main Nutrients
Milk group	4 servings or more a day	milk, cheese, yogurt	vitamin A, vitamin D; calcium; protein
Fruit-and-vegetable group	4 servings or more a day	leafy greens; red, orange, and yellow vegetables; potatoes; fruits	vitamin C, vitamin B_1, vitamin A; sugars and starches
Meat group	2 servings or more a day	meat; chicken; fish; eggs; peas; beans	protein; vitamin B_1, niacin; iron
Grain group	4 servings or more a day	breads, pastas, cereals; rice	vitamin B_1, vitamin B_2, niacin; iron; starches; some protein

doctor. Then follow the four food groups plan. You should take fewer and smaller servings. Your doctor will help you plan your food choices. Getting more exercise also helps you lose weight. The more active you are, the more calories you use up.

To stay the same weight, you can probably also have some extra servings. It depends on how active you are.

Review

I. Choose from the answer list the word that fits best. You may use words more than once.

nutrition   **balanced**   **nutritionists**   **four food groups**   **diet**

nutrients   **vitamins**   **more**   **fewer**

A _____ diet supplies all the _____ you

need. The study of how the body uses food is called _____ .

_____ are scientists that study how the body uses food.

For a balanced _____ , scientists have placed foods into

_____ . To lose weight, you would eat foods in all the

_____ , but you would eat _____ servings.

II. Use Table 1 to help you answer the following question. Write 1, 2, 3, or 4 for each of the statements below:

   1. Milk group   **3.** Fruit-and-vegetable group
   2. Meat group   **4.** Grain group

   A. _____ The food group that is missing from a lunch of chicken, potatoes, and ice cream.

   B. _____ Includes peas and beans

   C. _____ A source of both calcium and vitamin D.

   D. _____ Missing from a breakfast of egg, milk, and toast.

III. Choose the answer that completes the question. Write the letter of the answer in the blank.

   A. _____ A balanced diet includes   **a.** about two liters of water a day;   **b.** candy and snack foods.

   B. _____ To gain weight, you would   **a.** eat only the foods in the four food group plan;   **b.** eat the foods in the four food group plan plus some extra servings.

IV. Choose the answer that fits best. The body normally needs several classes of nutrients. These are supplied by the four food groups. When losing weight, the body probably needs   **a.** only one class of nutrients.   **b.** all classes of nutrients.

Review What You Know

A. Hidden in the puzzle below are the names of seven nutrients. Use the clues to help you find the names. Circle each name you find in the puzzle. Then write each name on the line next to its clue.

```
Y S T A R C H Z
W A S B M C P Y
A Q U P I R R X
T D G E N F O G
E F A T E H T I
R J R K R L E M
U V I T A M I N
I N O Q L R N Z
```

Clues:

1. It has a sweet taste. _____

2. Butter is a rich source. _____

3. Calcium is one example. _____

4. Drink it if you're thirsty. _____

5. Niacin belongs to this group. _____

6. Complex carbohydrate found in bread. _____

7. Builds and repairs tissues. _____

B. Write the word (or words) that best completes each statement.

1. The formula CO_2 stands for **a.** an element **b.** a compound **c.** a mixture

1. _____

2. Most of the body is made up of **a.** sugar **b.** starch **c.** water

2. _____

3. For photosynthesis, a cell needs carbon dioxide, water, and **a.** oxygen **b.** light **c.** heat

3. _____

4. During respiration, oxygen combines with **a.** sugar **b.** water **c.** nitrogen

4. _____

5. The tubes that carry water up through a plant's stem are **a.** xylem **b.** phloem **c.** pith

5. _____

6. A leaf's veins are part of the tissue called **a.** nonwoody **b.** pith **c.** vascular

6. _____

7. A plant's growth tissue is **a.** chlorophyll **b.** cambium **c.** phloem

7. _____

8. A nutrient that provides calories is
  a. fiber   **b.** vitamin A   **c.** protein

8. _____

9. Included among the fats is
  a. starch   **b.** cholesterol   **c.** sugar

9. _____

10. The weight of a person whose calorie intake is lower than his or her output will   **a.** increase
  b. decrease   **c.** stay the same

10. _____

C. Apply What You Know

  1. Study the drawing of the parts of a lunch you might have: hero sandwich, salad, milk, and banana.

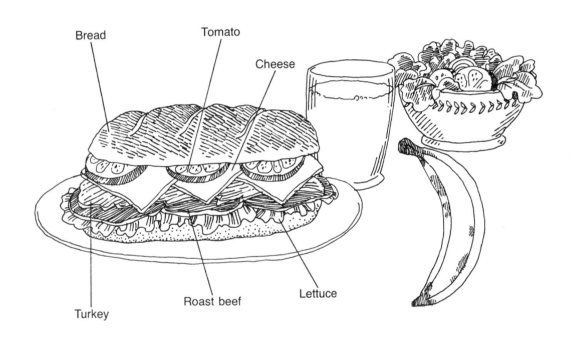

Bread   Tomato   Cheese   Turkey   Roast beef   Lettuce

For each food group below, write all the parts of the lunch that are good examples of that group.

a. Milk group _____

b. Fruit-and-vegetable group _____

c. Meat group _____

d. Grain group _____

  2. Make up another lunch that has none of the same foods. But be sure it includes each of the four food groups. Beside each food in your lunch, write the letter of the food group it belongs to.

D. Find Out More

1. A complete protein is one that supplies all eight amino acids we need from food. An incomplete protein supplies only some of the eight amino acids. Animal proteins are complete. Most plant proteins are incomplete. In the library, find out how different incomplete protein foods can be combined to make complete proteins. Plan some "vegetarian" menus that provide complete proteins.

2. Collect labels from foods such as cereals, canned goods, bread, and so on. Which things on the labels are not food but "food additives?" Do some research to find out. Are additives helpful or harmful? Find out the reasons for and against using additives.

A. Study the drawing. Write labels for the numbered parts. A clue for each label (with the same number) is given below. Use one of these words for each label:

respiration   carbon dioxide   photosynthesis   oxygen   consumer   producer   decomposer

1. The apple tree's link in a food chain _____

2. The girl's link in a food chain _____

3. Food-making process in the tree _____

4. "Burning" of food in the girl _____

5. Gas the tree gives off and the girl uses _____

6. Gas the girl gives off and the tree uses _____

B. Circle the word (or words) that makes each statement about the scene correct.

1. The cell parts in the tree's leaves that trap the sun's energy are (chloroplasts/vacuoles).
2. The clouds show part of the (oxygen-carbon-dioxide/water) cycle.
3. One-celled microbes present in the soil include (bacteria/vertebrates).
4. The rocks, grass, air, and girl are all parts of the same (ecosystem/population).
5. The apple is a rich source of (vitamins/proteins).
6. The girl is classified in the genus (*Felis*/*Homo*).
7. The biome shown is (deciduous forest/arctic tundra).
8. The tree's (xylem/phloem) tissue forms woody rings in its trunk.
9. A nonvascular plant growing near the tree might be a (mushroom/moss).
10. Before testing a hypothesis about the tree, a scientist would make (observations/theories).

DIGESTION AND TRANSPORT

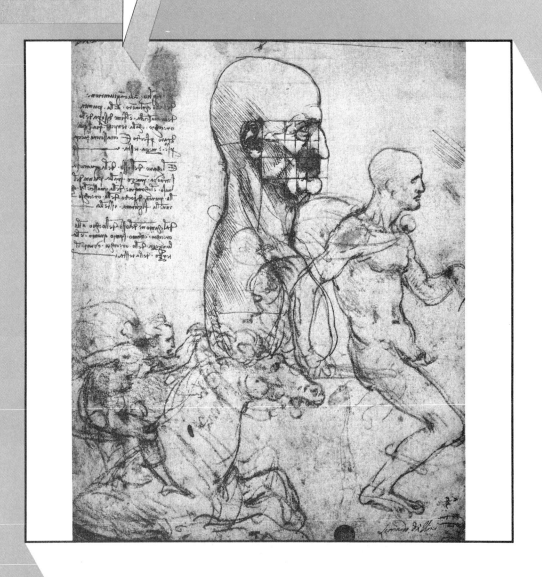

What Is the Job of Your Digestive System?

Exploring Science

The Hug of Life. Kim Lee was 14 years old when she saved her brother Larry's life.

One day not long ago, Kim and Larry were having lunch in a restaurant. While Larry was talking, he took a bite from his sandwich. Suddenly, he stopped talking and pointed to his throat. Kim asked what was wrong, but Larry could not speak. He also started to turn blue.

Kim could see that Larry was in danger. She knew at once what to do. In her first-aid class, she had learned the "Heimlich (HYM-lik) Hug." It was named after the doctor who first used it. "The hug" is part of courses in first aid.

Kim stood behind Larry and put her arms around his waist. She pressed his stomach, the way she had been taught. She heard a slight pop. Out came the piece of sandwich.

Larry took a deep breath. So did Kim, as she sighed with relief. Kim and Larry then went to see their family doctor. The doctor checked Larry over to be sure he was O.K. Larry was just fine!

● What do you think is the reason for taking a course in first aid before you try the Heimlich Hug?

The Heimlich "Hug"

The Heimlich "Hug" should be done only in an emergency when someone is choking.

Your Digestive System

Larry Lee's sandwich bite "went down the wrong way." What happens to food when it goes down the right way? It gets digested. The food, in a different form, goes inside your cells.

Chemically, foods are made up of compounds. The smallest parts of compounds are called **molecules** (MAHL-uh-kyoolz). Thus sugar, a food, is made up of molecules. So are starch, fat, protein, and other foods.

Only small molecules of foods can get into cells. During **digestion** (dih-JES-chun), your food is broken down into small molecules. Your cells then can use the food.

Your **digestive** (dih-JES-tiv) system is a group of organs whose job is to break down food.

Find each part of the digestive system on the diagram as you read on. You take food into your **mouth.** When you swallow, the food goes into the **esophagus** (ih-SOF-uh-gus). The esophagus is a short tube that carries food into the stomach.

The **stomach** is a bag-like organ shaped like a J. From the stomach, food moves into the small **intestine** (in-TES-tin). The small intestine is long and coiled. It connects to a shorter and thicker tube, the **large intestine.** Muscles in the walls of all these organs move the food along.

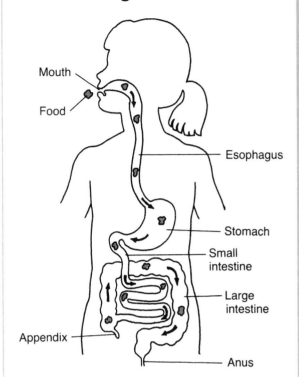

The Digestive Tract

Mouth

Food

Esophagus

Stomach

Small intestine

Large intestine

Appendix

Anus

Everything you eat passes through your digestive tract.

To Do Yourself Where Does Digestion Begin?

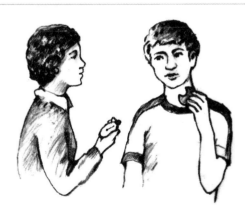

You will need:

Unsalted soda cracker, clock or watch with second hand

1. Take a bite of the cracker. Chew it.
2. Have a partner begin to time you.
3. Chew until the taste changes. Try not to swallow. Have your partner stop timing. Describe the taste of the cracker. How long did it take the change to happen?

Questions

1. How did the cracker taste at first? How did the taste change? _____

2. What caused this change? _____

3. Where does digestion begin? _____

The food your body cannot use collects in the large intestine as wastes. The wastes leave the body through an opening called the **anus.**

Attached to the large intestine is the **appendix** (uh-PEN-diks). The appendix is a worm-shaped sac through which food does not pass. It has no use in humans.

There are some organs, **glands,** that work with the digestive system. These are the **salivary** (SAL-uh-ver-ee) **glands,** the **pancreas** (PAN-kree-us), and the **liver.** Salivary glands are near the mouth. The pancreas is below the stomach. The liver is at the right of the stomach.

Food does not pass through the glands. The glands give off digestive juices. Chemicals in these juices help to digest foods. Many of these chemicals are **enzymes** (EN-zyms). Enzymes help break down large food molecules.

Each part of the digestive system has special jobs. You will learn about these jobs in lessons to come. You will see what happens to your food in each part.

Review

I. Write, in order, the names of the parts of the digestive system that a piece of food passes through. Start with the mouth. Find each part in the list below.

small intestine   pancreas   appendix   anus   large intestine

stomach   esophagus   liver   salivary glands

A. ___mouth___   D. _____

B. _____   E. _____

C. _____   F. _____

II. Write the names of the organs described.

A. Glands near the mouth _____

B. Gland below the stomach _____

C. Useless sac attached to the large intestine _____

D. Gland at the right of the stomach _____

III. State briefly what happens to food when it is digested. Use the word **molecule** in your answer. _____

IV. Glands give off digestive juices. What do these juices contain that help digestion? _____
_____

V. Study the drawing on page 90, then answer in sentences. Where do digestive juices of **(a)** the salivary glands, **(b)** the liver, **(c)** the pancreas do their work? Explain.

_____
_____
_____

How Does Digestion Begin?

Exploring Science

The Man With a Hole in His Stomach. One day in 1822, a hunter in Michigan accidentally shot himself. A U.S. Army physician, Dr. William Beaumont, was called in to save the man.

Under Beaumont's care, the hunter got well. But he was left with an opening into his stomach from the outside. In 1822, little was known about what happens to food in the stomach. Beaumont saw this opening as a chance to study digestion. The man agreed to this.

Beaumont placed bread in the man's stomach. Right away, a juice flowed from the stomach's walls.

Beaumont collected some of this juice. He put it in a test tube with some meat. After an hour, the meat fibers were swollen and separated. After a few hours, the fibers had turned into a liquid.

What Beaumont learned about the stomach is still useful. He was a pioneer in the study of digestion.

● Normally, food is chewed before it enters the stomach. Would chewed food become a liquid faster or more slowly than food left in chunks? Explain your answer.

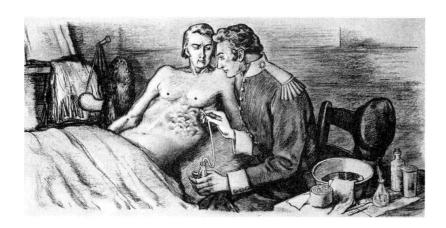

Dr. William Beaumont discovered the process of digestion by studying an accident victim.

How Digestion Begins

Suppose you eat a sandwich made of bread, meat, lettuce, and tomato. What happens to these foods?

Your teeth bite, tear, and grind the food. This chewing is part of mechanical (muh-KAN-ih-kul) digestion. **Mechanical digestion** breaks large pieces of food into small pieces.

At the same time, the salivary glands send **saliva** (suh-LY-vuh) into your mouth. Saliva wets food and makes it easier to swallow. Saliva also starts the chemical (KEM-ih-kul) digestion of starch. In **chemical digestion,** large molecules are broken down by enzymes into smaller molecules. There is an enzyme in saliva that acts on starch in the bread. It starts to break the starch

molecules down into smaller sugar molecules.

After the food is chewed and mixed with saliva, your tongue pushes it into your throat. You swallow, and the food enters your esophagus. Wavelike movements of muscles in the wall of the esophagus push the food downward.

From the esophagus, food enters the stomach. Digestion in the stomach is both chemical and mechanical. Lining the stomach are tiny glands. These glands give off **gastric** (GAS-trik) **juice.** The juice contains enzymes and an acid. The acid helps the enzymes do their work. The enzymes start to break down protein molecules. The enzymes go to work on the meat in your sandwich. Meat contains proteins.

Wavelike motions of muscles in the stomach wall mixes food with gastric juice. The motion also breaks the food into smaller pieces. After one to three hours, your sandwich has become a thick liquid. It is ready to go from the stomach to the small intestine.

To Do Yourself How Does Saliva Help Digest Food?

You will need:

Starch solution, saliva, water, test tubes, iodine solution, dropper, teaspoon, sugar-test tablets

1. Collect some saliva in a teaspoon.
2. Place one drop of starch solution in each of two test tubes one-fourth filled with water.
3. Add a drop of iodine solution to each tube. The starch should turn blue.
4. Add the saliva to one tube. Add an equal amount of water to the other tube. Shake the tubes.
5. Add a sugar-test tablet to each tube. Record your observations.

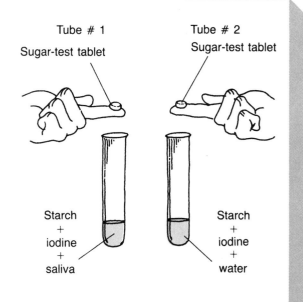

Questions

1. In which tube did the blue liquid turn clear? _____

2. Why did this happen? _____

3. What did the test for sugar show? _____

Review

I. Fill in each blank with the word that fits best. Use these words:

gastric   saliva   chemical   mechanical   esophagus

Chewing food is _____ digestion. Changing large

molecules to small molecules is _____ digestion. In the

mouth, _____ changes starch to sugar. In the stomach,

_____ juice acts on proteins.

II. Circle the correct ending to each statement:

A. Glands in the stomach produce enzymes and *(acid/saliva)*.
B. Digestion carried out by enzymes is *(mechanical/chemical)*.
C. When food leaves the stomach its digestion is *(only begun/finished)*.

III. In birds, food passes through a gizzard before it goes into the intestine. A gizzard has small stones in it that the bird has swallowed. What do you think the gizzard's job is?

How Does Digestion End?

Exploring Science

How to Live Without Eating. Nunzio Casillo lives a normal life . . . almost. Each day he goes to work. After work he often plays ball with his two sons. He looks lean and athletic. Each night, Casillo goes to his basement laboratory. There, he takes down bottles of substances from a shelf. He mixes together the right amount from each bottle. What is this mixture he is making?

Casillo is making his day's "meal." It contains all the nutrients he needs for a balanced diet. But the nutrients are already digested. They are ready to go directly into Casillo's blood. When he goes to bed, he plugs himself into a feeding machine. The machine pumps his "meal" into a vein near his heart.

Several years ago, Casillo became unable to eat. His small intestine was blocked. There was nothing doctors could do to get his intestine back in working order.

Luckily for Casillo, scientists can "digest" foods outside the body. And they invented the feeding machine. So, even though Casillo cannot eat, he can live.

● A hospital patient with normal intestines is fed sugar, water, and minerals through a vein. How does this feeding differ from Casillo's meal?

How Digestion Ends

Your small intestine is like a coiled tube. Stretched out, it would be 6 or 7 meters long. Most digestion takes place in the small intestine.

Digestive juices from three places work on foods in the small intestine. These juices come from the liver, the pancreas, and the small intestine itself.

The liver makes a juice called **bile** (BYL). Bile is stored in the **gallbladder** (GAWL-BLAD-ur). This is a small bag under the liver. When you eat fats, bile flows from the gallbladder into the small intestine. There, the bile breaks the fats into tiny droplets. The meat in the sandwich you ate (remember?) contained fats. After bile breaks the fats into small enough droplets, enzymes can act on them.

The small intestine has glands in its walls. These glands make enzymes. The pancreas also makes enzymes. One enzyme from the pancreas digests fats. It breaks fats into molecules of **fatty acids** and **glycerol** (GLIS-uh-rohl).

Other enzymes digest carbohydrates. Starch began to break down in the mouth. In the small intestine starch is broken down completely into simple sugars. Complex sugars are also broken down into simple sugars.

Protein began breaking down in the stomach. Enzymes in the small intestine finish digesting proteins. They are broken down into amino acids.

Digestion is now complete. Your sandwich has been changed into molecules your body can use.

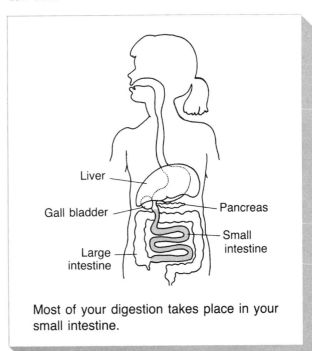

Most of your digestion takes place in your small intestine.

To Do Yourself How Does Digestion Change Fats?

You will need:

2 test tubes with stoppers, cooking oil, baking soda, dropper, teaspoon, water

1. Fill the two test tubes half full of water. Add a few drops of cooking oil to each tube.
2. Add one-fourth teaspoon baking soda to one tube of oil and water.
3. Stopper each tube and shake it well. Record your observations.

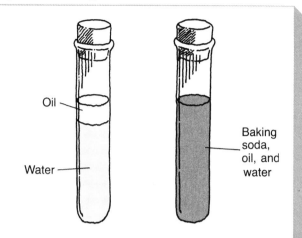

Oil

Water

Baking soda, oil, and water

Questions

1. Which test tube has fats that have not begun to break down? _____

2. Which tube has fats that were partly broken down? _____

3. What digestive juice did the baking soda act like? _____

Review

I. Complete the table below, which sums up digestion. Use words from the list to fill in the blanks.

small intestine amino acids glycerol stomach mouth fatty acids
simple sugars large intestine

Nutrients	Where Acted Upon	Final Forms
Carbohydrates	a. _____	c. _____
	b. _____	
Proteins	d. _____	f. _____
	e. _____	
Fats	g. _____	h. _____
		i. _____

II. Suppose you eat a piece of butter. Describe briefly what happens to its fatty part (which is most of it) until it is completely digested.

III. A person who has his or her gall bladder removed can still digest fats. Explain why.

What Happens After Food Is Digested?

Exploring Science

The King's Appendix. Edward was to be crowned king of England on June 25, 1902, and London was gaily decorated for the big show. People had come from all over the world.

But 12 days before the ceremony was to start, Edward got sick. His stomach was upset. He had a fever and a sharp pain in his right side. On June 24, word came from the palace: the crowning could not take place.

Edward had appendicitis. This means that wastes and bacteria become trapped in the appendix, a small organ attached to the large intestine. The appendix gets tender and starts to swell. If it bursts, the infection can spread to other parts of the body. The person may even die.

The doctors operated on Edward and removed his appendix. He recovered rapidly.

Note: Edward was finally crowned king of England on August 9, 1902.

● If you have the signs of appendicitis, you should not take a laxative. Can you think why?

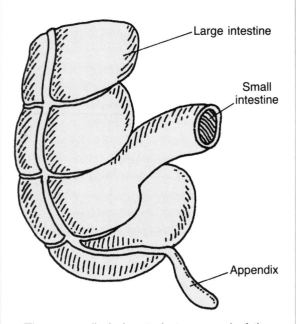

The appendix is located at one end of the large intestine.

Edward VII could not become king until he was cured of appendicitis.

After Digestion Is Complete

You ate a sandwich and digested it. The digested food is in your small intestine. It has been changed to molecules of amino acids, simple sugars, glycerol, and fatty acids. These molecules are small enough to move through the intestine walls into your blood.

The walls of the small intestine are lined with tiny bumps called **villi** (VIL-eye). There are many blood vessels in the villi. Digested food passes through the walls of the villi into the blood. The blood carries the food to all your cells. Each cell takes in, or **absorbs,** the food it needs.

Remember that sandwich? Its lettuce and tomato contain fiber. Your body cannot digest fiber. But fiber is an important part of your diet. Fiber keeps your intestines healthy. It makes it easier to eliminate, or get rid of, wastes.

Food parts you cannot digest become wastes. They pass into the large intestine, which absorbs water. In the large intestine, wavelike muscle motions move the waste material along.

Helpful bacteria live in the large intestine. The bacteria change the wastes into a solid. This solid waste is called **feces** (FEE-seez). Feces pass out of your body through the anus.

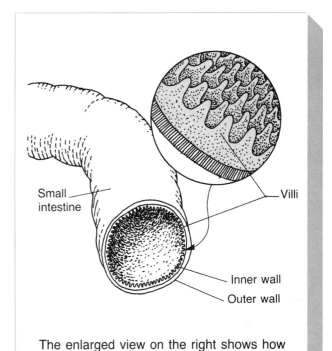

The enlarged view on the right shows how thousands of villi line the inner wall of the small intestine.

Review

I. In each blank, write the word that matches the statement. Use the words below.

villi   absorb   feces   fiber   blood vessels   appendix

A. _____ to take in

B. _____ solid waste

C. _____ cannot be digested

D. _____ found in villi

E. _____ bumps in the small intestine

II. Circle the correct ending to each statement:

A. Water is absorbed in the *(large/small)* intestine.
B. Bacteria in the large intestine are *(always harmful/usually helpful)*.

III. If you stand on your head after a meal, food still moves "down" your digestive system. Why? _____

_____

_____

What Is the Work of the Blood?

Exploring Science

Saving Lives With Blood Plasma. In 1940, World War II was being fought in Europe. One August day that year, Dr. Charles Drew in America got a cablegram from Dr. John Beattie, an old friend. Beattie was a doctor in Britain. The cable read:

CAN YOU GET 5,000 UNITS OF DRIED PLASMA FOR TRANSFUSION?

In a **transfusion** (trans-FYOO-zhun) one person's blood is given to another. **Plasma** (PLAZ-muh) is the blood's liquid part. Drew had found a way to dry blood plasma. When dried, plasma is easy to keep and to ship. Just before use, the dried plasma is mixed with water.

Drew answered Britain's call for help. He became head of the Plasma for Britain project. After the war, Drew directed a Red Cross blood bank. In peacetime, as in war, plasma saves lives. All hospitals today use plasma.

● Donors at a blood bank are given fruit juice and candy after they give blood. What two parts of the lost blood are partly replaced by these foods? Explain.

Dr. Charles Drew was a pioneer in blood transfusions.

The Work of the Blood

Has a doctor ever tested your blood? For many tests, a tube is filled with your blood. The tube is put in a machine that spins very fast. When the spinning stops, the blood is in two layers. At the top is the liquid part, or **plasma.** At the bottom is the solid part.

Plasma is 90 percent water. Dissolved in plasma are digested foods, wastes, and special chemicals. One chemical helps the blood **clot,** or stop flowing, when you get cut. Other chemicals help fight germs.

The solid part of the blood has two kinds of cells. **Red blood cells** are small and shaped like plates. They have no nuclei. **Hemoglobin** (HEE-muh-gloh-bin) in the red cells gives them their color. Hemoglobin has the job of carrying oxygen to all your body cells.

White blood cells are large and round. They have nuclei. There are many fewer white cells than red cells. The job of white blood cells is to fight germs.

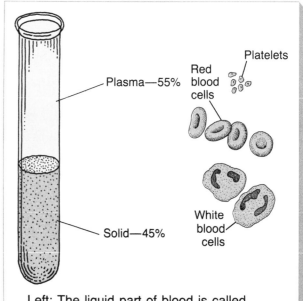

Left: The liquid part of blood is called plasma.
Right: The solid part is made of red blood cells, white blood cells, and platelets.

Tiny pieces of cells called **platelets** (PLAYT-lits) are also in the solid part of the blood. Platelets help form blood clots. A clot keeps blood from flowing from a wound. When you are cut, the platelets give out a chemical. This chemical works with part of the plasma to make a net of threads. This net catches red blood cells to form a clot. The dried clot is a **scab**.

To Do Yourself   What Are Some Parts of Blood?

You will need:

Prepared slide of human blood, microscope

1. Observe the prepared blood slide under low power. Then observe it under high power.
2. Identify the red blood cells and the white blood cells. Draw and label each kind of cell.
3. Select a section of the slide. Count the number of red blood cells and white blood cells you observe on this section.

Questions

1. Which kind of cells are larger? _____

2. Which kind of cells are present in the largest numbers? _____

Review

I. Fill in each blank with the word that fits best. Use the words below:

platelets   plasma   hemoglobin   clot   white   red

The liquid part of the blood is _____ . Blood cells that fight

germs are _____ blood cells. Round plate-shaped cells

without nuclei are _____ blood cells. The

_____ in red cells carries oxygen. Structures that help

form clots are _____ .

II. Circle the correct ending to each statement:

   A. A net of threads in a clot forms partly from *(plasma/white blood cells)*.
   B. A scab forms from dried *(platelets/red blood cells)*.

III. Blood clots sometimes form inside the body rather than where the skin is cut. Why could such a clot be harmful?

What Is the Job of Your Transport System?

Exploring Science

Birth of a Bloodstream. One night, early in this century, Dr. Florence Sabin worked late. Sabin was a professor at Johns Hopkins Medical School in Baltimore, Maryland. She later described that night in her lab as "the most exciting experience of my life."

What did Sabin see that was so exciting? As you might guess, it was something that was new to science. She had been watching an unborn chick, or embryo, as it grew. That night, under her microscope, tiny blood tubes formed. Blood cells then appeared, and the heart began to beat. She called what she saw "the birth of a bloodstream."

A chick's heart, blood tubes, and blood are in many ways like a human's. Seeing how these parts develop in a chick led to new knowledge of our own blood system. For example, Sabin showed where human blood cells are made. For the most part, these cells come from the center, or **marrow** (MAR-oh), of the long bones in the arms and legs.

Sabin also studied how certain blood cells help fight **tuberculosis** (too-bur-kyuh-LOH-sis), a lung disease that has killed many people. Some white blood cells can move like amebas.

They can move out of the blood and into the lungs. There they attack and kill the tuberculosis germs.

● What kinds of cells are probably found in a chick's blood? Why do you think so?

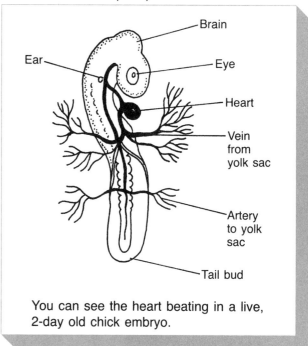

You can see the heart beating in a live, 2-day old chick embryo.

Your Transport System

The blood stream in Florence Sabin's chick was a transport system, just like a road or a railroad. So, too, is your bloodstream. It transports food, oxygen, and other materials. The main parts of this system are the blood vessels, heart, and blood. The blood goes in a complete path, or "circle," in the body. We say it **circulates** (SUR-kyuh-layts). Because of this, the transport system has another name: the **circulatory** (SUR-kyuh-luh-tohr-ee) **system.**

In the last lesson, you learned about the blood. In this one, we shall talk about the blood vessels and the heart.

Blood vessels are the tubes through which the blood moves. You have three kinds of blood vessels. **Arteries** (AR-tuh-rees) carry blood away from the heart. **Veins** (VAYNS) carry blood back to the heart. **Capillaries** (KAP-uh-ler-ees) connect arteries with veins.

The largest blood vessels are the arteries. And the largest artery in the human body is the **aorta** (AY-or-tuh). Blood leaving the heart goes through the aorta.

In the veins, valves let blood flow in only one direction—toward the heart. The valves are one-way doors.

The Transport System

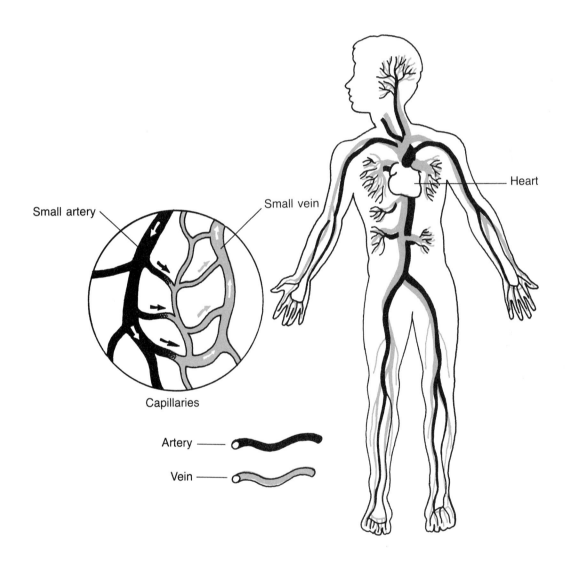

Small artery

Small vein

Capillaries

Artery

Vein

Heart

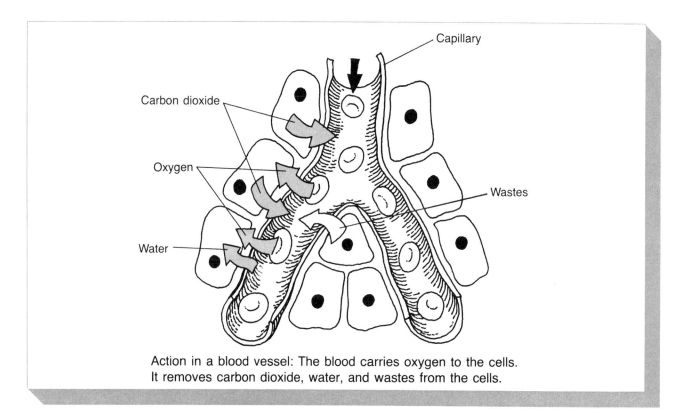

Action in a blood vessel: The blood carries oxygen to the cells. It removes carbon dioxide, water, and wastes from the cells.

You have millions of capillaries. These tiny blood tubes can be seen only with a microscope. They take the blood very close to every body cell.

The **heart** is a muscle whose job is to pump blood through the blood vessels. Your heart is about the size of a large fist. It lies at (or in) the center of your chest. The heart is two pumps in one. A wall of muscle divides the right pump from the left pump. Blood cannot flow from one side of the heart to the other.

Each side of the heart is divided into two chambers, or rooms. The upper chamber is an **atrium** (AY-tree-um). Veins carry blood to the atrium. The blood flows through the atrium to the lower chamber, which is called the **ventricle** (VEN-trih-kul). The job of the ventricle is to send blood out of the heart.

Between each atrium and ventricle is a **valve.** It keeps blood flowing in one direction: from the atrium to the ventricle. The valve prevents blood from flowing backward from the ventricle to the atrium.

Each time your heart beats, it **contracts,** or squeezes together. This pushes blood out of the heart into the arteries. The force of this muscle makes the arteries beat, too. The beating of the arteries is your **pulse.** Wherever an artery is close to the skin, you can feel your pulse.

To take your pulse, count the number of pulse beats for 6 seconds. Multiplying that number by 10 gives you your pulse.

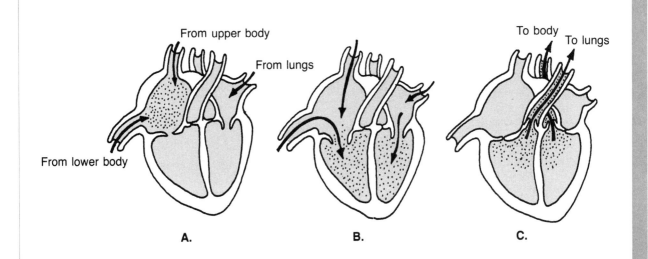

From upper body
From lungs
From lower body
To body
To lungs

A.

B.

C.

In A, blood enters the atria from the body and lungs. In B, the atria force the blood into the ventricles. In C, the ventricles send the blood to the body and the lungs.

Review

I. Write the names of the parts of the transport, or circulatory, system that match each clue below. Find each name in this list:

arteries   capillaries   ventricle   vein   atrium   valve   heart   cell

A. upper chamber in heart _____

B. lower chamber in heart _____

C. carry blood away from heart _____

D. carry blood toward heart _____

E. one-way door in heart or vein _____

F. smallest blood vessels in body _____

II. Circle the correct ending to each statement.

A. A blood vessel that has a pulse is *(an artery/a vein)*.
B. Because blood carries food and oxygen to cells, it *(contracts/circulates)*.
C. Blood flows from an atrium into a *(vein/ventricle)*.
D. Capillaries connect an artery with a *(vein/atrium)*

III. Unlike your veins, your arteries do not need valves. Can you explain why?

_____

_____

_____

What is the Path of Your Blood?

Exploring Science

Harvey the "Circulator." In the 1600s in England, quacks, or people who were not really doctors, sold remedies in medicine shows. These shows went around, or circulated, through the country. The quacks were called "circulators" (SUR-kyuh-lay-turs). When William Harvey, a real doctor, first announced that the blood circulates, people laughed at him. They called him a "circulator," as if he were a quack, too.

Before Harvey began his experiments on the blood's path, people thought the arteries were air tubes. They knew that the heart beats, but had no idea why. They also knew they had blood in their veins. But they thought the veins were two-way "streets," and that the blood moved in both directions.

Harvey showed that the heart beats because it is a pump. He showed that both arteries and veins carry blood. And he said that the blood tubes are one-way "streets." It was clear to Harvey that blood moves in only one direction, and that it goes in "circles."

Harvey was sure that somehow blood from the arteries moves into the veins. But he could find no tubes linking arteries with veins. Still, he predicted that someday the links would be found.

People did not want to believe in anything they could not see. They did not believe Harvey's theory. In 1661, only four years after Harvey died, Marcello Malphigi, in Italy, found the tubes Harvey could not see. Malphigi had a tool that Harvey did not have—a microscope. And, as you have already learned, capillaries are microscopic. That is, they can be seen only with a microscope. After that, everyone stopped laughing at Harvey.

● Circle the word (or words) that makes the statement true:

Harvey *(could/could not)* have predicted that the red blood cells carry oxygen to the body tissues. Explain your answer.

William Harvey discovered the circulation of the blood.

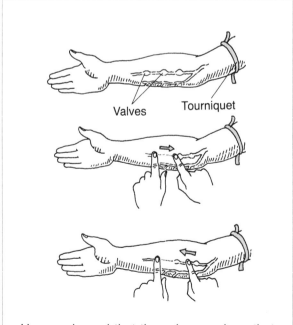

Harvey showed that the valves work so that blood flows in one direction only—toward the heart.

The Path of the Blood

Because of Harvey's pioneer work, you can trace the path of your blood through your body. To do so, use the diagram shown here. In the steps below, the numbers match those in the diagram.

(1) Blood in the right atrium has come from your body cells. This blood is high in carbon dioxide and low in oxygen. Its color is dark red.

(2) The right atrium contracts. Blood flows through a one-way valve into your right ventricle.

(3) The right ventricle contracts. This pushes the blood into the arteries that go to your lungs.

(4) The blood goes into the lung's capillaries. There, carbon dioxide moves out of the blood and oxygen moves into the blood. Now your blood is low in carbon dioxide and high in oxygen. Your blood is now bright red.

(5) The blood moves through veins from the lungs into the left atrium.

(6) The left atrium contracts. The blood goes through a one-way valve into your left ventricle.

(7) The left ventricle contracts. This pumps the blood into your body's largest artery, the aorta.

(8) The aorta divides into other arteries. Some arteries take blood into your upper body. Other arteries take blood to your lower body.

(9) The arteries divide again and again. Blood moves from the smallest arteries into capillaries all over your body. There, oxygen passes from your blood into your body cells. Carbon dioxide passes from your body cells into the blood.

Other materials also pass between the blood and the body's cells. When blood goes through the capillaries of your intestines, it picks up digested foods. The food molecules pass from the blood into all cells of your body. Besides carbon dioxide, other wastes also pass from your cells into your blood.

(10) From the capillaries, blood moves into the smallest veins. Small veins join together to form large veins. The largest veins take your blood back into your right atrium.

Your blood has completed a round trip—from the right atrium back to the right atrium.

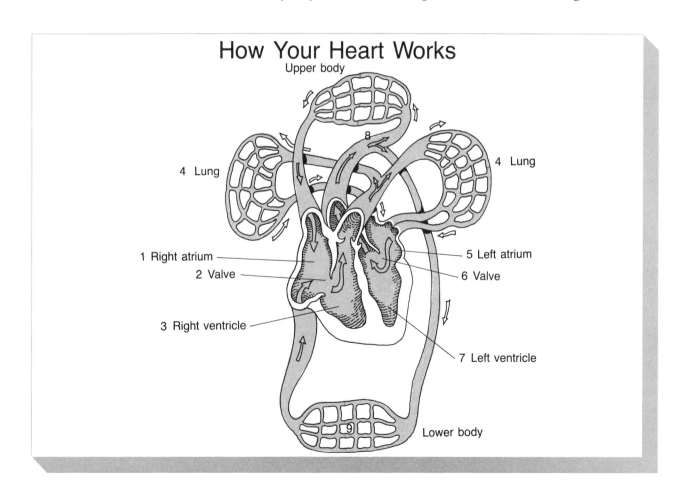

How Your Heart Works

Upper body

4 Lung

4 Lung

8

1 Right atrium

2 Valve

3 Right ventricle

5 Left atrium

6 Valve

7 Left ventricle

9

Lower body

To Do Yourself
What Is Inside a Heart?

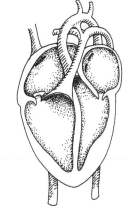

You will need:

Pig heart, sharp scissors or knife

1. Observe the pig heart. Find and count the blood vessels.
2. Cut the heart open. Your teacher may help you do this or show it.
3. Count the chambers and find the valves.
4. Find the section that has the most muscle—the thickest walls.

Questions

1. How many chambers does the heart have? What is the function of each? _____

_____

_____

2. Where are the valves? What is their function? _____

_____

_____

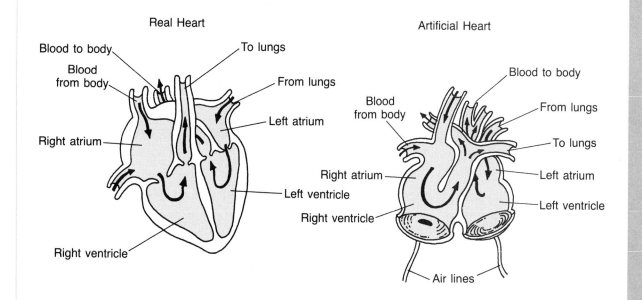

How Real and Artificial Hearts Work

Real Heart

Blood to body
Blood from body
Right atrium
Right ventricle

To lungs
From lungs
Left atrium
Left ventricle

Artificial Heart

Blood from body
Right atrium
Right ventricle

Blood to body
From lungs
To lungs
Left atrium
Left ventricle
Air lines

Blood flow through the heart is the same in both hearts. In an artificial heart, blood flows when compressed air pushes against a rubber diaphragm at bottom of each ventricle.

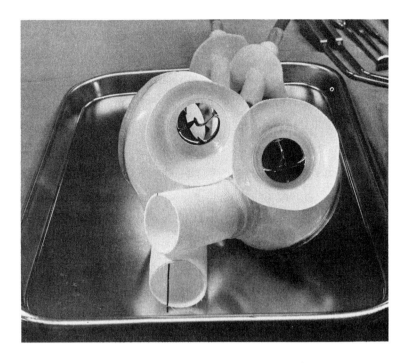

The Jarvik artificial heart can replace a real heart in humans.

Review

I. Write the names of the parts of the transport, or circulatory, system in the order in which blood passes through them. Start with the right atrium. Find the other parts in this list:

arteries to body
capillaries in lungs
veins from body
arteries to lungs
right ventricle

left ventricle
veins from lungs
capillaries in body
left atrium

A. __right atrium__

B. _____

C. _____

D. _____

E. _____

F. _____

G. _____

H. _____

I. _____

J. _____

II. Circle the correct ending to each statement:

A. The aorta is the body's largest *(vein/artery)*.
B. Carbon dioxide passes into the blood in the capillaries of the *(body/lungs)*.
C. Blood in the right ventricle is *(low/high)* in oxygen.
D. The color of the blood in the left atrium is *(dark/bright)* red.

III. The blood that goes through arteries to the body cells is rich in oxygen. If this blood is mixed with blood that is low in oxygen, the skin can look blue. One cause of the color of "blue babies" is a hole between the right atrium and left atrium.

A. Explain why such babies are "blue."
B. How can an operation save these babies?

A. Use the clues below to complete the crossword.

Across
   1. Sending chamber in heart
   5. Where digested food goes into the blood
   6. Formed with the help of platelets
   8. Liquid part of blood
   10. Vessels that carry blood toward the heart
   11. Blood cells that contain hemoglobin
   12. Dried net of threads and blood cells

Down
   1. Keeps blood flowing in one direction
   2. To go around in a circle
   3. Digested fats are glycerol and

   _____ acids
   4. To break down into small molecules
   7. They produce juices that contain enzymes
   9. Where feces leave the body

B. Write the word (or words) that best completes each statement.

   1. _____ A digestive juice made by the pancreas does its
      work in the **a.** esophagus **b.** stomach **c.** small intestine

   2. _____ Gastric juice helps to digest **a.** fiber **b.** meat
      c. oil

   3. _____ Bile is made in the **a.** liver **b.** villi **c.** appendix

   4. _____ Saliva starts to break starch into **a.** amino acids
      b. fatty acids **c.** sugar

   5. _____ Food and oxygen pass into cells through the
      walls of **a.** arteries **b.** veins **c.** capillaries

   6. _____ The heart's receiving chambers are its
      a. arteries **b.** atriums **c.** aortas

   7. _____ Carrying oxygen is the job of the **a.** red blood
      cells **b.** white blood cells **c.** platelets

   8. _____ Amino acids are formed by the digestion of
      a. fats **b.** proteins **c.** starches

   9. _____ Chewing food is part of digestion called
      a. gastric **b.** chemical **c.** mechanical

   10. _____ Blood returning to the heart from the lungs is
      a. high in carbon dioxide **b.** low in oxygen **c.** high in oxygen

11. _____ The longest part of the digestive system is the
  a. large intestine **b.** small intestine **c.** esophagus

12. _____ The most numerous cells in the blood are the
  a. white blood cells **b.** red blood cells **c.** platelets

13. _____ The gall bladder stores a liquid that helps to
  digest **a.** proteins **b.** starches **c.** fats

14. _____ Carbon dioxide passes out of the blood through
  the walls of **a.** veins **b.** capillaries **c.** the aorta

15. _____ Glycerol is formed from the digestion of
  a. fats **b.** proteins **c.** fiber

C. Apply What You Know

1. Study the drawing below of some body parts. Write labels for each
  numbered part. Use these labels:

  liver   large intestine   heart   salivary glands   esophagus   aorta

  small intestine   stomach

2. Some of the parts of two body systems are shown. What are those systems?

  _____

3. List the numbers of the parts that belong to each system named in question

  2. _____

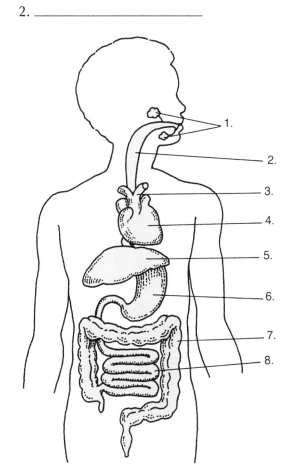

D. Find Out More

1. Obtain a fresh, whole fish. Using a source book from the library, find the following parts of its digestive system: pharynx (throat), stomach, intestine, liver, gallbladder. Also find the following parts of its circulatory system: heart (cut open to find its chambers), blood vessels (the larger ones can be seen). What are some differences between the fish's organs and yours?

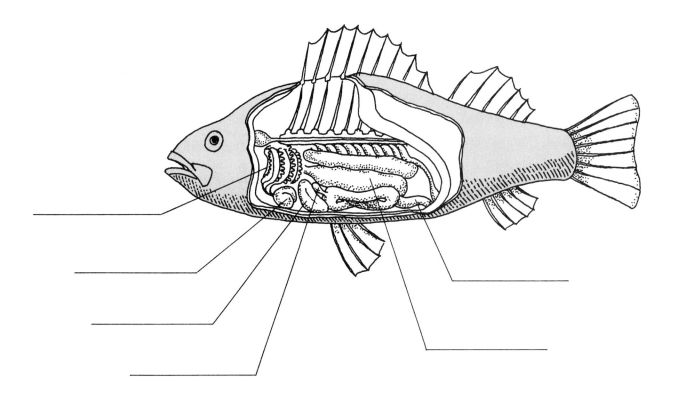

2. Plants, as well as animals, produce enzymes that digest foods. An enzyme that digests protein is found in papayas. A meat-tenderizer you can find in a supermarket contains this enzyme from papayas. To show how meat-tenderizer acts on the protein in egg white, try this. In one test tube, place bits of cooked egg white, water, and meat tenderizer. In another test tube, place only the egg white and water. Let stand several hours. What do you observe? Explain.

   Another protein-digesting enzyme is found in fresh pineapple juice. If the pineapple is cooked, as it is when it is canned, the enzyme is destroyed. Gelatin is a protein. People often add fruit to gelatin when making salads or desserts. Try this. Prepare one dish of gelatin to which fresh pineapple is added. Add canned or cooked pineapple to another dish of gelatin. What do you observe? Explain.

3. In the library, read about blood types. Why are blood types important? Visit a blood bank or a hospital laboratory. Ask to see how blood types are found. From your own doctor, you may find out what your blood type is. Make a bulletin-board display to explain what you have found out.

Careers in Life Science

Sports Medicine. Are you a sports fan? Join the crowd. So are 35 million Americans. Do you play sports or do daily exercise? Join an even bigger crowd. Close to half of all Americans—about 100 million—take part in physical activity every day. These numbers are getting larger all the time. So are the numbers of people with careers in sports medicine.

Athletic Trainers. Do you love both sports and science? Do you like helping people? Athletic trainers need these qualities. Their work helps both amateur and professional athletes perform better. Trainers help athletes prevent and recover from injury.

Some athletic trainers get started while still in high school. They work with more experienced trainers. Both the coach and the team doctor depend on the trainers—as do the athletes themselves—for many special tasks. To become a certified athletic trainer, four years of college are required.

Sports Physical Therapist. The same interests and talents that lead some people into careers as trainers lead others into careers as sports physical therapists. Athletes who have been injured, or who need surgery, are first treated by doctors. Then the physical therapist takes over. He or she plans and carries out treatments ordered by the doctor. The object: to relieve pain,

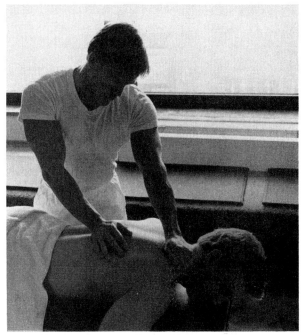

An athletic trainer applies a friction massage on injured player's back.

restore use of the injured parts, prevent further injury, and get the player back into action.

You can become a physical therapy assistant with two years of technical school. You need four years of college to become a licensed physical therapist. An assistant therapist works under the direction of a licensed therapist.

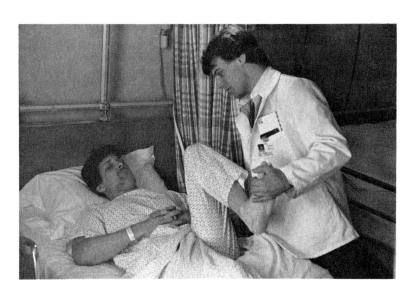

A physical therapist helps an athlete exercise an injured leg.

5

BREATHING AND MOVEMENT

What Is the Job of Your Respiratory System?

Exploring Science

Breath of Thin Air. In 1981, scientist Chris Pizzo set a record for the world's highest Frisbee throw. He did this while standing on top of the world's highest mountain, Mt. Everest.

Chris Pizzo on Mt. Everest. An oxygen mask and a gas sampler hang from his shoulder.

Of course, Pizzo didn't climb the mountain just to throw a Frisbee. He was part of the American Medical Research Expedition. Over 300 people carried scientific equipment to a camp two-thirds of the way up Mt. Everest. The air there is very thin. It contains only half as much oxygen as at sea level. Tests were done to learn how much work people can do while breathing so little air.

Pizzo climbed the rest of the way to Everest's top. The air up there is so thin that Pizzo needed extra oxygen. So he wore an oxygen mask. He also took along a gas sampler. As he climbed into thinner air, Pizzo went without the mask for a few minutes at a time. Before he put the mask on again, he breathed into the sampler. He took the air samples back to the camp, where they were studied by other scientists.

The scientists found out just how thin the air at the top of Mt. Everest is. They also found out how little oxygen is needed to keep a person alive and well. Doctors are using these findings to help people with breathing problems.

● Circle the word that makes the sentence correct:

People who live in very high places, such as the mountains of Peru, breathe (faster/slower) than people who live at sea level. Explain your answer.

Your Respiratory System

You need oxygen to keep alive. You get this oxygen from air, which is about one-fifth oxygen. But as you climb up from sea level, the air gets thinner. Your lungs have to work much harder to get the same amount of oxygen.

Your breathing organs take air into and let air out of your body. These organs make up your **respiratory** (RES-per-uh-tohr-ee) **system.**

When you breathe in, or **inhale,** you take air

into your nose. There the air becomes warm and moist. From your nose, air goes down your throat and into your **windpipe.** Rings of stiff tissue keep the windpipe open. You can feel these rings in your throat.

In both the nose and the windpipe, air is cleaned. **Cilia** (SIL-ee-uh), which are like little hairs, catch dust and other bits of dirt. **Mucus** (MYOO-kus), a sticky liquid, traps dirt.

The Respiratory System

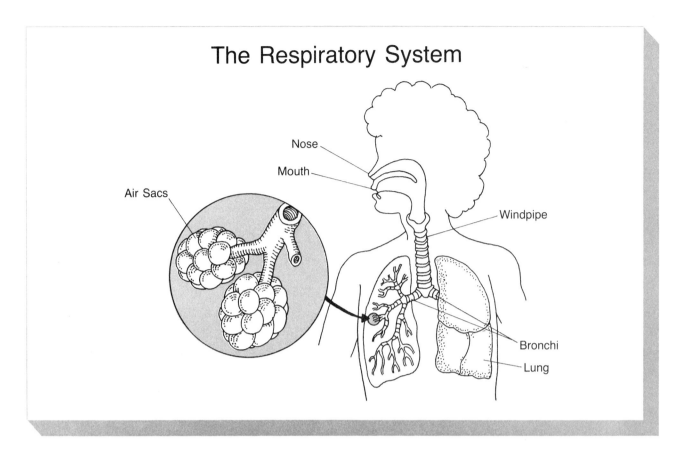

To Do Yourself What is Your Lung Capacity?

You will need:

Piece of rubber tubing, tank, water, saucer, measuring cup

1. Set up the bottle of water and the rubber tube as shown.
2. Inhale and fill your lungs with air. Exhale, blowing slowly through the rubber tube.
3. Slide the saucer under the mouth of the jar. Take the jar from the tank. Fill it with water, using the measuring cup. Record how much water you need to fill the jar. This is the amount of air you exhaled.
4. Make three more trials and take an average.

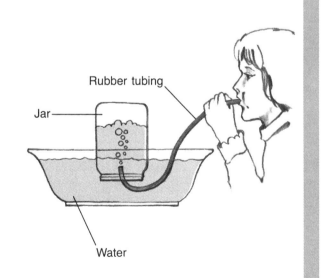

Questions

1. What is the air capacity of your lungs _____

2. How does this compare with others in your class? _____

The windpipe branches into two air tubes called **bronchi** (BRONG-ky) (the singular is **bronchus,** BRONG-kus). One tube, or bronchus, goes to each lung. In the lung, the bronchus branches like a tree, into smaller and smaller tubes. The tubes end in millions of tiny **air sacs** (SAKS).

Each air sac has tiny blood vessels called **capillaries** around it. Oxygen goes from the air in each sac into the blood. At the same time, carbon dioxide goes from the blood into the air. Some water also goes from the blood into the air.

When you breathe out, or **exhale,** the air passes back through the same parts that it came in. But the air you exhale has less oxygen and more carbon dioxide than the air you inhale. Do you know why? There also is more water in the air that you exhale. Where do you think the water comes from?

Review

I. Fill each blank with the word that fits best. Use these words:

mucus   exhale   respiratory   cilia   inhale   bronchus   oxygen

Your _____ system takes air into and lets air out of your

II. body. When you _____ , you breathe in. When you

_____ , you breathe out. Hairlike parts that clean the air

are _____ . A sticky liquid that traps dirt is _____ .

List, in order, the body parts that oxygen passes through during respiration. Start with the nose. Use these parts:

bronchi   throat   capillaries   windpipe   air sacs

A. ___nose___   C. _____   E. _____

B. _____   D. _____   F. _____

III. Circle the word that makes each statement correct.

A. Air that you exhale contains (more/less) carbon dioxide than air you inhale.
B. Capillaries that take blood into the lungs contain (more/less) oxygen than those carrying blood out of the lungs.

IV. Smoking can destroy cilia. How might this lead to lung disease?

_____

_____

_____

What Happens When You Breathe?

Exploring Science

The Boy Who Did Not Drown. One January day, not long ago, Jimmy Tontlewicz went sledding with his dad along the shore of Lake Michigan. Four-year-old Jimmy threw his sled onto the frozen lake. His dad walked onto the ice to bring back the sled. Jimmy followed. He jumped onto the ice . . . and both of them fell through.

Jimmy's dad was able to stay afloat until help arrived. But Jimmy went under. When divers finally pulled Jimmy out, there were no signs of life.

A few years ago, Jimmy would have been another boy who drowned. Scientists used to think that no one could be alive after more than 4 minutes under water. Jimmy had been under for 20 minutes. It is now known that people may be alive even after 30 minutes in cold water.

The rescue team used CPR—a method anyone can learn—to help Jimmy's heart to beat and start his breathing again. In the hospital doctors used special new ways to help Jimmy. Soon he was on the way to being well again.

Jimmy Tontlewicz, 10 days after he almost drowned.

● Explain how Jimmy's case shows that the body can store oxygen for use at a later time.

 ## To Do Yourself — How Can You Measure The Carbon Dioxide You Exhale?

You will need:

Methylene blue solution, straw, glass jar, clock or watch with second hand

1. Fill the jar half full with methylene blue solution.
2. Take a deep breath and exhale through the straw into the solution.
3. When enough carbon dioxide is bubbled through methylene blue solution it turns yellow. Have a partner time how long it takes for you to do this.

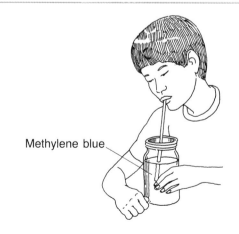

Methylene blue

Questions

1. How long did it take for the methylene blue to change to yellow? _____

2. How did this time compare with other students? _____

Respiration and Breathing

When Jimmy went under the water, he could no longer take oxygen into his lungs. But there was already enough oxygen in his body to keep him alive for a while. His breathing and even his heartbeat stopped. But a process that keeps the cells alive did not stop. That process was **cell respiration.**

Like the cells of most living things, your cells take in both oxygen and food. When the food, in the form of simple sugar, combines with the oxygen, energy is released. Carbon dioxide and water are given off. This process is respiration.

Breathing means getting air into and out of the lungs. Muscles in your chest help you breathe. One of your breathing muscles is the **diaphragm** (DY-uh-fram). The diaphragm is like a sheet. It lies below the lungs. At rest, the diaphragm is curved like a bowl upside down. When you breathe in, your diaphragm moves down and becomes less curved. At the same time, rib muscles move your ribs up and out. As a result, the space inside your chest gets larger. Air rushes from the outside into your lungs to fill the larger space.

When you breathe out, your diaphragm moves up, becoming more curved. At the same time, your ribs move down and in. The space inside your chest gets smaller. The air is pushed from your lungs to the outside.

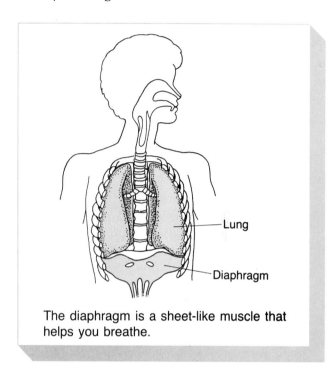

The diaphragm is a sheet-like muscle that helps you breathe.

Review

I. Fill each blank with the word that fits best. Use these words:

breathing   **respiration**   **CPR**   **diaphragm**   **ribs**   **bronchi**

In cell _____ ,sugar combines with oxygen. In the process

of _____ , air moves into and out of your lungs. Muscles

move your _____ up and out when you breathe in. When

your _____ moves up, air is pushed out of your lungs.

II. Circle the word or phrase that makes each statement correct.

   A. The diaphragm becomes (more/less) curved when you inhale.
   B. When you exhale, your ribs move (up and out/down and in).
   C. A process that takes place in every body cell is (breathing/respiration).

III. Some bacteria can live only *without* air.

   A. Do they carry on respiration?
   B. How do you think they survive?

How Does Your Body Get Rid of Wastes?

Exploring Science

Going for the Gold. In the 1984 Olympics at Los Angeles, cyclist Connie Carpenter "went for the gold." And she won it—the gold medal for coming in first. The race itself was a "first." It was the first Olympic women's bicycle road race ever held.

Only 12 centimeters behind Carpenter was Rebecca Twigg, who won the silver medal. Nearly as close was Sandra Schumacher, who won the bronze medal. Also very close was Unni Larson, who came in fourth.

After the race ended, Carpenter, Twigg, Schumacher, and Larson each had to give a urine sample for drug tests. So did the top four athletes in every other Olympics event. In all, 1500 urine samples were tested. A machine able to find tiny amounts of dozens of different drugs was used.

Why were the urine tests done? Some athletes think certain drugs help them do better. Some drugs give a person more "pep." Some drugs can make muscles bigger and stronger. But it has been shown that these drugs, and others, also harm the body. So Olympic athletes may not use such drugs, in the interests of both health and fair play. The urine tests help make sure that every medal winner is drug-free.

Connie Carpenter, winner of the 49-mile bicycle race at the Los Angeles Olympics.

● Circle the word that makes the second sentence correct:

The kidneys are the organs that produce urine. One job of the kidneys is to take (harmful/useful) materials out of the blood. Explain your answer.

Getting Rid of Wastes

If someone takes drugs, the drugs enter his or her bloodstream and are carried to the cells. Remains of the drugs will be given off by the cells as wastes. Tests are used to find the wastes and tell what drugs were used, as at the Olympics.

Your cells give off many wastes. These include water, carbon dioxide, salts, and urea. **Urea** (yoo-REE-uh) is formed when amino acids are broken down. All of these wastes must be removed from your body or you will get very sick. Getting rid of wastes is called **excretion** (ik-SKREE-shun).

The cells pass their wastes into the blood. The blood carries the wastes to the lungs, kidneys, and skin. Excretion takes place through these organs.

LUNGS. Your lungs remove carbon dioxide and some water from your body. When you breathe out, your lungs **excrete** (ik-SKREET), or get rid of, these wastes. If a person drinks alcohol, some of the alcohol will be given off by the lungs. Police sometimes test automobile drivers' breath to see if they have been drinking.

KIDNEYS. Water, urea, and other wastes are removed from the blood by your two kidneys.

The kidneys are in the back part of your body, just above your waist. Each is about the size of your fist.

In each kidney there are thousands of tiny filters. As the blood passes through the filters, the wastes are removed. These wastes, plus water, form a liquid called **urine** (YOOR-in).

The urine flows from the filters into a tube called the **ureter** (yoo-REE-tur). One ureter from each kidney carries the urine into the **bladder.** The bladder is an elastic sac that stores urine until it is excreted. The urine leaves your body through a tube called the **urethra** (yoo-REE-thruh).

SKIN. Your skin covers and protects your body. It is also an organ of excretion. Your skin contains two million tiny **sweat glands.** Capillaries carry blood close to each sweat gland. Waste water, salts, and some urea move from the capillaries into the sweat glands. These wastes make up a liquid called **sweat.**

At the top of each sweat gland is an opening in the skin. This opening is called a **pore.** Sweat leaves your body through the pores.

Your skin also helps to control your body's temperature. When your body is too warm, more blood flows to the skin. You sweat more. Sweat on the skin evaporates, or turns into water vapor. This uses heat, and helps cool your body.

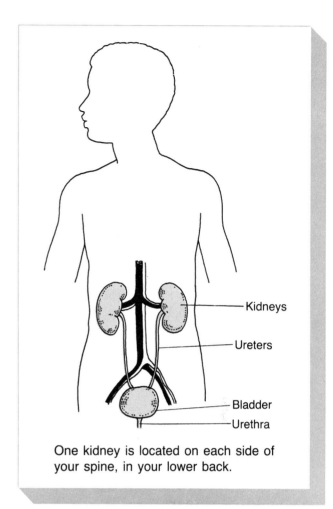

Kidneys
Ureters
Bladder
Urethra

One kidney is located on each side of your spine, in your lower back.

Paul Van Winkel of Belgium won the 1,500-meter wheelchair race in the Los Angeles Olympics.

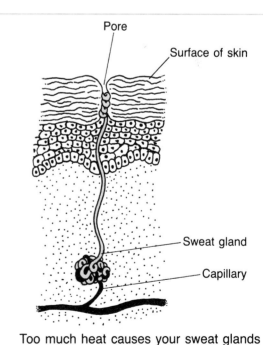

Pore
Surface of skin
Sweat gland
Capillary

Too much heat causes your sweat glands to make sweat, which goes through the pores to the surface of the skin. The sweat cools the skin.

To Do Yourself How Does Sweating Cool the Body?

You will need:

Water, 2 thermometers, piece of cardboard, cotton

1. Use wet cotton to cover an area of your skin with water.
2. Fan both the wet area and a dry area with cardboard. Record which area feels cooler.
3. Place one thermometer in a ball of wet cotton. Place the other thermometer next to it. Take and record the temperatures.
4. Fan both thermometers for several minutes. Again, take and record the temperatures.

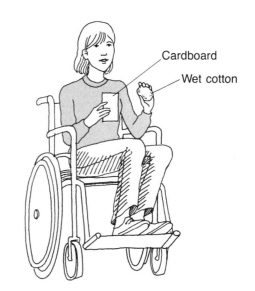

Questions

1. Which area of the skin was cooler? _____

2. Which thermometer recorded a lower temperature? _____
3. Besides getting rid of wastes, why is sweating important to your body?

_____

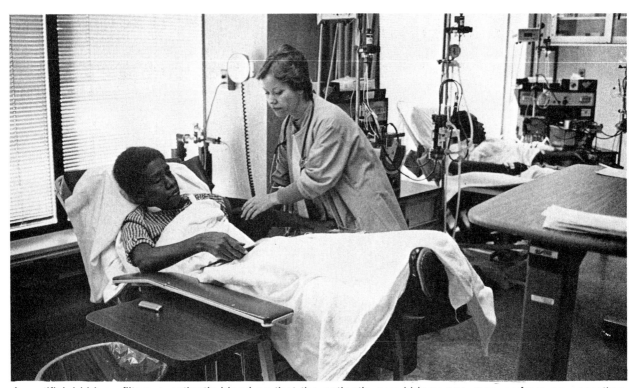

An artificial kidney filters a patient's blood so that the patient's own kidney can recover from an operation.

Review

I. Fill in each blank with the word that fits best. Use these words:

urea   bladder   pores   urethra   filter   sweat   ureter
excretion   urine

The process of getting rid of cell wastes is _____ . The

kidneys _____ wastes from the blood. The waste made by

the kidneys is called _____ . A big tube called a

_____ carries urine from each kidney to the _____ .

Urine passes from the bladder through the _____ to the

outside of the body. The _____ glands excrete wastes

through _____ in the skin.

II. For each organ in the list below, write the names of the wastes that are
excreted through that organ. (Some wastes will be listed more than once.) Use
this list of wastes:

urea   salts   water   carbon dioxide

A. lungs _____

B. kidneys _____

C. skin _____

III. When you go for a checkup, your urine is tested. If the doctor finds sugar in
your urine, this can be a sign of disease. Can you tell why?

IV. Label the organs of excretion on the lines below.

1. _____
2. _____
3. _____
4. _____

What Is Your Body's Framework?

Exploring Science

New Faces for Old Bones. What did humans look like 50,000 years ago? One group of people of that time were the Neanderthals (nee-AN-dur-thawls). Parts of their skulls and other bones have been found in both Europe and Asia. Were the Neanderthals rough, savage, and apelike? They are often shown that way in comics and movies.

Scientists' models and paintings of the Neanderthals also used to make them look animal-like. You may have seen them in science museums and books. Now, the same old bones of these early humans are being given new faces. The scientists who draw and shape the new faces are also artists.

To make a model, a scientist-artist starts with a plaster cast of the bones of a Neanderthal. The bones, and the casts made from them, have ridges and grooves on them. These are muscle scars. The scars show where muscles were once attached to the bones. They also provide clues as to what the muscles looked like.

Now the scientist-artist has an idea of what Neanderthal's muscles looked like. The next step is to model the muscles on the bones. The scientist-artist uses clay for this purpose. Clay is also used to shape the tip of the nose and the ears. Next, a thin layer of clay "skin" is added over the whole model.

Finally, the model is painted. The result looks much more like a modern-day human than do the crude, apelike models that used to be made from the same old bones. Most scientists agree that this new model is more accurate than the old one was.

● What part of the model face is probably made mostly by guesswork?   (A) nose (B) chin (C) forehead. Explain your answer.

To Do Yourself   What Does a Bone Look Like?

You will need:

Chicken bones, large beef bone sawed in half, hand lens

1. Scrape the outside of the bones and describe what you find.
2. Look for cartilage at the ends of the chicken bones.
3. Use a hand lens to examine the inside of the beef bone. Draw and label the parts you can identify.

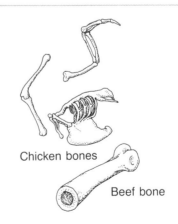

Chicken bones

Beef bone

Questions

1. How is the outside of the bone different from the inside? _____

_____

2. How is cartilage different from bone? _____

_____

Your Body's Framework

BONES. Like the Neanderthals of long ago, your body gets its shape from your bones. There are 206 bones in your body. Together, they make up your **skeleton** (SKEL-ih-tun).

The skeleton does much more than give shape to your body. It also provides the body's basic framework, much as wooden beams provide the framework for a house. Without the skeleton, you would not be able to stand upright.

Another job of your skeleton is protecting vital organs. Your skull protects your brain.

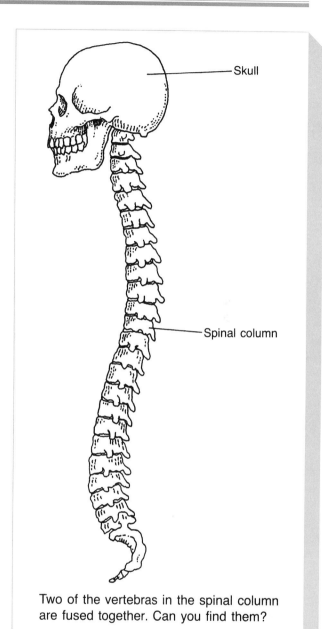

Two of the vertebras in the spinal column are fused together. Can you find them?

The Human Skeleton

How are your lower arms similar to your lower legs?

Your breastbone and ribs protect your heart and lungs. Your backbone, made of 33 **vertebrae,** encloses and protects your **spinal cord.** The spinal cord carries messages between your brain and the rest of your body.

Some bones have the job of making new blood cells. This work goes on in the soft center, or marrow, of the long bones in your arms and legs.

Your skeleton also enables you to move your body. Muscles that are attached to bones work with the bones when you move. You need both

Kinds of Joints

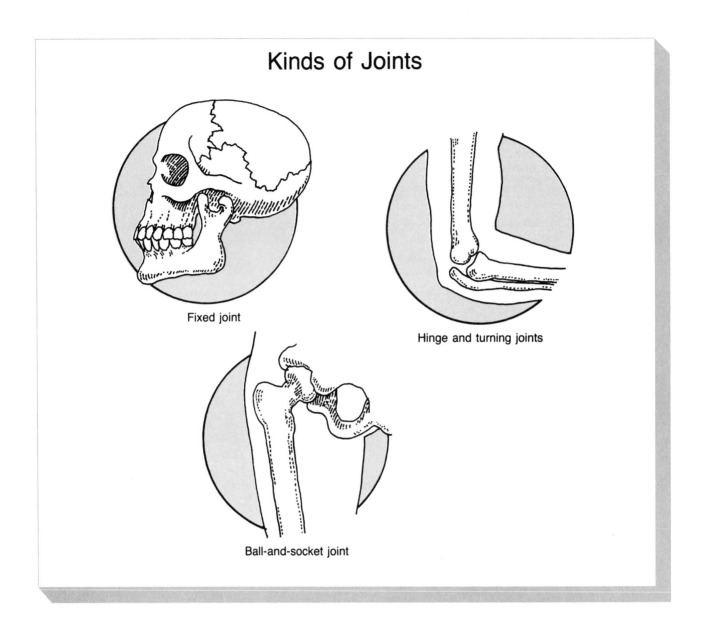

Fixed joint

Hinge and turning joints

Ball-and-socket joint

muscles and bones to walk, stand, sit, write, eat, speak, play sports or music, and so on.

Some parts of your skeleton are not made of bone. They are made of **cartilage** (KAR-tuh-lij). Cartilage is softer than bone. The outside of your ears and the tip of your nose are made of cartilage.

JOINTS. A place where two or more bones meet is a **joint** (JOYNT). Those joints that you can move are tied together by tough bands called **ligaments** (LIG-uh-munts).

You have several kinds of joints. The joint at your shoulder is a **ball-and-socket joint.** Your upper-arm bone has a ball at its end. This ball fits into a cup, or socket, in your shoulder blade. Your hip joint also is a ball-and-socket joint. At both the shoulder and the hip you can

make twisting movements. You also can swing an arm or a leg around in a full circle.

A **hinge joint** moves back and forth like a door on its hinge. Your knees and fingers have hinge joints.

Your elbow has two joints. Its hinge joint works when you raise and lower your forearm. Its **turning joint** works when you turn your hand over. With this joint you can move your lower arm in a half-circle.

Some joints are called **fixed joints** because they do not move. The "cracks" in your skull are fixed joints. When you were born, your skull bones were small. You had a soft spot on your head where the bones did not come together. As you grew, the skull bones grew too, until they finally joined.

Review

I. Fill each blank with the word that fits best. Choose from these words:

vertebrae   skeleton   supports   ligament   protects   shape   move

The body's inside frame is its _____ . The skeleton gives

your body its _____ and holds it up, or _____

it. Muscles attached to bones _____ the body. The bones

of the backbone are the _____ .

II. If the statement is true, write *T*. If it is false, write *F* and correct the underlined words.

A. _____ New blood is made in the <u>spinal cord</u>.

B. _____ The shoulder joint can be moved in a <u>full</u> circle.

C. _____ The vertebrae enclose and protect the <u>heart and lungs</u>.

D. _____ The tough bands that tie bones together are the <u>muscles</u>.

E. _____ The tip of your nose is made of <u>bone</u>.

F. _____ The cracks in your skull are <u>fixed</u> joints.

G. _____ <u>Ligaments</u> carry messages from the brain to the rest of the body.

H. _____ The knee is an example of a <u>hinge</u> joint.

III. Your wrist contains a type of joint called a sliding joint. Where else in the body are sliding joints found? Describe their movement.

_____

_____

_____

How Do Your Muscles Work?

Exploring Science

Tommy John's Elbow. One July day in 1974 the Los Angeles Dodgers were playing the Montreal Expos. Tommy John was pitching for the Dodgers. He had already won 13 games that season. Now, in the top of the fifth, it looked like another win. The score was Dodgers–4, Expos–0.

Suddenly, something snapped in John's elbow as he threw the ball. John was out of the game and in great pain. The elbow was seriously injured. Dr. Frank Jobe, the team doctor, was afraid that John might never use his arm again.

But Jobe tried a new way to operate on the elbow. It worked. Two years later, John was playing professional baseball again. By 1980, he was a star pitcher for the New York Yankees. That year, he had 22 wins.

How had the pitcher injured his elbow? What made it right again? Tommy John had torn a ligament in his pitching arm. Ligaments are bands of tissue that tie bones together where they meet. Dr. Jobe knew that **tendons** (TEN-duns) are made of nearly the same kind of tough tissue as ligaments. Tendons are bands that attach muscles to bones. Dr. Jobe's new idea was to use a piece of tendon to replace the torn ligament.

First, the doctor took a piece of tendon from John's right arm. Then he cut away the torn ligament in the left arm and put the tendon in its place. The operation was only meant to let John move his arm again. Dr. Jobe did not think it would let John pitch in a major-league game again. But John would not give up. As soon as his pitching arm healed, he began to practice. Slowly but surely, the arm became as good as new.

● Circle the word or words that makes the sentence correct:

If muscles were not attached to bones, you (could/could not) move your arm to throw a ball. Explain your answer.

Pitcher Tommy John had an unusual operation.

Your Body's Movers

When you throw a ball, you move your bones. But bones cannot move by themselves. Your body's movers are your muscles.

There are more than 600 muscles in your body. Many muscles are attached to bones by tendons. A **tendon** is a strong band of tissue. When a muscle shortens, or **contracts** (KON-trakts), it pulls on the tendon. At the same time, the tendon pulls on the bone. This causes the bone to move.

Muscles work in pairs. The two muscles of a pair cause opposite movements. In your upper arm the **biceps** (BY-seps) and **triceps** (TRY-seps) muscles are a pair. Try this: Squeeze the biceps on one upper arm. It is on the top side of the arm. Now squeeze the triceps. It is on the underside of the arm. Now bend the elbow. Feel how your biceps gets firm as it contracts. At the same time, you can feel how the triceps gets soft as it relaxes. Now straighten the elbow. The triceps contracts. You can feel how it gets firm. How does the biceps feel as it relaxes?

You can control your arm muscles. In fact, you can control all muscles that are attached to bones. These muscles are **voluntary** (VOL-un-ter-ee). The muscles in your arms, hands, legs, feet, face, neck, and trunk are voluntary. These muscles are made of a kind of muscle tissue

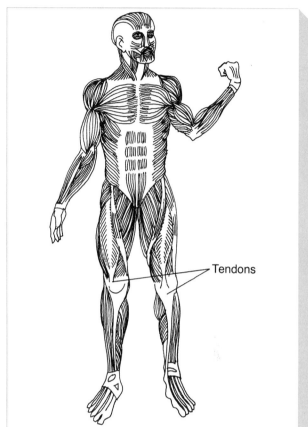

A tendon connects a bone to a muscle. What is the best known tendon in the human body, and where is it?

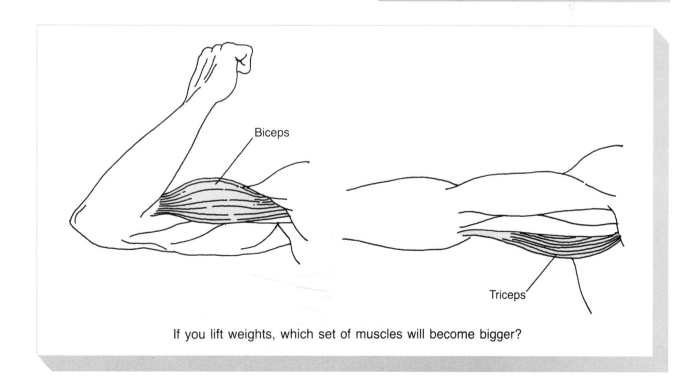

If you lift weights, which set of muscles will become bigger?

called **skeletal** (SKEL-ih-tul) **muscle** because they are attached to the skeleton.

Some muscles are not under your control. These muscles are **involuntary** (in-VOL-un-ter-ee). Certain involuntary muscles, such as those in your stomach and blood vessels, are made of a kind of tissue called **smooth muscle.**

Your heart is made of a kind of involuntary muscle tissue called **cardiac** (KAR-dee-ak) **muscle.** "Cardiac" means "of the heart." Cardiac muscle works harder than any other kind of muscle. Among other things, it must pump food and oxygen to those arm muscles so they are strong enough to throw a ball.

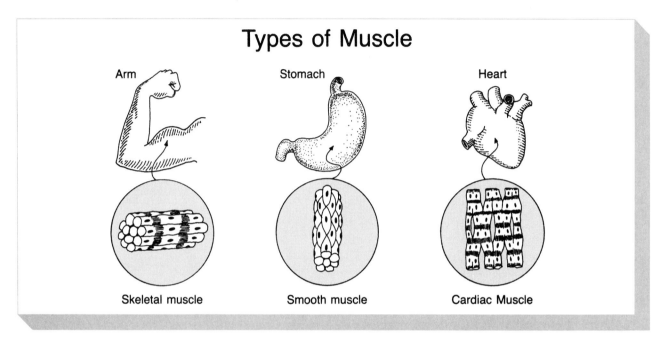

Types of Muscle

Arm

Stomach

Heart

Skeletal muscle

Smooth muscle

Cardiac Muscle

To Do Yourself   Where Are Your Muscles and Tendons?

You will need:

Chicken leg, including a thigh, hand lens, dissecting needle or probe, scissors

1. Skin the chicken leg and thigh.
2. With the dissecting needle or probe, pull apart the muscle layers. Look for tendons.
3. Pull on the tendons. Describe what happens.
4. Now find the muscles in your upper leg. Straighten your knee, as you feel the muscles work. Bend your knee and find the muscles that make this happen.

Dissecting needle

Chicken leg

Questions

1. Where are the muscles attached? _____

2. What attaches the muscles to the bones? _____

3. Which muscle bends the knee? Which straightens it? _____

Review

I. Fill in each blank with the word that fits best. Choose from these words:

**involuntary   biceps   contracts   triceps   voluntary   tendons
ligaments   relaxes**

Muscles are attached by _____ to bones. When a muscle

_____ it shortens. A pair of muscles in your upper arm are

your _____ and _____ . Muscles under

your control are _____ . Muscles not under your control

are _____ .

II. Write the name of the kind of muscle in list **B** that matches each body part in
list **A**.

	A		B
A.	_____ stomach		**1.** cardiac
B.	_____ heart		**2.** smooth
C.	_____ leg		**3.** skeletal
D.	_____ blood vessel		
E.	_____ finger		

III. Circle the word that correctly completes each statement.

A. When the biceps muscle contracts, the triceps (contracts/relaxes).
B. The muscles of your legs are (voluntary/involuntary).

IV. A pair of muscles in your upper leg are attached by tendons, called
hamstrings, to a bone in your lower leg. Describe the action of these muscles.

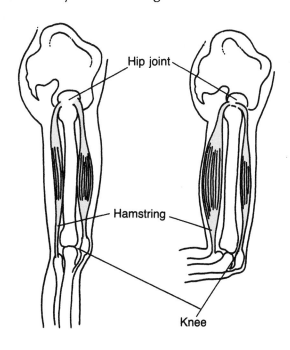

A. Unscramble the groups of letters to form science words. Write the words in the blanks.

1. P Y R R A T E S O I R (system that moves air) _____

2. N I R U E (produced in the kidneys) _____

3. K N L E S E O T (the body's framework) _____

4. C D A A I C R ("of the heart") _____

5. X I T E E N O C R (getting rid of wastes) _____

6. G E R T L I A C (found in outer ear) _____

B. Write the word (or words) that best completes each statement.

1. _____ Oxygen enters the blood through **a.** pores
b. cilia **c.** air sacs

2. _____ A joint in the elbow is called **a.** fixed **b.** hinge
c. ball-and-socket

3. _____ The biceps is made of muscle that is
a. skeletal **b.** smooth **c.** cardiac

4. _____ Bones are tied together at joints by **a.** tendons
b. ligaments **c.** triceps

5. _____ A waste excreted through sweat glands is
a. carbon dioxide **b.** mucus **c.** urea

6. _____ A tube that carries urine from a kidney to the
bladder is a **a.** ureter **b.** bronchus **c.** capillary

7. _____ An example of a voluntary muscle is one in the
a. leg **b.** stomach **c.** heart

8. _____ Carbon dioxide is excreted when we **a.** inhale
b. exhale **c.** sweat

9. _____ New blood cells are made in **a.** cartilage
b. hard bone **c.** marrow

10. _____ Salt is excreted through the **a.** kidneys
b. windpipe **c.** joints

11. _____ The muscle in a blood vessel is **a.** cardiac
b. skeletal **c.** smooth

12. _____ A muscle that bends the elbow when it contracts
is the **a.** triceps **b.** diaphragm **c.** biceps

13. _____ A waste produced by cell respiration is **a.** urea
b. carbon dioxide **c.** salt

C. Apply What You Know

1. Study the drawing of some of the parts of the body below. Write labels for each numbered part. Choose from these labels:

   ureters   windpipe   diaphragm   nose   bronchus   liver
   kidneys   urethra   lung   bladder

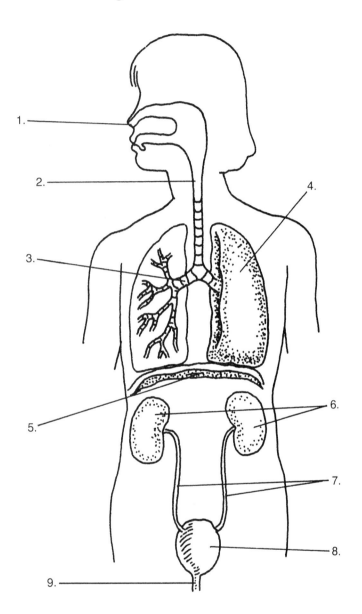

2. On each blank below, write the name of the correct part. Choose from the labels you used on the drawing in 1.

   a. Becomes more curved when air leaves the body. _____

   b. Made up of many tiny filters. _____

   c. Carries air from windpipe into lungs. _____

   d. Passes urine out of the body. _____

   e. Made up of many tiny air sacs. _____

3. Study the drawing of some of the parts of a human leg. Write labels for each numbered part. Choose from these labels:

tendon   lower leg bones   knee joint   ligaments   calf muscle   hip

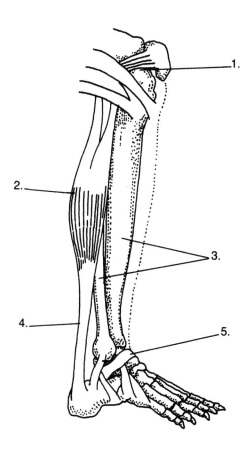

Write the number of the part that matches each statement below.

a. _____ Attaches a muscle to a bone.

b. _____ Has an action like a hinge.

c. _____ Are joined by ligaments to thigh bone.

d. _____ Tie lower leg bones to ankle bones.

e. _____ Contracts when you stand on tiptoe.

D. Find Out More

1. Calcium and other minerals make bones hard. What would a bone be without minerals? Try this with two chicken leg bones. Place one bone in a jar of vinegar. Keep the other one in the air. After a week, try to bend both bones. What happens? What can you do to be sure there is enough calcium in your bones?

2. Part of a physical checkup is to have your urine tested. Visit a hospital laboratory to see how test are done. What can doctors find out by testing urine?

3. In the library, find out what causes acne. Or talk to a dermatologist—a doctor who specializes in skin diseases. How can acne be cured? Report your findings.

A. Study the pictures. Each item is shown as it looks under the microscope.

   1. On the line below each picture, write its name. Choose from these names:

   cork   villi   diatoms   air sacs   smooth muscle   green leaf
   polio viruses   sweat gland   blood   skeletal muscle

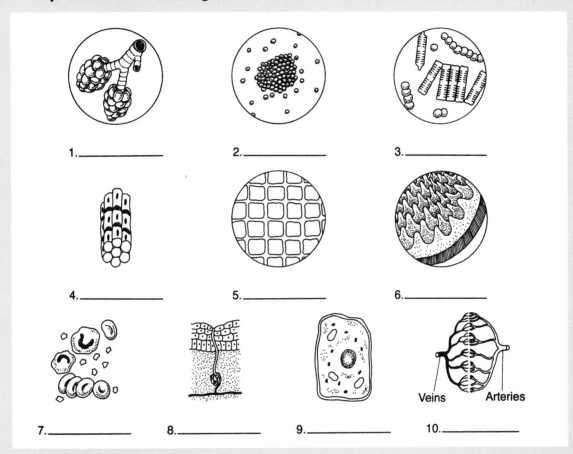

1._____   2._____   3._____

4._____   5._____   6._____

7._____   8._____   9._____   10._____

Veins   Arteries

B. Each statement below refers to one of the items shown. The number of the statement is the same as the number of the item. Circle the word (or words) that makes each statement correct.

   1. The gas that goes into the blood through their walls is (oxygen/carbon dioxide).
   2. Scientists do not all agree as to whether they (are living things/can reproduce).
   3. These are golden (fungi/algae) with glassy shells.
   4. This tissue is part of muscles that are (involuntary/voluntary).
   5. The scientist who called these "cells" was (Leewenhoek/Hooke)
   6. Digested food passes through their walls from the (large/small) intestine.
   7. These cells float in a liquid called (plasma/mucus).
   8. When the waste it excretes evaporates, the body is (warmed/cooled).
   9. The cytoplasm of these cells has parts that contain (cellulose/chlorophyll).
   10. They connect veins with (arteries/atriums).

BEHAVIOR AND CONTROL

Why Do Living Things Act as They Do?

Exploring Science

"Mother" Konrad Lorenz. Konrad Lorenz is a scientist who lives in Austria. One day Lorenz went for a walk in his garden. He crouched down and began to waddle. He flapped his arms. He called "gork-gork." After a while he stood up. Over the fence, a row of people stared at him. Why was a grown man acting like a duck?

While studying animal behavior, or how animals act toward their environment, Lorenz made an important discovery about ducks. For a short time after hatching, the first moving object a baby duck sees becomes its "mother." This kind of animal behavior is called **imprinting** (im-PRIN-ting).

Lorenz had let himself be imprinted by a group of baby ducks. They became attached to him and followed him everywhere. But, by quacking, they let him know that he also had to act like a duck. If he didn't, they became afraid and upset. That day in the garden, he wanted the baby ducks to feel happy. So he acted like a good mother to his "family." Tall grass, however, hid the baby ducks from view. The people could only see Lorenz. No wonder they stared!

● Before a baby duck hatches it can hear, but not see, through the egg shell. How might a duck become attached to its mother even before birth?

Konrad Lorenz walks with some of his imprinted geese.

The Behavior of Living Things

All the actions of a duck, a person, or any living thing make up its **behavior** (bih-HAYV-yur). What makes living things act, or **behave,** as they do? The behavior of living things helps them survive. It helps them get food, protection, and other things they need.

Like all living things, ducks receive many messages from their environment. These messages are called **stimuli** (STIM-yuh-ly). For Lorenz's ducks, the sight and sound of him were stimuli. (One message is a **stimulus.**)

A reaction to a stimulus is a **response** (rih-SPONS). The ducks' response to "Mother" Lorenz was to follow him everywhere. How is this behavior useful to baby ducks in the wild?

If you touch a hot stove, you pull your hand away quickly. The painful heat is a stimulus. Pulling away your hand is a response. This act protects you. It prevents your hand from being badly burned. When you are thirsty, your dry mouth is a stimulus. What will be your response? How is this response useful?

bright light

dim light

In bright light, the pupils become small; in dim light, the pupils become larger.

Some responses happen without your knowing about them. Digestive juice starts to flow when food enters your stomach. When you go into dim light, the openings of your eyes—called pupils—get larger. Why are these useful responses?

Some of your responses are not under your control. These are called **involuntary** responses. Pulling away from painful heat is involuntary. So are the flow of digestive juices and changes in the size of your pupils. Can you think of some other involuntary responses?

Some responses are under your control. These are **voluntary** responses. If you are at bat in a softball game, you decide whether or not to swing at a ball. This response is voluntary. Can you name some other voluntary responses?

Plants also respond to stimuli. Have you ever raised a plant on a windowsill? If so, you have seen how a plant's leaves grow toward light.

To Do Yourself How Do Some Animals Respond to Stimuli?

You will need:

Earthworm, shoebox lid, pencil, board, damp paper towels, flashlight, aluminum foil

1. Observe the earthworm as it responds to the touch of your hand.
2. There are nerve endings in each segment of the earthworm. Gently touch the top of the earthworm. Observe its response.
3. Place the earthworm on a wood board covered with a damp paper towel. Tap the board with a pencil. Observe the earthworm's response to the sound.
4. Place the earthworm on a damp paper towel in the shoebox lid. Cover half the lid with aluminum foil. Shine a flashlight on the earthworm. Observe its responses.

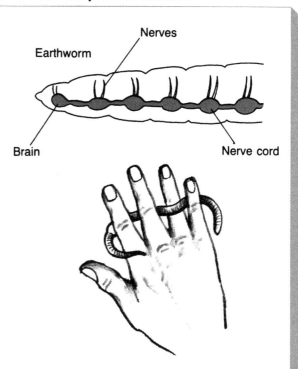

Questions

1. Which stimuli did the earthworm respond to? How did it respond? _____
2. How does the earthworm's body receive the messages of the different stimuli.

_____

Light is a stimulus. The plant's turning toward light is a response. How is this behavior useful to the plant? (Hint: Plants use light in the food-making process, which takes place in their leaves.)

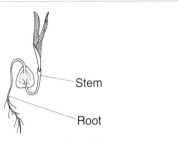

Stem

Root

If a seed is planted upside down, roots will still grow down and stem will still grow up. This response of plants is called geotropism.

A plant's stem bends so that the leaves of the plant always face toward the light.

Review

I. Fill each blank with the word that fits best. Choose your answers from these words:

survive   response   behave   involuntary   stimuli   stimulus

behavior   voluntary

The _____ of a living thing includes all of its actions. A message, such as heat or light, is a _____ . A reaction, such as a movement, is a _____ . The responses of living things helps them to _____ . The flow of gastric juice is a(n) _____ response. Hitting a softball is a(n) _____ response.

II. For each stimulus in list **A** draw a line to the correct response in list **B**. (One item in **B** does not match any in **A**.)

A Stimulus	**B** Response
(1) dog barks	**(a)** dog's ears lift
(2) odor of food	**(b)** pupils get smaller
(3) bright light	**(c)** person sneezes
(4) whistle	**(d)** plant's leaves turn away
(5) pepper in nose	**(e)** cat's hair stands on end
	(f) saliva flows in mouth

III. A willow tree is planted near a river. The roots of the tree grow toward the river. Why do you think they do this?

How Does Your Body Receive Messages?

Exploring Science

Does ET Really Exist? Stories and movies tell about intelligent beings on distant planets. These creatures are called **extraterrestrials**—(ek-struh-tuh-RES-tree-uls)—or ETs. "Extra" means "outside," and "terrestrial" comes from a word that means "earth." So an ET is a being from outside the earth. Do ETs really exist? Some scientists think so. They also think that we may someday "talk" to ETs.

How might we do this? One way is to send messages into space. In 1977, the spacecraft *Voyager I* was launched. Its main mission was to send back TV pictures of planets in our sun's family. Then it was to pass into deep space.

After thousands of years, it may reach a planet of another star.

If that planet has living creatures on it, they may receive messages that scientists have placed on *Voyager I*. Those messages are on a special phonograph record. On it are recorded voices in 55 languages. There are sounds of rain, a train whistle, the greeting call of a whale, and music. Other messages on the record can be used to form pictures of people, animals, and plants.

● By sending a record into space, what do scientists think must be true of intelligent ETs?

Voyager I has taken spectacular pictures of the outer planets.

Receiving Messages

How do you know what is going on around you? People and animals receive stimuli, or messages, through **sense organs.** These include the skin, tongue, nose, eyes, and ears. Each sense organ is sensitive to certain kinds of stimuli.

TOUCH. Your skin is a sense organ that covers your whole body. Suppose you gently touch your skin with a wire. Under each point where you feel the wire, there is a **nerve ending** sensitive to touch. Your skin has special nerve endings that receive five kinds of stimuli: touch, pressure, heat, cold, and pain.

Messages from your skin go through bundles of fibers called **nerves** to your **spinal cord.** The spinal cord relays messages from the skin and other parts of the body to the brain. The brain interprets those messages. Only then, when the messages reach your brain, can you feel what you touch.

TASTING AND SMELLING. Suppose you close your eyes, hold your nose, and have someone place a slice of apple or pear in your mouth. Your sense of taste will tell you if the fruit is sweet or sour. But you may have trouble telling whether it is an apple or a pear unless you let go of your nose. Why is this?

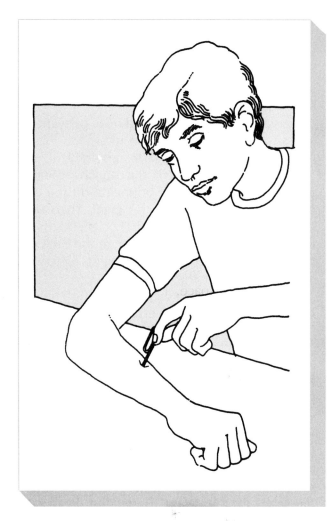

Your nose helps you taste food.

On the tongue there are four kinds of nerve endings sensitive to taste. The four tastes are: sweet, sour, salty, and bitter.

Many foods have one or more of the four kinds of taste. But part of what we call a food's taste is actually its odor or smell. The nose senses odors. It can identify many different food flavors and other smells.

Nerves from the tongue and nose carry messages to the brain. The brain interprets these messages so that you can taste and smell.

SEEING. When you look at a cat, what causes you to see the cat? Light bouncing off the cat enters your eye through the **pupil.** Then the light goes through the **lens.** The lens focuses light on the **retina** (RET-uh-nuh), at the back of the eye. The retina is sensitive to light. A picture of the cat forms on the retina.

From the retina, messages pass along a nerve to the brain. The brain interprets the messages so that you see a picture of the cat.

HEARING. When a friend speaks to you, what happens that causes you to hear what is said? He or she makes sound waves when speaking. Sound waves that enter your **outer ear** strike your **eardrum** and cause it to vibrate.

Attached to the eardrum are three tiny bones in the **middle ear.** When the eardrum vibrates, so do the three bones. The vibrations then pass to the **inner ear.** From the inner ear, nerves carry messages to your brain. There, the messages are interpreted so that you hear the sound of your friend's voice.

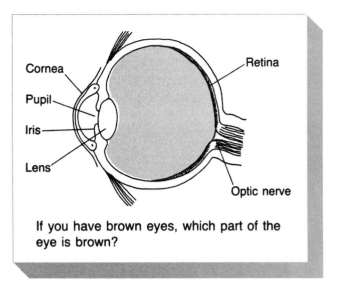

If you have brown eyes, which part of the eye is brown?

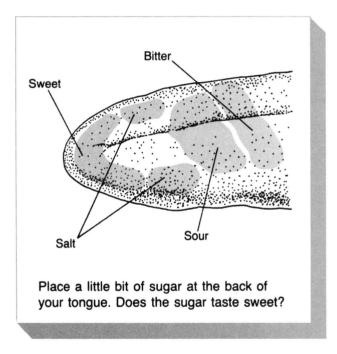

Place a little bit of sugar at the back of your tongue. Does the sugar taste sweet?

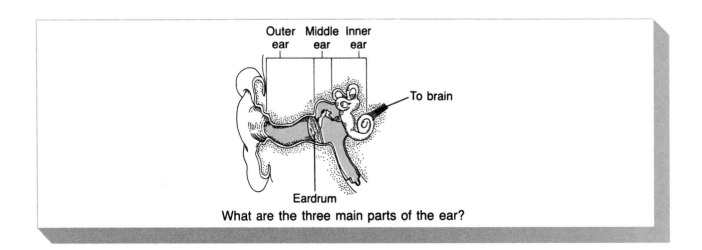

What are the three main parts of the ear?

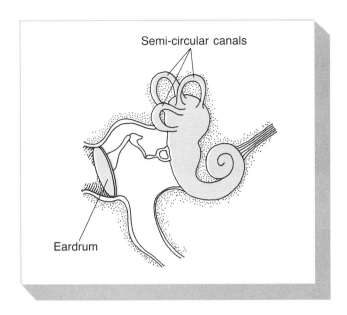

Semi-circular canals

Eardrum

Three tubes in the inner ear are filled with fluid. These tubes, called semi-circular canals, help you keep your balance. Astronauts floating in outer space may upset their semi-circular canals. This causes them to get motion sickness.

Review

I. Fill each blank with the word or phrase that fits best. Choose your answers from these words:

brain   stimuli   spinal cord   nerves   sense organs   responses

Through your _____ you receive messages from around

you. From each sense organ, _____ carry messages.

Messages from the skin are relayed by the _____ . In the

_____ messages from each sense organ are interpreted.

II. Name the five kinds of stimuli received by the skin. _____

III. What are the four kinds of tastes? _____

IV. Circle the word or phrase that makes each statement true.

   A. In the eye a picture of what you see is formed on the (lens/retina).
   B. From the eardrum vibrations pass to the bones of the (middle/inner) ear.
   C. When you touch something hot you feel the heat when messages reach the (spinal cord/brain).

V. Why might it be dangerous if you lost your sense of smell?

What Is the Job of Your Nervous System?

Exploring Science

Nan Davis Graduates—Walking and Standing Up. When Nan Davis was 18, she lost the power to move her legs. An auto accident left her lower body paralyzed. Nan had a break in her spinal cord that would never heal.

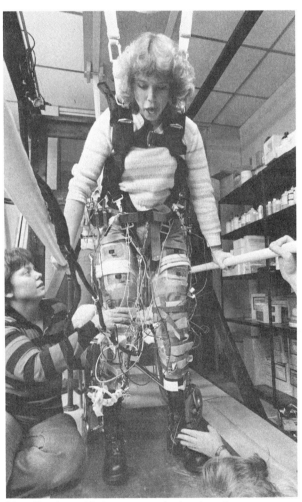

Nan Davis, with her computerized walker.

The spinal cord carries messages that tell muscles how to move. When the spinal cord is cut, it is like cutting a telephone wire. No messages can get through. In the past, people with Nan's kind of spinal injury were told, "You'll never walk again."

Nan arrived at Ohio's Wright State University in a wheelchair. There, Dr. Jerrold Petrofsky was experimenting with a computer to help people like Nan.

Using wires, Petrofsky connected Nan's muscles to the computer. He connected every muscle that Nan needed to stand and walk. The computer did the work of Nan's spinal cord. Now Nan could make her muscles move!

Nan's first computer "nervous system" was a large mass of wires. "When she walked, she looked like she was carrying her own telephone switchboard," said Petrofsky. But once he was sure all the connections were correct, he made the machine much smaller. Tiny computer chips replaced the wires. Then Nan could carry the whole thing in a school bag.

On graduation day in 1983, Nan stood up and walked to receive her diploma. And she stood while she made her graduation speech. In so doing, she made history. For Nan, and many other spine-injured people, the future looks brighter.

● In a computer, messages are carried by electricity. A computer can replace human nerves. What does this tell you about the messages that your nerves carry?

Your Nervous System

For Nan Davis the connection between her brain and her nerves was cut when her spinal cord was cut. Your nervous system is built to send and receive messages. Cells that are part of the nervous system are called nerve cells.

The centers of control in your nervous system are your **brain** and your **spinal cord.** Nerves branch out from the brain and the spinal cord. A **nerve** is a bundle of nerve cell **fibers** (FY-burs). Nerves have many branches that spread

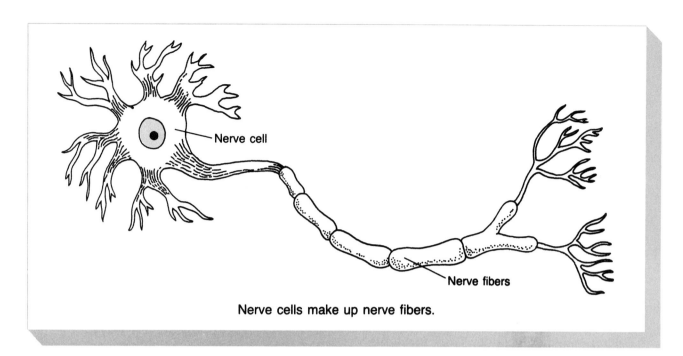

Nerve cells make up nerve fibers.

throughout every part of your body.

Each nerve is a one-way street. It carries messages in only one direction. **Sensory** (SEN-suh-ree) **nerves** carry messages from the sense organs to the spinal cord and brain. They tell the spinal cord and brain what is happening to your body. **Motor nerves** carry messages from the spinal cord and brain to other parts of the body.

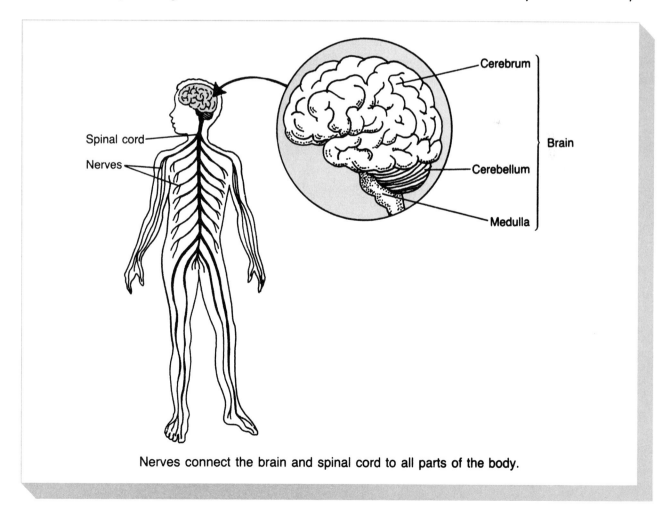

Nerves connect the brain and spinal cord to all parts of the body.

The messages tell the body what to do. Some motor nerves take messages to muscles to tell the muscles how to move. Other motor nerves take messages to glands, telling them to make chemicals.

Suppose you stub your toe on a sharp rock. What happens? Nerve endings in the toe pick up a stimulus of pain. This message is carried by a sensory nerve to your spinal cord. The spinal cord passes the message to motor nerves. The motor nerves carry the message to your muscles. "Pull away!" Your muscles pull away. They move your foot away from the rock. This is your first response to the stimulus.

Meanwhile, the spinal cord also sends a message to your brain. Your brain interprets the message. Only then do you feel the pain and say "ouch!"

Pulling away your foot is an involuntary action. You do it before you know what you have done. This kind of involuntary action is called a **reflex** (REE-fleks). Can you name some other reflexes?

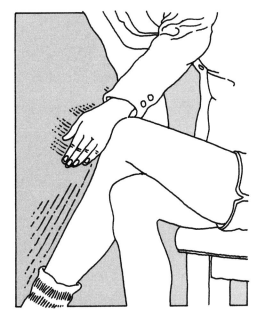

A doctor tests a patients involuntary reflex action.

To Do Yourself   What Are Some Parts of a Fish's Nervous System?

You will need:

Fresh fish which has been cut in half, paper plate, paper towels, large pins, hand lens

1. Place a fresh fish on a paper towel. Use the drawing to help you locate the backbone. Then locate the dark spinal cord, below and inside the backbone. Trace it from the tail to the head of the fish. Use the pins to mark its location.

2. Follow the spinal cord to where it enters the head. Locate the brain at the end of the spinal cord with a pin. Since the fish was cut in half, only part of the brain may be present. Use the hand lens and the drawing to help you observe the brain.

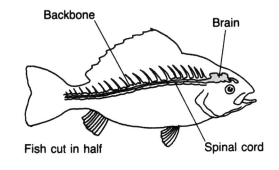

Backbone   Brain

Fish cut in half   Spinal cord

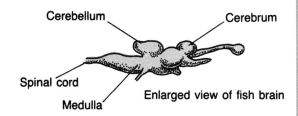

Cerebellum   Cerebrum

Spinal cord

Medulla   Enlarged view of fish brain

Questions

1. Why is the spinal cord located inside the backbone? _____

2. How do messages get from body surfaces to the spinal cord? _____

Your spinal cord is the center of control for many involuntary actions. The brain controls some involuntary actions. It also controls all your voluntary actions. Deciding to stand or walk is a voluntary action. So is watching out for sharp rocks!

Review

I. Fill each blank with the word or phrase that fits best. Choose your answer from these words:

sensory   nervous   brain   spinal cord   reflex   motor   voluntary stimulus

Receiving and sending messages is the job of your _____

system. Your _____ and _____ are

centers of control. Messages from sense organs go through _____

nerves. Messages to muscles or glands go through _____

nerves. A _____ is an involuntary action.

II. If you put your hand into water that is too hot, a reflex action takes place. Use numbers 1 through 6 to indicate in what order the following things happen.

A. _____ spinal cord relays message

B. _____ you feel the hot water

C. _____ hot water touches skin

D. _____ message goes through motor nerve

E. _____ hand pulls away from hot water

F. _____ message goes through sensory nerve

III. Some motor nerves carry messages to glands, such as the salivary glands. (These are the glands that make your mouth water.) Has the smell of food ever made your mouth water? This is a reflex centered in the brain. Describe what happens in your nervous system during this reflex.

_____

_____

_____

_____

What Are the Jobs of Your Brain?

Exploring Science

Down Memory Lane on the Operating Table. The patient on the operating table has her brain exposed. But she is awake. Pain-killing medication keeps her comfortable. Dr. Wilder Penfield touches a spot on her brain with an electric probe. The patient says, "I hear music. The band is playing a tune I know, loud and clear."

The doctor takes away the probe. The music stops. Then he touches the spot again. The patient reports that the music starts again. She "hears" the same tune as before. This patient, like many others treated by Penfield, relived a past experience. The memory of that experience was somehow stored in her brain.

Penfield was treating the patient for epilepsy. This is a brain disorder in which the person can suddenly pass out. The doctor was using his probe to locate unusual brain cells. His discovery of the total recall of "forgotten" events amazed him. Some patients could "hear" voices or even traffic noises from the past. Others "saw" people and scenes from the past. Each of these experiences seemed to be stored at an exact spot in the brain.

● Do you think some sort of change takes place in brain cells when you learn something? Explain.

To Do Yourself   What Are the Parts of the Vertebrate brain?

You will need:

Sheep brain from a butcher, tray, large pins, paper, drawing of fish and human brains

1. Place the sheep brain in the tray. Use the drawing of the human drain to locate the different parts.
2. Label the cerebrum of the sheep's brain. How does it compare to that of the human brain?
3. Label the cerebellum of the sheep's brain. Compare it to that of the human brain.
4. Label and compare the medulla of the sheep's brain to that of the human.

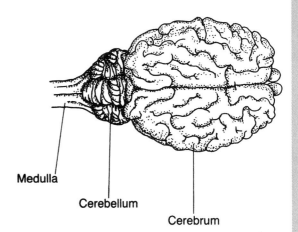

Sheep's Brain
(Top View)

Medulla

Cerebellum

Cerebrum

Questions

1. How are the sheep's brain and human brain alike and different? _____

2. What part of the brain connects to the rest of the body? What does it attach to?

_____

3. How does the sheep brain compare with the fish brain? _____

Your Brain

The work of Dr. Penfield helped make it possible to draw maps of the human brain. Different parts of your brain have special jobs.

The brain's largest part is the **cerebrum** (SER-uh-brum). The top of your skull covers and protects the cerebrum. You use most of your cerebrum to think, reason, and remember. Like a computer, your cerebrum sorts and stores information. But no computer can do what your cerebrum can do.

Messages from each sense organ go to certain areas of the cerebrum. There the messages are interpreted. You can find these control centers in the brain map. You do not "see" anything until nerve messages reach your brain's center for sight. The same is true for your senses of hearing, smell, taste, and touch.

You can find these areas on the brain map. Other areas of the cerebrum control your voluntary muscles. (Remember that these muscles are attached to your bones. You can move them at will.)

The **cerebellum** (ser-uh-BEL-um) is part of the brain below the cerebrum. It is in the back of your head. The cerebellum helps your muscles work together. It also helps you keep your balance.

The **medulla** (mih-DUL-uh) is the part that connects your brain to the spinal cord. Your heart rate and breathing rate are controlled by the medulla. So are the movements of involuntary muscles, such as those in your digestive system. Some reflex actions, such as blinking and yawning, are centered in the medulla.

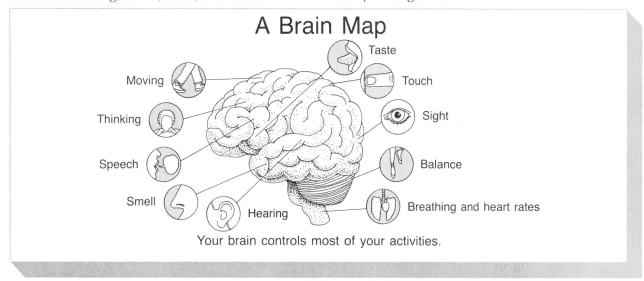

A Brain Map

Your brain controls most of your activities.

Review

I. Write the name of the part of the brain (cerebrum, cerebellum, medulla) that controls each of the following:

A. balance _____

B. stomach contractions _____

C. heart rate_____

D. memory _____

E. hearing _____

F. voluntary movement _____

G. reason_____

H. yawning _____

II. When you swallow, the action starts as voluntary. Then it continues as an involuntary action. What parts of the brain control (a) the start of swallowing (b) the rest of the action?

III. A person may "see stars" after a blow on the head. Explain.

How Do You Learn New Behavior?

Exploring Science

Goodbye to Cold Hands. People usually have a hand temperature of about 32° Celsius. But one woman who came to Dr. Keith Sedlacek had a hand temperature of only 22° Celsius. She wore heavy gloves. But her hands were still cold and very painful.

The woman had Raynaud's disease. This can be caused by stress. When a person is tense or upset, nerves cause blood vessels in the hand to narrow. Not enough warm blood can get into the hands.

Sedlacek taught the woman special exercises to relax. As she did the exercises, her hands were connected to a machine. The machine recorded her hand temperature. This let her see the effect of the exercises. When she relaxed, the blood vessels in her hands opened. Her hands got warmer. The machine showed a rise in temperature. Eventually, the woman learned to increase her hand temperature to above 32° Celsius.

Sedlack is an expert in **biofeedback** (by-oh-FEED-bak). In biofeedback, patients are trained to do exercises to relax the part of the body that is tense.

● Some persons with high blood pressure can use biofeedback to lower their blood pressure. What seems to be one cause of high blood pressure? Why?

Your brain produces certain kinds of brain waves when you are relaxed. A biofeedback machine measures these waves.

Learned and Inborn Behavior

Biofeedback exercises are a type of **learned behavior.** One of the first people to study learned behavior was the Russian scientist Ivan Pavlov. Pavlov observed how a dog's mouth waters when the dog smells food. He tried an experiment. He rang a bell each time he fed a dog. He repeated this many times. Pavlov always rang the bell when he gave food to the dog.

Then Pavlov rang the bell without giving the dog any food. Still the dog's mouth watered.

The dog had learned to connect the sound of the bell with being fed. Before the experiment, the dog's response (mouth-watering) was made to one stimulus (smell of food). The dog now made the same response (mouth-watering) to a new stimulus (a bell).

The dog had learned a new response. A response (or behavior) learned in this way is called a **conditioned** (kun-DISH-und) **response.** This kind of learning is called **conditioning** (kun-DISH-un-ing). Can you give an example of how

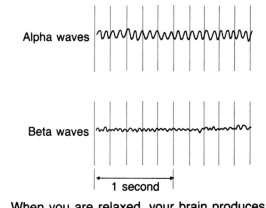

When you are relaxed, your brain produces alpha waves. They are slow and high. When you are excited, your brain produces beta waves. They are fast and flat.

you have been conditioned to respond to a bell?

Another way of learning is by trial and error. In **trial-and-error learning,** you learn something by trying different ways of doing it. You learn skills—such as riding a bicycle—by trial and error. The more you practice, the better you become at avoiding mistakes.

Animals also use trial and error. A mouse was put in a maze. A food reward was placed at the end of the maze. Each time the mouse ran the maze, it made fewer mistakes. In time, it found the way to the food without any mistakes. It had learned the correct pathway.

Reasoning (REE-zuh-ning) is learned behavior in which you think things through. Your ability to solve a math problem depends on reasoning. So does doing a puzzle or finding a lost object.

Many animals also use reasoning. A chimpanzee was put in a room with a bunch of bananas too high to reach. Three boxes were also in the room. The chimp looked over the situation for some time. Then it piled the boxes on top of each other. Climbing up, it was able to reach the bananas.

Behavior that does not have to be learned is **inborn** (IN-BORN) **behavior.** At this moment, your heart is beating. Your digestive system is breaking down food. You are breathing. You may also be coughing, sneezing, or yawning. Every few seconds, your eyes blink. All these behaviors are reflexes. Remember that a reflex happens outside your control. Reflexes are examples of inborn behaviors.

"Pavlov's dog" was trained to salivate when a bell rang, even though no food was present.

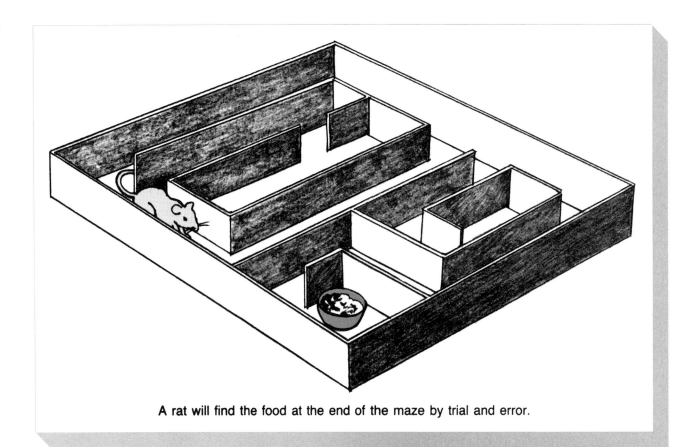

A rat will find the food at the end of the maze by trial and error.

The chimpanzee uses reasoning to get to the bananas.

To Do Yourself   Can Animals Learn?

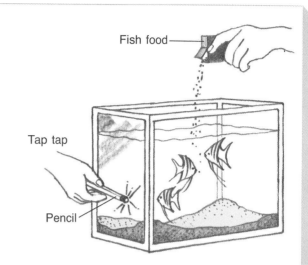

You will need:

A fish tank, goldfish, fish food, pencil

1. Set up a simple fish tank with several fish of one kind in it.
2. Before you feed the fish, tap the side of the tank several times with the pencil. Do this each time you feed the fish. Feed them at the same time each day. Also, feed them at the same place in the tank.
3. After a week or so, tap the side of the aquarium, but do not feed the fish. What happens?

Questions

1. What was the stimulus in the fish experiment? What was the response? _____

2. How long did it take for your fish to learn the behavior? _____

3. What kind of response is this an example of? _____

Review

I. Fill each blank with the word that fits best. Choose your answer from these words:

**trial and error   response   learned   stimulus   reasoning   inborn
conditioning**

A reflex is _____ behavior. A conditioned response

is _____ behavior. Pavlov's dog's mouth still watered when

the _____ was changed. An animal learns a maze by

_____ . Thinking things through is

_____ .

II. For each statement, write the kind of learning described. Choose from this list: conditioning, reasoning, trial and error.

A. You figure out where to find a lost sweater._____

B. Your dog comes when you call its name._____

C. A chick at first pecks at both the ground and at its feed. Later, it pecks only at the feed._____

What Are Chemical Messengers?

Exploring Science

No Joking Around. When you visit sick friends, you try to cheer them up. Perhaps you tell them funny stories or jokes. Almost everyone has heard that making people laugh can help them get well.

Recently, scientists have begun to understand how . . . and why.

In one hospital, a comedian often performs for the patients. After laughing for 45 minutes, patients say their pain has gone away or become less. How does this happen?

When you laugh, the body's chemical messenger system gets going. Chemicals set free by this system have many good effects. One group of these chemicals are called **endorphins** (en-DAWR-finz). They are the body's own pain killers. They kill pain—like drugs do, but without the bad effects of drugs.

So: no joking around—laughter really is good for you!

● What other feelings, besides the pleasure that makes you laugh, do you think might set free chemical messengers? Explain.

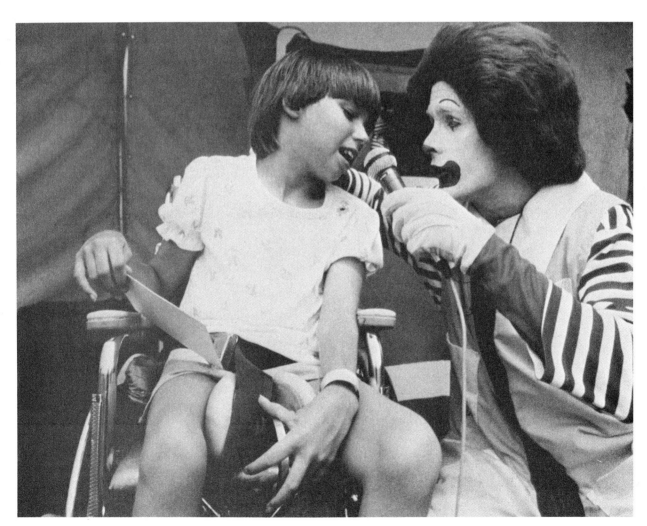

A laugh a day may keep the doctor away.

Chemical Messengers

The endorphins that are released when you laugh are a kind of hormone. **Hormones** (HOR-mohns) are chemical messengers. They control many activities in your body.

How tall you grow to be depends on **growth hormone.** This hormone is made by your **pituitary** (pih-TOO-ih-ter-ee) **gland.** A giant has too much growth hormone. A midget has too little. The pituitary also makes other hormones. These control many body activities. Some even control other glands. For this reason, the pituitary is called the "master gland."

The **thyroid** (THY-roid) **gland** produces the hormone **thyroxin** (thy-ROK-sin). Thyroxin controls the rate at which your body produces energy. An adult with too little thyroxin may be tired and gain weight. Too much thyroxin can make a person nervous and cause weight loss.

You have two **adrenal** (uh-DREEN-ul) **glands.** They make a hormone called adrenalin (uh-DREN-ul-in). When you feel angry, excited, or afraid, your adrenals send adrenalin into your bloodstream. Adrenalin makes you breathe faster, so that you take in extra oxygen. Adrenalin also causes more sugar to go into the blood. And adrenalin makes your heart beat faster, so that oxygen and sugar get to your cells faster. All these changes give you an extra burst of energy. In an emergency, this energy can help you do things you would not be able to do at other times. For example, if you were in real danger you could probably run faster than you normally could.

Your pancreas makes digestive juice. The

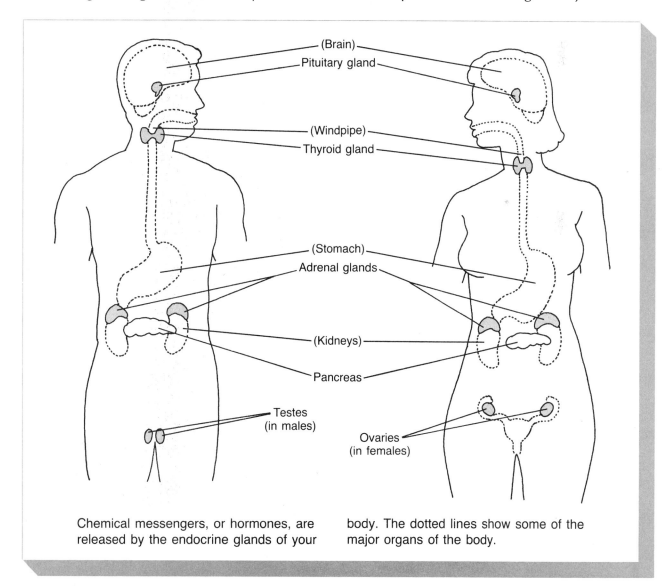

Chemical messengers, or hormones, are released by the endocrine glands of your body. The dotted lines show some of the major organs of the body.

pancreas also makes **insulin** (IN-suh-lin). Insulin is a hormone that controls the use of sugar by the body cells. If the pancreas makes too little insulin, the person has diabetes (dy-uh-BEE-tis). In this disease, extra sugar builds up in the blood. The kidneys remove some of this sugar, so that the urine has sugar in it. Diabetes can be controlled by proper diet and exercise, or by taking insulin.

If you are a girl, you have two **ovaries** (OH-vuh-rees). If you are a boy, you have two **testes** (TES-teez). These organs, the ovaries and testes, are part of the reproductive system.

Ovaries produce female sex hormones that cause many changes during adolescence. As a girl becomes a woman, her breasts develop and her hips widen. Testes produce male hormones. These also have many effects during adolescence. As a boy becomes a man, his beard grows, his voice deepens, and his muscles grow larger and stronger.

When you get excited, what hormone does your body release?

All these glands are part of your **endocrine** (EN-duh-krin) **system.** The endocrine glands produce hormones that pass directly into the bloodstream. The blood carries the hormones to the parts of your body where they are needed.

To Do Yourself   How Are Hormones Helpful?

You will need:

Two plastic bags with ties, two green bananas, one orange

1. Place a green banana into each plastic bag. Tie one tightly and set it aside.
2. Add an orange to the other bag. Tie it tightly.
3. Place the bags where they will not be disturbed. Fruits produce a hormone in the form of a gas that causes them to ripen.
4. Examine the bags each day. After the second day take the bananas from the bags and compare them to see which one has ripened most.

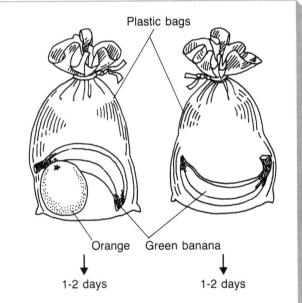

Plastic bags

Orange   Green banana

1-2 days   1-2 days

Questions

1. Why do you think banana in the bag with the orange ripened first? _____

2. Which bag had the most hormone in it? _____

3. Where did this hormone come from? _____
4. How is this kind of hormone different from hormones in the human body?

_____

Review

I. Fill each blank with the word that fits best. Choose your answer from these words:

thyroxin   insulin   endocrine   adrenalin   testes   ovaries
hormones   pituitary

The body's _____ system is made up of glands that

produce _____ . The "master gland" is the

_____ . The hormone that helps you meet an emergency

is _____ . Diabetes is caused by not enough

_____ . Hormones that cause female body changes

are made by the _____ .

II. If the statement is true, write T; if it is false, write F. Place your answer after the sentence. Then correct the underlined word.

A. _____ Not enough of a hormone from the pancreas can cause a person to become a midget.

B. _____ A hormone made by the adrenals speeds up the heart.

C. _____ Too much insulin can make a person nervous and cause loss of weight.

III. Explain why **athletes sometimes** perform better in a game or race than they can in practice **sessions.**

_____

_____

_____

IV. Write the name of the endocrine gland that matches the number in the diagram.

1. _____

2. _____

3. _____

4. _____

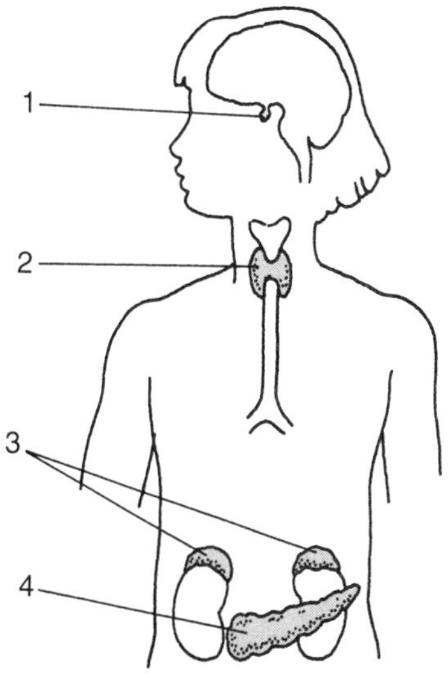

Review What You Know

A. Hidden in the puzzle below are the names of seven parts of the body. Use the clues to help you find the names. Circle each name in the puzzle. Then write each name on the line next to its clue.

```
M O T O R O D S
Z B H F E V H G
I J Y L N A P P
C E R E B R U M
N Q O M O I P R
O T I X Q E I S
S W D A V S L K
E M E D U L L A
```

Clues:

1. Has nerves sensitive to odors. _____

2. Where light enters the eye. _____

3. Brain's center for involuntary acts. _____

4. Controls rate at which body uses energy. _____

5. Type of nerve that carries messages to muscles. _____

6. Make female sex hormones. _____

7. Brain's center for memory. _____

B. Write the word (or words) that best completes each statement.

1. _____ When a bell rings near your ear, you hear the sound when messages reach your **a.** eardrum **b.** inner ear **c.** brain

2. _____ An example of inborn behavior is **a.** blinking **b.** trial-and-error **c.** reasoning

3. _____ The brain's center for balance is in the **a.** medulla **b.** cerebrum **c.** cerebellum

4. _____ Light that enters the eye is focused as it passes through the **a.** retina **b.** lens **c.** nerve

5. _____ When you touch a hot object, you pull your hand away when messages reach your **a.** sensory nerve **b.** spinal cord **c.** brain

6. _____ An example of learned behavior is **a.** yawning **b.** conditioning **c.** sneezing

7. _____ A hormone that can speed up your breathing rate is **a.** adrenalin **b.** insulin **c.** thyroxin

8. _____ Male sex hormones are produced in the
   a. thyroid **b.** pancreas **c.** testes

9. _____ Diabetes is caused by too little **a.** insulin
   b. thyroxin **c.** adrenalin

10. _____ The body's master gland is the **a.** thyroid
   b. adrenal **c.** pituitary

C. Apply What You Know

Study the drawings of three steps in teaching a puppy its name. In a few sentences, explain what is happening. Use these words in your answer:

stimulus   response   brain   conditioned.

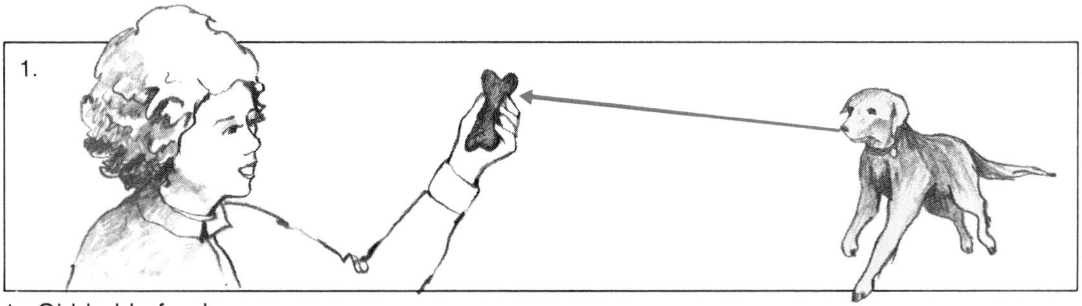

1. Girl holds food; puppy comes.

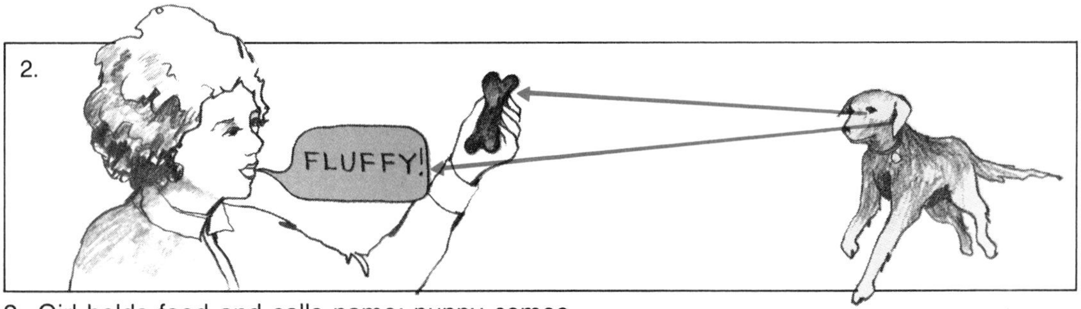

2. Girl holds food and calls name; puppy comes.

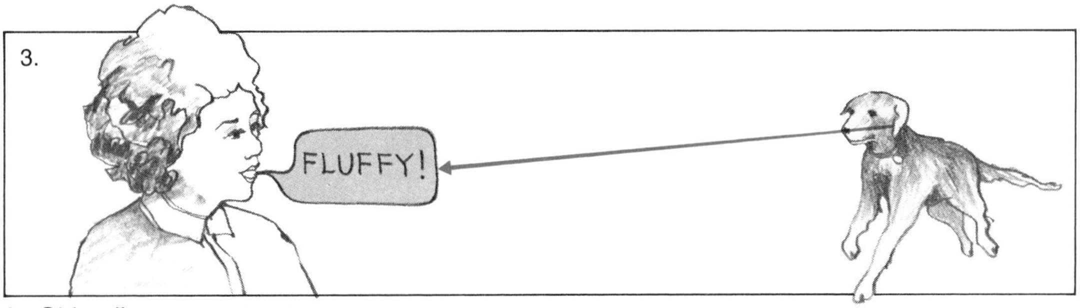

3. Girl calls name; puppy comes.

_____

_____

_____

_____

_____

D. Find Out More

1. Do you know you have a blind spot in each of your eyes? Try this. Close your left eye. Look at the square with your right eye. Slowly bring the page closer. Stop when you cannot see the circle. You have found the blind spot in your right eye. Now close your right eye and look at the circle. Bring the page closer until you cannot see the square. In the library, find out why you have blind spots.

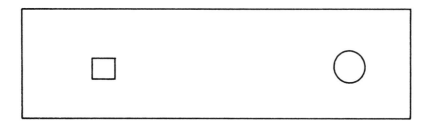

2. Plan how you would train a pet to do a trick. Then carry out your plan.
3. To find nerve endings for hot and cold in the skin, try this. You will need a partner. Use a ball-point pen to mark off a 2-centimeter square on the back of your partner's wrist. Make 16 evenly spaced dots within the square.

   Place one iron nail in hot water. Place another nail in ice water. Blindfold your partner. Touch 8 scattered dots lightly with the hot nail. Then touch the other 8 dots with the cold nail. Have your partner tell you what he or she feels with each touch. Make a map of the nerve endings for hot and cold. Use red pencil or ink for hot and blue for cold. Trade places with your partner and repeat the investigation.

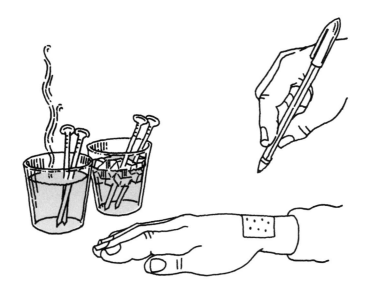

4. Blinking is a reflex that can sometimes be hard to control. Work with a partner to test your blinking reflex. Hold a clear sheet of glass or plastic in front of your eyes. Have your partner throw wads of paper so they hit the glass. Can you keep from blinking each time a wad hits the glass? Trade places with your partner. Can she or he avoid blinking?

Careers in Life Science

A Healthy Mind in a Healthy Body. "Health is wealth" is an old saying. So is "A healthy mind in a healthy body." It reminds us that health is not only physical well-being. Health is also mental and emotional well-being.

People with emotional problems often go to mental health professional for help. Are you interested in what makes people "tick"? Are you able to "tune in" to other people's feelings? Are you in touch with your own inner self? Then you may want a career in mental health.

Mental Health Technician. A mental health, or psychiatric, technician is part of the team of "helpers" in a mental health center. As a mental health technician, you might be the first person seen by new patients. Your job would include listening to them and observing their behavior.

The mental health technician's relationship with patients is the start of their treatment, or

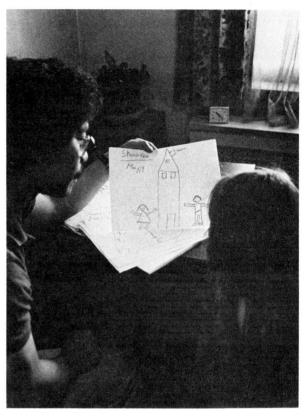

A social worker helps a young patient.

A psychiatric technician helps a patient in a mental-health center.

therapy. The therapy continues in patients' relationship with other members of the team. A two-year training program after high school can prepare you for a career as a mental health technician.

Clinical Social Worker. The main therapy for mental or emotional problems may be conducted by a clinical, or psychiatric, social worker. The worker helps patients gain a thorough understanding of themselves. Patients use their new self-knowledge to cope better with problems.

Four years of college, followed by two years of social work school, are needed to become a clinical social worker.

All mental health careers demand that you give a great deal of yourself. But the rewards of helping people are also very great.

REPRODUCTION IN SIMPLE ORGANISMS AND PLANTS

How Do Living Things Reproduce?

Exploring Science

Kelly's Unlikely Baby. Horses can only give birth to horses—right or wrong? If you let nature take its course, the answer is "right." But when scientists take a hand in the matter, the answer can be "wrong." Kelly is a horse at the Louisville Zoo in Kentucky. She gave birth to a baby zebra. How did this happen?

The baby zebra's real parents were, of course, zebras. The baby began its life in the body of its real mother. At a very early stage of growth, the unborn zebra was moved from its mother into Kelly's body. For 12 months, the baby zebra grew in its substitute mother's body. Then it was born.

Kelly is the first horse to have a zebra baby. But she is just one of a number of animal mothers at zoos that have unlikely babies. For example, a cow has given birth to a wild ox, an endangered animal similar to a cow. Using substitute mothers will increase the population of wild oxen.

Some rare species of zebras also are endangered. Scientists plan to use more horses as substitute mothers for these zebras.

● Why do you think scientists chose a horse instead of a cow or other animal as the substitute mother for a zebra?

Kelly, the horse, with her newborn baby zebra.

This cow has given birth to the baby wild ox shown.

How Living Things Reproduce

When zebras and other living things reproduce, they make more of their own kind. The young are called **offspring** (AWF-spring). The offspring of zebras are zebras. Those of humans are humans. Those of trees are trees.

Like the zebra in the experiment, you came from two parents. One parent, the father, is male. The other parent, the mother, is female. A dog, a cat, a fish—nearly any living thing you can name—comes from two parents. Reproduction from two parents is called **sexual** (SEK-shoo-ul) **reproduction.**

Some living things reproduce from only one parent. Reproduction from one parent is called **asexual** (ay-SEK-shoo-ul) **reproduction.** Protozoans and many other one-celled organisms can reproduce asexually.

The simplest kind of asexual reproduction is called **fission** (FISH-un), which means "splitting." Remember that a cell has a center of control called the nucleus. During fission, the nu-

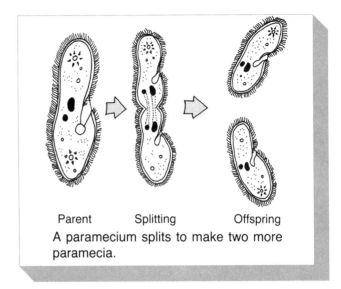

| Parent | Splitting | Offspring |

A paramecium splits to make two more paramecia.

cleus splits into two equal parts. So does the cytoplasm—the part of the cell around the nucleus. Each half of the parent cell becomes a new cell, enclosed by its own cell membrane.

To Do Yourself   How Do Yeast Cells Reproduce?

You will need:

Sugar, 1 package dry yeast, 3 glass jars, medicine dropper, warm water, cold water

1. In one jar place ½ cup warm water, ⅓ package dry yeast, and ½ spoonful of sugar. Label.
2. Set up the second jar the same way but use cold water. Label.
3. Set up the third jar the same as the first, but omit the sugar. Label.
4. Stir each jar and allow to stand.
5. After 5 to 10 minutes, examine the jars. When yeast reproduces, it produces alcohol and carbon dioxide. Carefully smell each jar and determine the one or ones in which yeast reproduced.

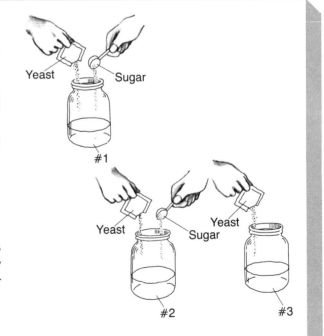

Questions

1. In which jar did the yeast grow best? _____

2. What does a yeast cell need in order to reproduce? _____

3. How could you tell your yeast was reproducing? _____

The two new cells are called **daughter cells.** Each daughter cell is just like the parent cell but half its size. Each daughter cell grows until it reaches full size. Then it may also reproduce by fission. Two organisms that can reproduce this way are amebas and paramecia.

Another way that some living things can reproduce asexually is by **budding.** Yeasts, the one-celled organisms used in making bread, can reproduce by budding.

When a yeast cell buds, a part of its cell wall pushes out. This is the start of the **bud.** The cell nucleus moves toward the bud. The nucleus then splits into two equal parts. One part goes into the bud. The other part stays in the parent cell.

The yeast bud grows larger while attached to the parent cell. When the bud becomes large enough, a new cell wall grows between the parent cell and the bud. Then the bud may break away. The newly formed yeast cells can also reproduce by budding.

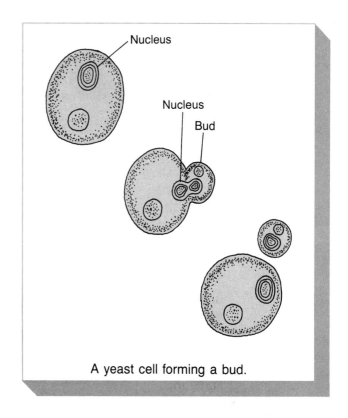

A yeast cell forming a bud.

Review

I. Fill each blank with the word that fits best. Choose from the words below.

**daughter   parent   budding   fission   cytoplasm   sexual
asexual   bud   nucleus   offspring**

The young that result from reproduction are the _____ of the parents. Two parents are needed for _____ reproduction. Only one parent is needed for _____ reproduction. During _____ , the whole cell divides into two equal parts. During _____ a small part of the parent cell becomes a new cell. Two _____ cells form as a result of fission. A _____ forms as a result of budding. In both fission and budding the cell _____ divides equally.

II. "Tree green" is a kind of alga (*Protococcus*) that grows on the bark of trees. It reproduces by fission. Circle the word that makes each statement true.

A. The new alga cells that form are (equal/unequal) in size.

B. Each new cell is called a (bud/daughter) cell.

C. The form of reproduction of the alga is (sexual/asexual).

III. Bacteria reproduce by fission. If a single bacterium reproduces once every 20 minutes, how many bacteria would be formed at the end of 1 hour? 2 hours? 3 hours?

How Do Molds Reproduce?

Exploring Science

Dr. Fleming's Lucky Find. In September of 1928, it was warm in London. Dr. Alexander Fleming kept the windows of his laboratory open, hoping to cool off. Fleming was studying disease-causing bacteria. He grew the bacteria in glass dishes. As he examined one dish of bacteria with its cover off, something happened that he could not see. The breeze from his windows blew something into the open dish.

A few days later, Fleming examined the dish again. The bacteria were still growing in the dish. But so was a green mold! The mold had "spoiled" the dish. Fleming's first thought was to throw the dish away. But something unusual caught his eye. All the bacteria near the mold had died. Why?

Fleming did some studies. He discovered that the mold made a substance that killed deadly bacteria. Fleming named this substance **penicillin** (pen-ih-SIL-in).

Fleming's discovery was a "lucky" find, indeed. Penicillin became a famous medicine. Its power to kill bacteria has saved countless lives.

● What do you think the "something" was that blew in Fleming's windows? Where did it come from?

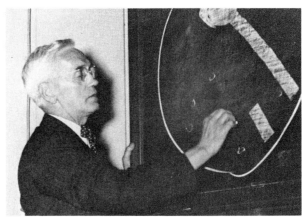
Sir Alexander Fleming discovered penicillin.

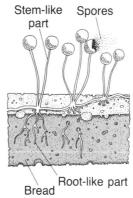
Bread mold reproduces by spores.

Reproducing by Spores

Have you ever seen green mold growing on an orange or a lemon? Its name is *Penicillium* (pen-ih-SIL-ee-um). It is the same mold that grew in Fleming's dish of bacteria. The first penicillin was made from this common mold. How did the mold get into Fleming's laboratory? Let's look at its structure.

Under a microscope, you can see that *Penicillium* has root-like parts. These are attached to the food it grows on. The mold takes in food through these "roots." The mold's stem-like parts grow up into the air. At the ends of the "stems" are strings of tiny reproductive cells, called **spores** (SPOHRS). The spores are made in great numbers.

Each spore can grow into *Pencillium* mold. It has only one parent, so this is a kind of **asexual reproduction.** The spores are so tiny and light that the slightest breeze carries them away from the parent mold. They go everywhere and fall on everything. They fell in the dish in Fleming's laboratory.

Another kind of mold grows on old bread. The mold looks like white fuzz filled with tiny black dots. Under a microscope, you can see that the fuzz is the mold's "stems." You can also see that the black dots are balls at the tips of the bread mold's "stems." Each ball breaks open and releases thousands of spores. Each spore can grow into another bread mold.

To Do Yourself — How Can We Slow Down the Growth of Mold?

You will need:

Potato, apple-coring tool, cotton balls, household disinfectant, soapy water, hand lens, 3 test tubes

1. Use the apple-coring tool to take cylinders, or cores, from a potato.
2. Roll each potato core on a dusty table.
3. Spray one potato core with disinfectant. Wash one with soapy water. Leave the third alone.
4. Place a wad of moistened cotton in the bottom of each tube. Put a potato core inside and label tubes.
5. Mold grows best in a dark, warm place. Place your labeled tubes where the mold can grow for several days. Observe the potato cores each day with a hand lens. Record your observations.

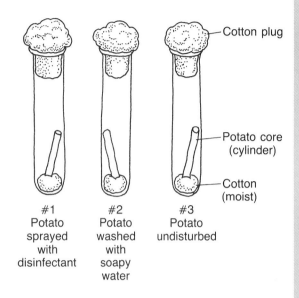

#1 Potato sprayed with disinfectant

#2 Potato washed with soapy water

#3 Potato undisturbed

Questions

1. In which test tube did you first observe mold growing? _____
2. Which mold grew the most? The least? _____
3. What could you do to slow down the growth of mold? _____

Review

I. Fill each blank with the word that fits best. Choose from the words below.

"stems"   *Penicillium*   **"roots"**   **fission**   **spores**   **mold**   **buds**

A mold that grows on oranges and lemons is called _____ .

A mold reproduces by _____ . A mold takes in food

through its _____ . Spores form on a mold's

_____ . One spore can grow into a whole new

_____ .

II. Explain how making spores is like fission and budding. Explain how it is different from fission and budding.

How Do Animals Grow Back Lost Parts?

Exploring Science

A Tale of a Lizard's Tail. What good is a tail? For many lizards, a tail can be used for self-defense. When a snake attacks a lizard, the lizard's tail breaks off. While the snake pays attention to the tail, the lizard tries to escape. The snake may not catch on to what's happened until the lizard is far away. As for the lizard, it simply grows itself a new tail!

This defense works better for some lizards than for others. Scientists in Texas observed how snakes react to the broken-off tails of two kinds of lizards: anoles (un-NOH-lees) and skinks (SKINGKS).

After an anole's tail comes off, the tail doesn't move very much. But a skink's broken-off tail keeps thrashing about. The more the broken-off tail moves, the longer the snake "thinks" it has caught the whole lizard.

In an experiment, snakes caught many more anoles than skinks. For fooling snakes, it is good for a lizard to have a tail that can both come off and keep moving.

● Which kind of lizards—skinks or anoles—do scientists think have a special way to store energy in their tails? Explain your answer.

Skink escapes while snake goes after skink's thrashing tail.

Growing Back Lost Parts

Like lizards, some other animals can grow back a lost part. This power to replace lost parts is called **regeneration** (rih-jen-uh-RAY-shun). A lizard whose tail breaks off can **regenerate,** or grow back, a new tail. Lobsters and crabs can regenerate lost claws.

Can your body regenerate itself? You cannot grow back a lost part like a finger or toe. But to some extent your body can repair itself. If you cut your skin, new skin cells grow to replace the cells that are lost or damaged. If you break a bone, it can repair itself, too. Your body's power of self-repair is a kind of regeneration.

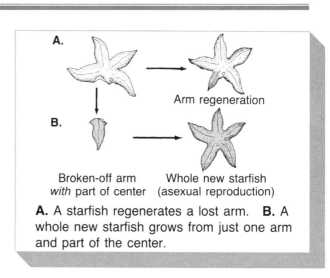

A.

Arm regeneration

B.

Broken-off arm *with* part of center

Whole new starfish (asexual reproduction)

A. A starfish regenerates a lost arm. **B.** A whole new starfish grows from just one arm and part of the center.

The starfish has an unusual ability to grow back lost parts. If a starfish loses an arm, it can grow a new arm. This is regeneration. But a cut-off arm can also grow into a whole new starfish. This is a kind of asexual reproduction.

The planarian (pluh-NAIR-ee-un) is a kind of flatworm. It also can reproduce asexually from a cut-off part. Cut a planarian in half, and two new worms will form. Cut the worm into four pieces, and four new worms will form!

To Do Yourself   Is Regeneration a Form of Reproduction?

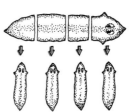

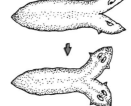

You will need:

Planaria, single-edged razor blade, petri dish and cover, hand lens or microscope, medicine dropper, aged tap water

1. Use a medicine dropper to transfer a planarian to your petri dish.
2. Use a single-edged razor blade to dissect your planarian, as done in one of these figures.
3. Add aged tap water to your petri dish. Label and cover.
4. Observe your planarian each day with the hand lens. Record any regeneration that you observe.

Questions

1. How is some type of regeneration a kind of reproduction? _____

2. Is this kind of reproduction sexual or asexual? _____

Review

I. For each statement, write if it is an example of <u>regeneration</u> or (asexual) <u>reproduction</u>.

A. Your body makes 1 billion new blood cells each day. _____
B. A snake grows a new skin under its old skin, then sheds the old

   skin. _____
C. A sponge animal cut into 3 parts grows into three new sponge

   animals. _____

D. A deer sheds its antlers, then grows new antlers. _____
E. A small piece of a ribbon worm grows into a whole new ribbon

   worm. _____

II. Starfish like to eat oysters. Oyster fishers used to cut up starfish and throw the pieces back into the water. They thought they were destroying the starfish. What really happened?

How Do Plants Reproduce Asexually?

Exploring Science

Shooting Trees for Science. Forester Steve Jolly sets off for a morning's hunt among the giant redwoods. His weapon, a shotgun. His target, trees!

Yes, part of Jolly's job is to shoot trees. Most of the trees around him are tall, about 40 meters high. But he is seeking the few trees that are still taller, 60 meters high or even higher. When he finds an extra tall tree, he selects a small branch just 1 meter long. It must be near the tree's top. A well-aimed shot from Jolly's gun brings down the branch.

Jolly's "catch" of branches will go to a laboratory. From small pieces of the parent trees, scientists will grow new young trees. Scientists expect that the offspring will grow as tall as their parents. The aim: to grow whole forests of such "supertrees." The scientists have found that many more redwoods can be grown from pieces of young branches than can be grown from seeds.

Why do we need supertree forests? People need trees for wood. Without wood, we would have no paper or lumber. We also need wood for fuel and many other products. Baseball bats, charcoal, and cellophane are made from wood. Wood is already in short supply. And scientists predict that our need for wood products will double in the next 50 years.

● Is the reproduction of trees from parts of branches asexual or sexual? Explain.

Steve Jolly works in his tree laboratory.

Asexual Reproduction in Plants

The tree branches that scientists use to reproduce supertrees are "growing parts." It takes only a piece of stem or a leaf cut from a redwood branch to grow a whole new tree. Many other kinds of plants can also be reproduced from their stems, leaves, or roots. Reproducing plants from growing parts is called **vegetative propagation** (VEJ-ih-tay-tiv prop-uh-GAY-shun). This is a kind of asexual reproduction. Do you see why?

Vegetative propagation can happen in nature. Two ways that plants propagate in nature are by bulbs and tubers (TOO-burs). People also use bulbs and tubers to grow new plants.

BULBS. A **bulb** is a short, thick underground stem. It has thick leaves on it that store food. Onions are bulbs. Other bulbs you may know are tulips and garlic. When conditions are right, a bulb will grow into a new plant like its parent. The food stored in the bulb is used by the young plant until it starts to make its own food.

TUBERS. A **tuber** is another kind of underground stem. It has a fleshy part that looks like a root. A white potato is a tuber. The fleshy part of the potato is stored food. The "eyes" are stem buds. Each eye can grow into a new potato plant.

Farmers use cut-up potatoes to grow new crops of potato plants. First, the potatoes are cut into pieces. Each piece has a bud on it. When the pieces are planted, a new potato plant grows from each bud. The fleshy part of

The onion you eat is an underground stem with fleshy leaves.

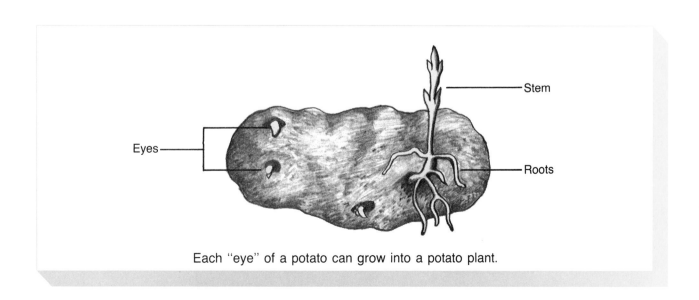

Eyes

Stem

Roots

Each "eye" of a potato can grow into a potato plant.

the potato provides food for the developing young plants.

Two other ways that people propagate plants are by cutting and grafting.

CUTTING. Some plants can be reproduced from a cut-off piece of stem with a few leaves on it. The piece of stem is called a **cutting.** Ivy and geraniums are plants that you can propagate from stem cuttings. When the cutting is put in soil, it grows into a whole new plant.

Some plants can be reproduced from leaf cuttings. A leaf, or even a piece of a leaf, placed in moist sand can grow into a new plant. Begonias (bih-GOHN-yuhs) and African violets are plants often propagated from leaf cuttings.

GRAFTING. Plant growers use grafting to produce large numbers of plants with certain traits. In **grafting,** a stem cutting with leaves on it is taken from one plant. The cutting is joined with the stem of a related plant. The first plant may produce beautiful flowers. The second plant may have strong roots.

By grafting, the good features of both plants are combined. Grafting is a way to reproduce large numbers of plants more quickly than by planting seeds.

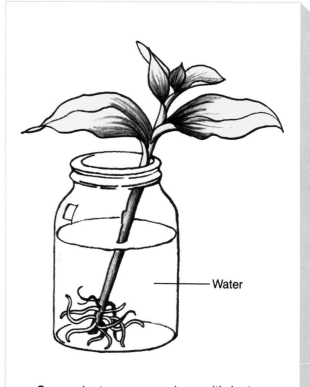

Water

Some plants can reproduce with just a stem and a leaf, placed in soil or water.

Three Kinds of Grafts

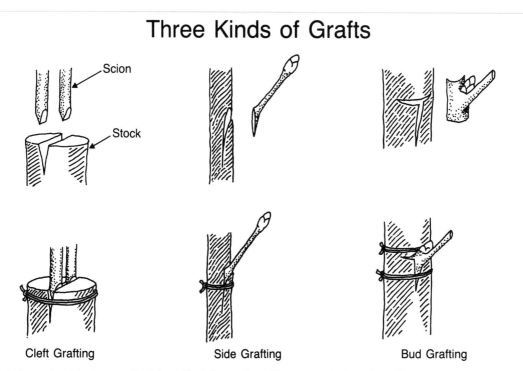

Scion

Stock

Cleft Grafting

Side Grafting

Bud Grafting

The twig or bud being grafted is called the *scion.* The rooted plant is called the *stock.* After the graft is made, the scion is tied to the stock. Soft wax is then placed over the cut to prevent infection.

To Do Yourself   How Can Tubers Be Used To Reproduce Plants?

You will need:

Plastic knife, toothpicks, 2 white potatoes, water, paper cups

1. Place toothpicks around the middle of one of the white potatoes. Place it in a cup of water.
2. Cut the second potato into sections.
3. Place toothpicks into each section.
4. Suspend each section in a cup of water.
5. Label each cup and place it in a dark, warm place to grow.
6. After a week, observe the whole potato and each section of potato. Record the number of "eyes" on each potato section.

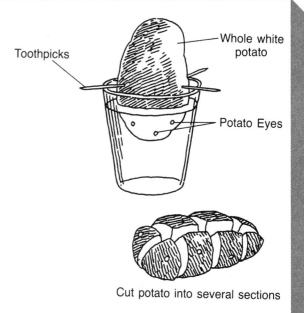

Cut potato into several sections

Questions

1. On which potato sections did a new potato plant begin to grow? _____

2. Why would a farmer cut potatoes into sections and plant them? _____

Review

I. Fill each blank with the word that fits best. Choose from the words below.

cutting   asexual   sexual   grafting   tuber   bulb   spore

Vegetative propagation is a kind of _____ reproduction. An

underground stem with fleshy leaves is a _____ . An

underground stem with buds is a _____ . A piece of stem

or leaf may be a _____ . In _____ a
branch of one plant is joined to the stem of another.

II. Circle the word that makes each statement true.

A. Potatoes can be reproduced from (tubers/bulbs).

B. A stem cutting is a way to propagate (onions/ivy).

C. Joining an orange tree branch to a lemon tree stem is a kind of (leaf cutting/grafting).

D. A bulb is a way to reproduce (onions/geraniums).

III. The thick part of a carrot is its main root. If planted, it can grow into a new carrot plant. Is this a kind of vegetative propagation? Explain.

What Is the Work of a Flower?

Exploring Science

The Ranchers, the Clover, and the Bees. Do you like lamb chops? Lambs are the young of sheep. They need a lot of good hay for their feeding. Today, some of the best lamb comes from New Zealand. This is a country in the Pacific near Australia.

There is plenty of red clover, which makes very good hay, in New Zealand. But years ago, there was no red clover in New Zealand at all. The sheep ranchers wanted to improve their hay crops. So they imported red clover seeds from Europe and planted them.

The seeds grew into healthy clover plants with sweet-smelling purple flowers. The clover crop was a big success. Then something went wrong. The second year, there was no clover. In other parts of the world, red clover forms plenty of seeds. The seeds drop to the ground. They grow into the next year's crop. Why didn't this happen in New Zealand?

The ranchers soon solved the mystery. Red clover cannot produce seeds without bumblebees. But there were no bumblebees in New Zealand! The ranchers imported more seeds and planted a new crop. They also imported 100 bumblebees. They set the bees free in the clover fields. After the bees got to work, the clover plants made lots of seeds. The clover grew richly, year after year. The bees also reproduced. Soon there were several hundred and then several thousand of them.

What do bees have to do with seed-making in clover? When a bee visits a clover flower, the bee picks up grains of something called **pollen** (POL-un). The bee also drops off pollen that it picked up from other clover flowers. This transfer of pollen from flower to flower must happen before clover seeds can form.

● Which seems most likely to be true? Explain your answer.

A. The transfer of pollen is a step in the asexual reproduction of plants.

B. The transfer of pollen is a step in the sexual reproduction of plants.

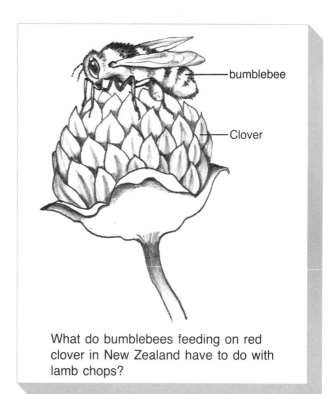

bumblebee

Clover

What do bumblebees feeding on red clover in New Zealand have to do with lamb chops?

The sheep of New Zealand needed red clover and bumblebees.

The Work of a Flower

Like red clover, most plants with flowers reproduce by seeds. Reproduction by seeds is a kind of sexual reproduction. For a seed to be made, a male sex cell and a female sex cell must join together. A male sex cell is called a **sperm** (SPURM). A female sex cell is called an **egg.** The joining together of a sperm and an egg is called **fertilization** (fur-tuh-lih-ZAY-shun.)

The sperm and eggs in a plant join together in a flower. Let's first take a look at the parts of a flower.

PARTS OF A FLOWER. Look at the diagram of a flower. The numbers below match those in the diagram.

(1) Green leaf-like parts are called **sepals** (SEE-puls). They cover and protect the flower bud before it opens. After the bud opens, you may see the sepals where the flower is attached to the stem.

(2) The colored parts of the flower are the **petals** (PET-uls). Like sepals, they help protect the inner parts of the flower. Petals also attract bumblebees or other insects.

(3) Inside the petals are the flower's male parts, called **stamens** (STAY-muns). Each stamen is a thin stalk with a knob at the top. The knobs

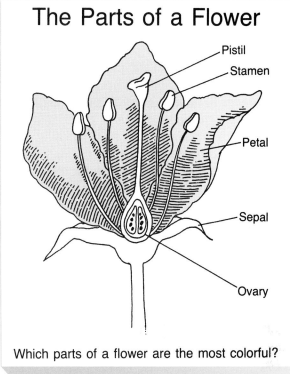

The Parts of a Flower

Pistil
Stamen
Petal
Sepal
Ovary

Which parts of a flower are the most colorful?

produce a fine yellowish powder, called **pollen.** Pollen is made of many tiny pollen grains. Pollen grains contain sperm.

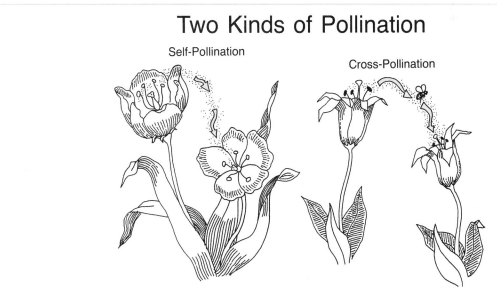

Two Kinds of Pollination

Self-Pollination

Cross-Pollination

Self-pollination occurs when pollen from one flower is carried or falls to another flower on the same plant. Cross-pollination occurs when pollen from one flower is carried to a flower on a different plant.

(4) At the center of the flower is the **pistil** (PIS-til). This is the flower's female part. The pistil has a sticky top that helps trap pollen. At the lower part of the pistil is a bulge called the **ovary** (OH-vuh-ree). Inside the ovary are the eggs.

POLLINATION AND FERTILIZATION. Remember the bees and the clover? Bees, other insects, birds, or the wind may carry pollen from flower to flower. The way pollen is carried depends on the kind of plant. The transfer of pollen from a stamen to a pistil is called **pollination** (pol-uh-NAY-shun).

When a pollen grain lands on top of a pistil, the grain starts to grow. It grows a long tube down through the pistil. The tube grows until it reaches the ovary. Then a sperm that was inside the pollen tube joins with an egg inside the ovary. This is fertilization—the joining of the sperm cell with the egg cell.

After fertilization, the flower can form seeds. Soon, young plants start to form inside the seeds.

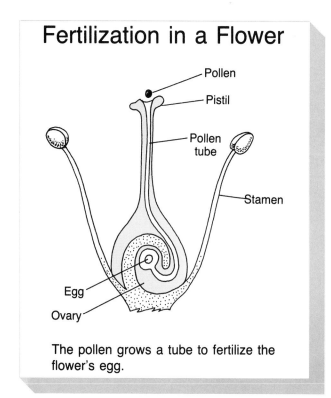

Fertilization in a Flower

The pollen grows a tube to fertilize the flower's egg.

To Do Yourself   **What Are the Parts of a Flower?**

You will need:

A flower such as a tulip, scissors, hand lens, drawing paper, pencil

1. Carefully examine your flower. Compare it to the drawing in this lesson.
2. Use the hand lens to observe the stamens and find the pollen.
3. Use the scissors to cut off some of the petals. Locate the pistil. Then carefully cut through the ovary at the base of the pistil.
4. Make a drawing of your flower and label the parts that you observe.

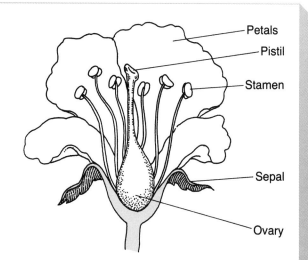

Questions

1. What are the male parts of your flower? _____

2. What are the female parts of your flower? _____

3. What part of your flower attracts insects for pollination? _____

Review

I. Match the flower part in column A with its description in column B.

A	B
_____ **1.** stamen	**a.** attract insects and help protect inner parts
_____ **2.** pistil	**b.** produces pollen
_____ **3.** petals	**c.** has ovary at its lower end
_____ **4.** sepals	**d.** cover flower bud before it opens

II. Circle the word that makes each statement true.

  A. Egg cells are found inside the (pollen/ovary).

  B. Moving pollen from a stamen to a pistil is (propagation/pollination).

  C. Male sex cells are called (sperm/egg) cells.

  D. The joining of a male cell and a female cell is (fertilization/propagation).

III. Corn flowers are pollinated by the wind rather than by insects. Which parts, petals or ovaries, are missing in the silks (female flowers) of corn? Explain.

IV. Some plants, such as corn, have male flowers (called tassels) and female flowers (called silks) on the same plant. Which flower parts are present on a tassel, but not on a silk—and vice versa? Explain your answer.

Flowers on a Corn Plant

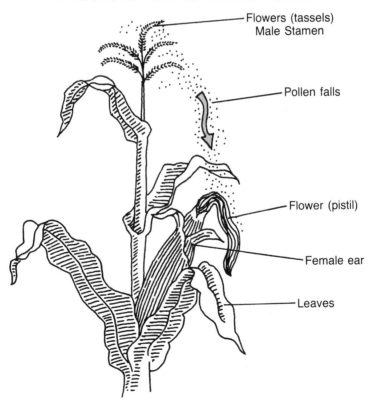

Flowers (tassels)
Male Stamen

Pollen falls

Flower (pistil)

Female ear

Leaves

What are Seeds and Fruits?

Exploring Science

The Seeds That Lived 1,000 Years. A thousand years ago in China, seeds from the sacred lotus were buried in mud. The mud dried. For a lack of water, the seeds did not sprout. These seeds had coats that were very hard, like marble. They stayed buried for 1,000 years. Then they were found by scientists. The scientists used a special test to find out how old the seeds were. Later, they put the ancient lotus seeds in a museum.

Then the scientists had an idea. They knew that some seeds stay alive only for days or weeks. Others stay alive for many years. Could the ancient seeds with the "marble" coats still be alive? They decided to find out.

First, the scientists softened the hard seed coats with an acid. Then they planted the seeds. The seeds sprouted! Even more amazing, the new lotus plants bloomed. On July 29, 1952, they had beautiful pink flowers!

Now, each July, visitors to the Kenilworth Aquatic Gardens in Washington, D.C., get a special treat. They see the blossoms of lotuses whose seeds lived for 1,000 years. For each year since 1952, the lotuses have continued to bloom.

● Wheat seeds have much softer coats than lotus seeds. Which claim is more likely to be true:

A. Lotus seeds from Japan that were 3,000 years old were sprouted.

This lotus flower is from a seed that was buried for a thousand years.

B. Wheat seeds from Egypt that were 3,000 years old were sprouted.

Explain your answer.

Seeds and Fruits

The story of the 1,000-year-old seeds starts with the lotus flowers that produced them. After the flowers were pollinated, they lost their petals. Inside each flower's ovary, a number of eggs were fertilized by sperm that were in the pollen. Then each ovary began to grow. It grew until it became a large seed pod. Each section of the pod contained a seed.

Just what is a seed? After an egg in a flower is fertilized, it develops into a tiny young plant called an **embryo** (EM-bree-oh). At the same time, other cells within the ovary form a food supply for the embryo. The embryo and its food supply are the seed. Around the seed is a **seed coat.** The seed coat protects the embryo during its resting stage. This resting stage, as you have read, may last a short time or a long time. The time that a seed rests depends on the kind of seed it is. It also depends on whether conditions are right for the embryo plant to start growing again.

Remember the seed pod of the lotus? It may come as a surprise to you that a seed pod is the plant's fruit. A **fruit** is a ripened, enlarged ovary that contains seeds. You have eaten many kinds of fruits. Think about what you find when you bite into a fruit such as a peach or an apple. There is a fleshy part. And there are one or more seeds.

Many foods that we call vegetables or nuts are really fruits. Some are fleshy and some are dry. Tomatoes, cucumbers, and squash are fleshy fruits. Walnuts and acorns are dry fruits.

All fruits, fleshy or dry, contain seeds. Seeds usually have a better chance of growing if they are some distance away from the parent plant. (Why?) The fruit protects and helps to scatter the seeds. Animals and people eat the fleshy parts of fruits and throw away the seeds. A bird may eat a cherry and drop the seed far away.

The seeds of a maple have wings, and those of a dandelion have parachutes. The wind carries them far from the parent plants. Other seeds, such as the burdock, have hooks that stick to fur or clothing. Have you ever helped to scatter seeds that stuck to your clothes?

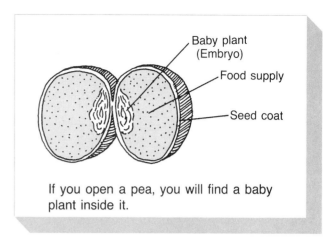

If you open a pea, you will find a baby plant inside it.

Plants make many more seeds than they need. Most will never grow into new plants. But scattering the seeds does help some of them to land where conditions for growth are good.

When a seed starts to sprout, its seed coat breaks open. The embryo plant starts to grow again. In time, it develops into a mature plant. When the new plant produces its own flowers, the cycle of reproduction and growth begins again.

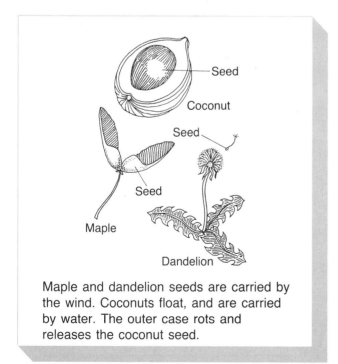

Maple and dandelion seeds are carried by the wind. Coconuts float, and are carried by water. The outer case rots and releases the coconut seed.

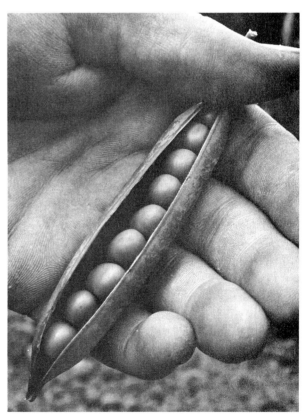

Which is the fruit—the pea or the pod?

How a Flower Becomes a Seed

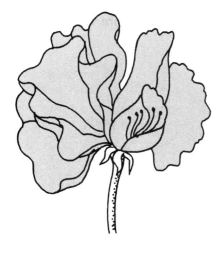
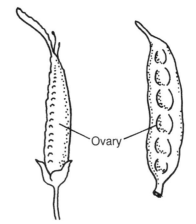
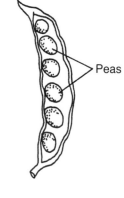

Sweet Pea Flower   Undeveloped Pod   Developed Pod   Open Pod

When the flower dies, its ovary becomes the pod. The pod, when developed, contains seeds.

To Do Yourself   Where Can You Find the Seeds of Plants?

You will need:

Seeds of dry fruit such as lima bean, pea, peanut in shell; fleshy fruit such as tomato, orange, apple, grapefruit, grape, pepper; water; hand lens

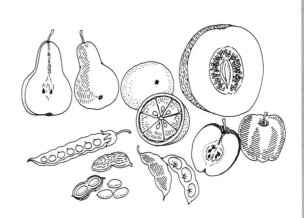

1. Soak the lima bean and pea in water overnight. Carefully remove the seed coats and open the seeds. Use a hand lens to examine and identify the seed parts.
2. Draw and Label what you observe.
3. Open the peanut shell. Remove the seed coat carefully and examine the parts of the peanut. Compare with the bean and pea. Draw what you observe.
4. Open the fleshy fruits. Locate and collect the seeds.

Questions

1. How did the peanut compare with the pea and the bean? _____

2. What do each of the fruits have in common? _____

Review

I. Fill each blank with the word or phrase that fits best. Choose from the words below.

**ovary   fruits   animals   wind   eggs   stamens   embryo
seed coat**

A fertilized egg develops into an _____ . Pea pods and

tomatoes are kinds of _____ . An embryo and its food

supply are covered by a _____ . A fruit is a ripened

_____ . Seeds can be scattered by _____

or by _____ .

II. Circle the word that makes each statement true.

A. An example of a fleshy fruit is (squash/peanut).

B. A seed that travels by the wind is (maple/cherry).

C. After a flower is pollinated it loses its (ovary/petals).

III. Seed coats are often so tough that an animal's digestive system cannot break them down. How does this help some plants to scatter seeds? (Think, for example, of a bird eating a berry, seeds and all.)

IV. Pines and other conifers have cones instead of flowers. Some cones are male and others are female. Male cones usually grow in clusters; female cones usually grow alone. Female cones are also larger than male cones. In the drawings below, write "male" under the male cone. Write "female" below the female cone.

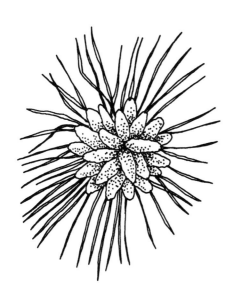

_____   _____

Review What You Know

A. Use the clues below to complete the crossword puzzle.

Across

1. A sperm _____ an egg.
4. A tulip or garlic
5. Tiny cell of a mold
7. Can grow into a whole potato
9. Found in a fruit
11. Root-like stem
12. Reproduction from one parent

Down

1. How one paramecium becomes two
2. Tiny plant inside seed
3. To transfer pollen
6. Sex cells found in ovaries
8. Reproduction from two parents

10. A sperm is a male sex _____ .

B. Write the word that best completes each statement.

1. _____ Two daughter cells of the same size result from
   a. budding **b.** fission **c.** grafting

2. _____ The black dots in bread mold are its **a.** stems
   b. roots **c.** spores

3. _____ The regrowth of a lizard's tail is
   a. reproduction **b.** regeneration **c.** propagation

4. _____ Onions reproduce in nature from **a.** bulbs
   b. stems **c.** tubers

5. _____ Pollen grains contain cells called **a.** eggs
   b. buds **c.** sperm

6. _____ A male flower part is a **a.** stamen **b.** pistil
   c. sepal

7. _____ Vegetative propagation can be used to
   reproduce **a.** worms **b.** starfish **c.** geraniums

8. _____ An example of a fruit is **a.** mushroom
   b. tomato **c.** potato

9. _____ A flower's female part is a **a.** petal **b.** pistil
   c. stamen

10. _____ A seed contains a food supply and a(n) **a.** egg
    b. embryo **c.** sperm

11. _____ Asexual reproduction can result from
   a. pollination   **b.** regeneration   **c.** fertilization

12. _____ A mold reproduces by   **a.** buds   **b.** spores
   c. seeds

13. _____ Potatoes reproduce in nature from   **a.** tubers
   b. grafts   **c.** bulbs

C. Apply What You Know

1. On the line below each picture, write the term that describes the picture
   best. Choose from these terms:

   Budding   **Vegetative propagation**   **Regeneration**   **Spore formation**
   Seed Scattering   **Fission**

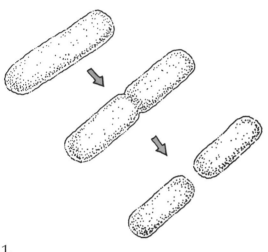

1. _____

2. _____

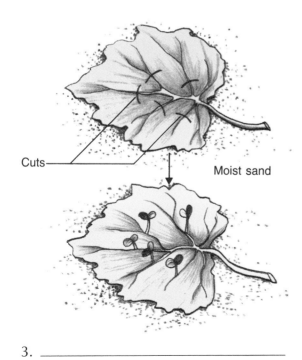

Cuts

Moist sand

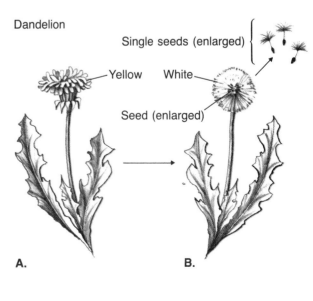

Dandelion

Single seeds (enlarged)

Yellow   White

Seed (enlarged)

A.   **B.**

3. _____

4. _____

2. Each statement below refers to one of the pictures on page 181. The number of the statement is the same as the number of the picture. Circle the word (or words) that makes each statement true.

   a. The offspring of a bacterium are called (buds/daughter cells).

   b. A broken-off claw of a lobster (can/cannot) grow into a whole new lobster.

   c. Young begonias grow from (cuttings/tubers).

   d. When a dandelion turns from yellow to white, it loses its (petals/embryos).

3. How many fruits can you identify in the drawing below?

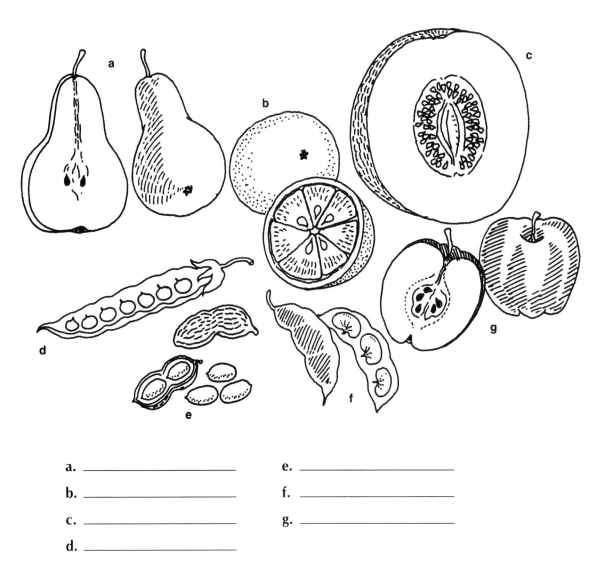

a. _____   e. _____

b. _____   f. _____

c. _____   g. _____

d. _____

D. Find Out More

   1. Make a seed collection. Get real seeds from nature or from foods. You can use pictures of some (don't forget coconuts). Make a display of your collection. Label each seed to tell how it is scattered.

   2. All "vegetables" that contain seeds are fruits. But not all fruits contain seeds. Find out how seedless oranges, grapes, and so on first came to be. How are they propagated?

A. On the drawing of a plant, write labels for each numbered part. Use these labels:

stem   root   leaf   flower

Each statement below refers to one of the plant parts shown. The number of the statement is the same as the number of the part. Circle the word (or words) that makes each statement true.

1. After fertilization, the (ovary/stamen) ripens into a fruit.
2. Plant cells that make food give off (carbon dioxide/oxygen) during daylight.
3. A tissue that can store food is (pith/cambium).
4. Water moves upwards through (phloem/xylem) tissue.

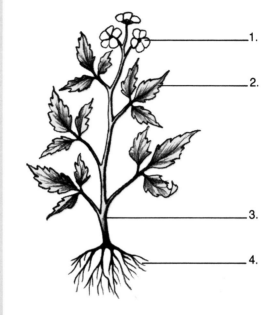

B. On the drawing of the body, write labels for each numbered part. Use these labels:

heart   small intestine   thyroid gland   large intestine   cerebrum

blood vessels

The number below refers to one of the human parts shown. The number of the statement is the same as the number of the part. Circle the word or words that makes each statement true.

1. The brain's largest part contains the control center for (thought/breathing).
2. Too little of the hormone thyroxin may cause (tiredness/diabetes).
3. Blood in the right atrium is (high/low) in oxygen.
4. Enzymes digest proteins by breaking them into (fatty/amino) acids.

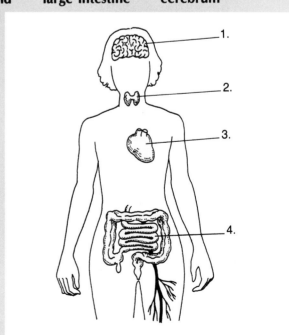

REPRODUCTION IN HIGHER ANIMALS

How Do Animals Reproduce Sexually?

Exploring Science

Dr. Just and the Sea Urchin. Look at the picture below. You might not think so at first, but the "pin cushion" in the picture is an animal. It's a sea urchin, a spiny-skinned relative of the starfish.

Sea urchins produce eggs that are fertilized by sperm. Much of what scientists know about how an egg changes when it is fertilized they have learned from sea urchins.

In the early 1900s Dr. Ernest Just experimented with sea-urchin eggs. Just knew that the centers, or nuclei, of sperm and egg join at fertilization. He discovered that the nuclei needed

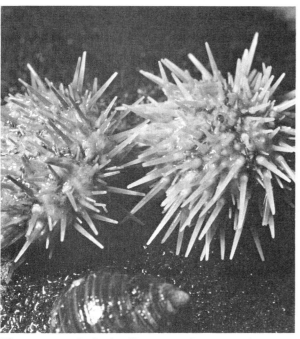

The sea urchin looks like an underwater pin cushion. Its mouth is on the under side.

Ernest Just did basic research in the fertilization and development of the eggs of marine animals.

something else when they joined. They needed cytoplasm. This is the part of the cell around the nucleus.

There are still many mysteries about how animals reproduce. If eggs are fertilized in outer space, do they develop normally? This question may be answered by sending sea-urchin eggs aboard spacecraft. Today's scientists, like Dr. Just, are still learning from the lowly sea urchin.

● Do sea urchins reproduce sexually or asexually? Explain your answer.

Sexual Reproduction in Animals

Like the sea urchin, most animals reproduce sexually. There are two parents, one male and one female. In animals, the male parent has organs called **testes** (TES-teez), which produce sperm cells. The female parent has organs called **ovaries,** which produce egg cells.

The egg cells of most animals are much larger than sperm cells. Some eggs have a stored food supply, called **yolk** (YOHK).

A sperm cell has a head and a whiplike tail. The head is mainly the cell's nucleus. Sperm are released into water or are produced in a liquid.

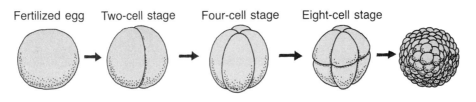

Fertilized egg   Two-cell stage   Four-cell stage   Eight-cell stage

How a fertilized egg develops.

They use their tails to swim towards eggs. Thousands of sperm may reach one egg, but only one sperm can enter it.

When a sperm **fertilizes** (FUR-tuh-lyz-is) an egg, its head enters the egg. The tail is left outside. The sperm nucleus and egg nucleus join to make one nucleus. This cell, the fertilized egg, is called a **zygote** (ZY-goht).

The zygote then divides into 2 cells, which do not separate. This two-celled young animal, or **embryo,** divides again, forming 4 cells. These cells divide forming 8 cells, and so on. Soon, the embryo is a ball of many cells.

The pictures show how a sea-urchin embryo develops from an egg into a ball of cells. Other animal embryos, including humans, look very much the same at these early stages. The ball of cells then curls and folds, and continues to develop. Its later growth turns it into an animal like its parents.

How Animals Develop

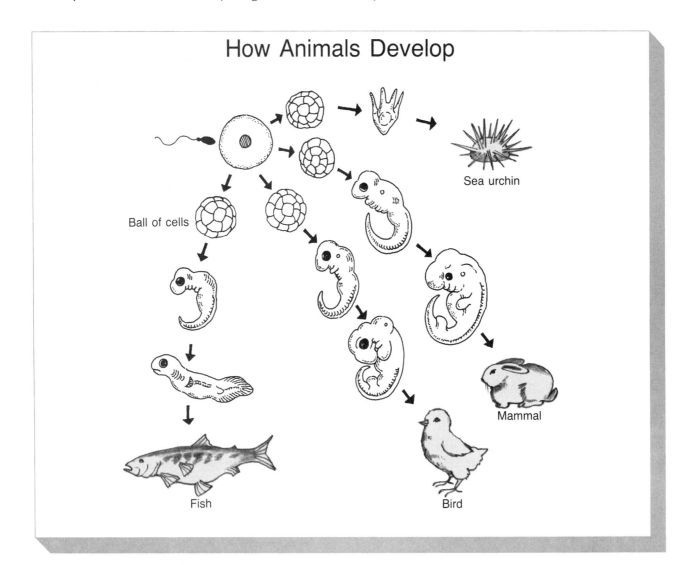

Ball of cells

Sea urchin

Mammal

Bird

Fish

To Do Yourself How Do Snails Reproduce?

You will need:

Small aquarium with sand and a few plants, several snails, hand lens, lettuce

1. Place some snails in an aquarium.
2. Feed you snails some small pieces of lettuce. Remove uneaten portions that begin to decay.
3. Observe your snails to find out when they being to lay eggs. Carefully observe the aquarium glass with your hand lens.
4. Use the hand lens to observe the eggs' development.

Questions

1. Where did your snails lay their eggs? _____

2. What did the eggs look like? _____

3. How long did it take for the eggs to develop and hatch? _____

Review

I. Fill in each blank with the word that fits best. Choose from the words below.

fertilizes   divides   yolk   ovaries   cytoplasm   nucleus   zygote

testes

The male organs of an animal are the _____ . The female

organs are the _____ . The _____ is a

stored food supply. A fertilized egg, or _____ , is a single

cell that _____ into two cells. The sperm

_____ joins with the egg nucleus during fertilization.

II. Circle the word that makes each statement true.

    A. The nucleus of a sperm cell is in its (head/tail)

    B. In fertilization, a (testis/sperm) joins with an egg.

    C. A ball of cells is a stage of development of the (embryo/ovary).

III. In the drawing on page 186, which two embryos look the most alike in their later stages? Why do you think this is so?

How Do Fish Reproduce?

Exploring Science

Fish that Change Sex. It is easy to see how clown fishes got their name. They are bright yellow with bands of black-and-white "make-up" and sad mouths.

One species of clown fish live in family groups. The family home is near a giant sea anemone (uh-NEM-uh-nee), a flower-like animal related to the jellyfish.

The clown fish and the anemone help each other get food. The fishes swim nearby and attract other fishes into the anemone's deadly "arms" (tentacles), which sting and then catch them. Meanwhile, the clown fishes that attracted the food stay safe inside those same arms. Later, the anemone and the clown fishes share the meal.

The largest member of the clown-fish family is an adult female. She is about five centimeters long. There are also an adult male and several "children"—younger and smaller fishes.

The sex life of these fish is unusual. If the female dies or is taken away, the male grows larger and turns into a female! Then the largest "child" grows up and becomes and adult male. There is always just one adult of each sex.

Other kinds of fish sometimes change sex, too. A stoplight fish, as it grows larger and older, changes from female to male. The female is red. What color do you think the male is? That's right—the male is green.

Why do fish change sex? In each case—and in different ways—the change helps the fish to have more young. You will soon see why fish need as many young as they can produce.

● You have learned that eggs are larger than sperm. In a fish couple, why might it be better for the female to be larger than the male?

The clown fish is not harmed by the poisonous sting of the sea anemone.

The Life Cycle of a Fish

The fishes are a group of vertebrates, or animals with backbones. They spend their lives in the water. A fish breathes through its **gills.** Water that goes into a fish's mouth goes out through its gills. In the gills, oxygen from the water passes into the fish's blood. Carbon dioxide passes from the blood into the water.

Most species of fish, such as tuna or trout, have the same sex all their life. In a male fish, the testes produce sperm. From each testis, a **sperm**

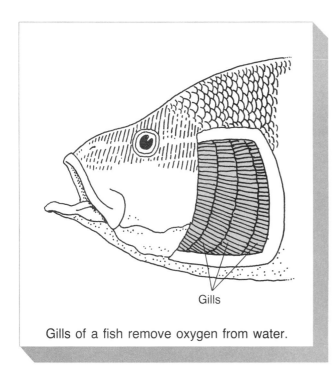

Gills of a fish remove oxygen from water.

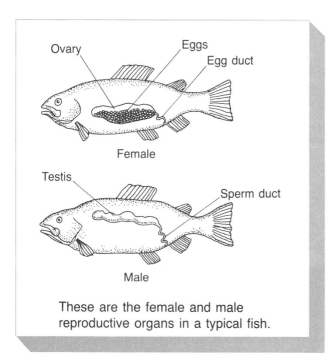

These are the female and male reproductive organs in a typical fish.

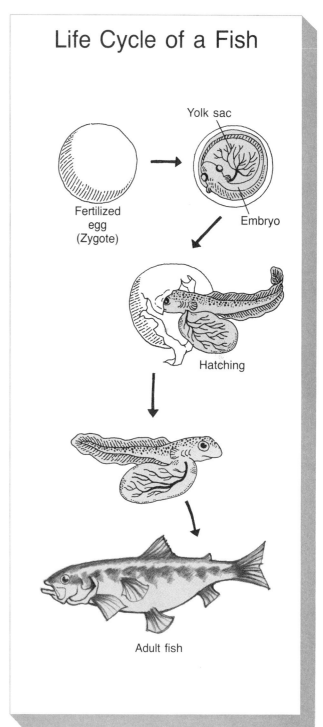

Life Cycle of a Fish

tube carries the sperm out of the body. In a female, the ovaries produce eggs. From each ovary, an **egg tube** carries the eggs out of the body.

When fishes mate, the female lays a mass of jelly-coated eggs in the water. The male releases sperm over the eggs. Then fertilization takes place. This is called **external** (ik-STUR-nul) **fertilization,** because the eggs are fertilized outside the female's body.

The fertilized eggs, or **zygotes,** develop into **embryos.** A **yolk sac** forms around the yolk, which is the embryo's food supply. After the egg hatches, the embryo lives off the yolk until it grows big enough to catch food.

In a few kinds of fish, such as guppies, the male deposits sperm into the female's body. This is called **internal** (in-TUR-nul) **fertilization,** because the eggs are fertilized inside the female. The embryos develop inside the mother. When the young are born, they are able to catch food for themselves.

Fish lay thousands or millions of eggs at a time. Those that have live babies produce hundreds. Why so many? Most parent fishes give no care to their eggs or young. Not all eggs will be fertilized in the water, and most of those that are will be eaten by enemies. So will the embryos and little fishes. To make sure that even a few will grow to be adults, large numbers of eggs must be laid. Those that do grow up complete their **life cycle** when they produce their own eggs and sperm. A life cycle is the pattern of an organism's growth—from birth, through growth and reproduction, to death.

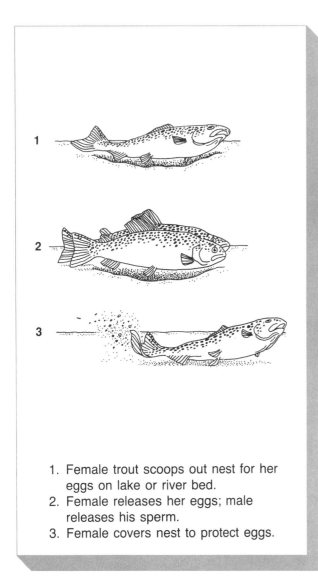

1. Female trout scoops out nest for her eggs on lake or river bed.
2. Female releases her eggs; male releases his sperm.
3. Female covers nest to protect eggs.

A stickleback fish nest is shown at top. Below it, the nest of a sunfish.

Review

I. Fill in each blank with the word or words that fits best. Choose from the words below.

internal   blood   external   zygote   egg tube   sperm tube
yolk sac   gills

Oxygen moves into a fish's blood through its _____ . A

testis connects to a _____ and an ovary to an

_____ . Fertilization outside the female is

_____ . Fertilization inside the female is _____ .

The fish embryo's food supply is in the _____ .

II. Some fish build nests and lay their eggs in them. Would you expect these fish to lay more or fewer eggs than those that lay eggs in open water? Explain.

To Do Yourself   How Do Some Types of Fish Reproduce?

You will need:

Small tank or fishbowl, sand, aquarium plants, several guppies, hand lens, aged tap water, fish food

1. Set up an aquarium with sand, plants, aged tap water, and guppies.
2. Feed the guppies, as instructed on the food container.
3. Observe the guppies: Males are smaller and more colorful than females. After mating and fertilization of the eggs, the female gives birth to 50 to 200 young in two weeks.
4. Observe and record the reproduction of your guppies over a period of time.

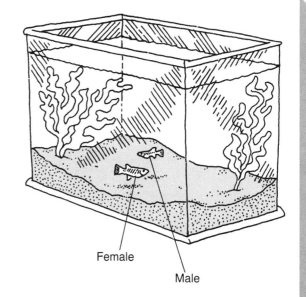

Female

Male

Questions

1. How often did your guppies produce offspring? _____

2. How could you tell that the female was about to give birth? _____

3. How many young were born? Why do you think there were so many? _____

How Do Amphibians and Reptiles Reproduce?

Exploring Science

Herp Facts and Fables. What is a herp? Any frog or other amphibian is a herp. So is any snake of other reptile. Scientists called **herpetologists** (hur-pih-TOL-uh-jists) study herps. These scientists must often help correct the many false ideas, or fables, that people have about herps. At the HERPlab, in the National Zoo at Washington, D.C., you can get close to herps. You can also learn many facts about herps and find out which ideas about herps are fables.

Here's a herp quiz for you. Which sayings are facts? Which are fables? (Answers below.)

1. In South America, Indians make poison for arrows from frogs.
2. A snake can hold its tail in its mouth and roll like a hoop.
3. A bullfrog can jump nine times its own length.
4. Toads cause warts.
5. Snakes steal milk from cows.

Answers: **1.** fact; **2.** fable; **3.** fact; **4.** fable; **5.** fable.

Here's another fact about herps. Some snakes and some lizards do not lay eggs. They give birth to live young, instead. But most herps do lay eggs, as you will see.

● Almost all herps are harmless. Why, then, do you think so many people believe the opposite, that most herps are harmful?

Youngsters meet some reptiles in the classroom.

Life Cycles of Amphibians and Reptiles

The **amphibians** (am-FIB-ee-uns) are a group of vertebrates. They include frogs, toads, and salamanders. Most amphibians live part of their life in water as **tadpoles.** Like fish, tadpoles breathe with gills. As adults, on the land, amphibians breathe with lungs. They reproduce sexually.

The **reptiles** (REP-tils) are another group of vertebrates. They include snakes, lizards, turtles, crocodiles, and alligators. Most reptiles live on the land, and all reptiles breathe with lungs. They also reproduce sexually.

Let's follow the life cycle of animals from each of these groups.

LIFE CYCLE OF A FROG. Frogs mate in the water. A female frog lays hundreds—or thousands—of eggs in the water. Fertilization is external, or outside the female's body. As the eggs are laid, the male deposits sperm on them. The sperm fertilize the eggs. Each egg has a lot of yolk, the food supply for the embryo. A covering of jelly protects the eggs while they develop.

A frog's egg hatches into a tadpole. It looks like a fish, with a tail and gills. Slowly, it grows

The Life Cycle of a Frog

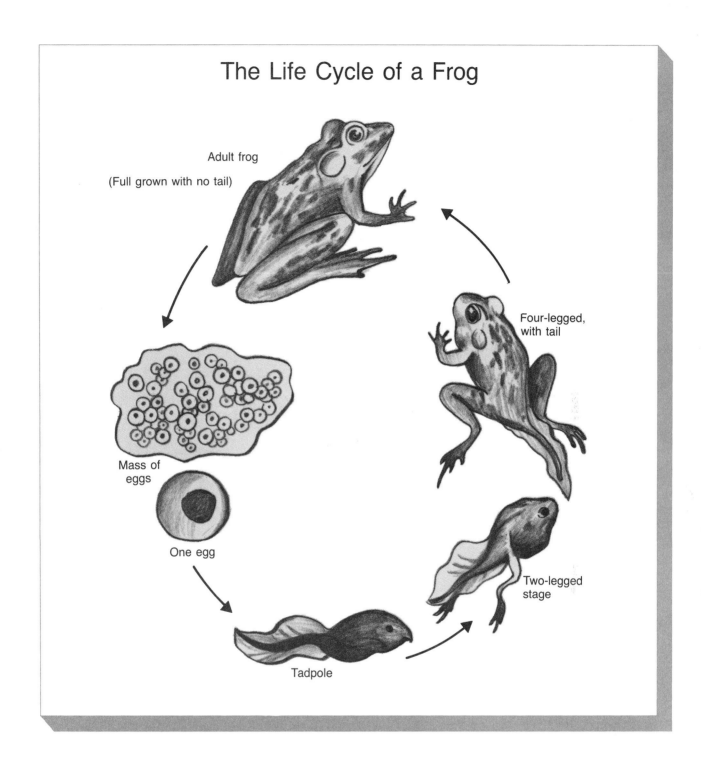

Adult frog
(Full grown with no tail)

Four-legged, with tail

Mass of eggs

One egg

Two-legged stage

Tadpole

hind legs and then front legs. It loses its gills and its tail. It develops lungs and then hops onto the land. There it grows into an adult frog. It has gone through a complete change in body form. This change is called **metamorphosis** (met-uh-MOR-fuh-sis)—from *meta*, which means "change," and *morph*, which means "form."

LIFE CYCLE OF A REPTILE. Reptiles mate on the land. In reptiles, fertilization is internal, or inside the female's body. After the eggs are fer-

tilized, they become coated with a large amount of yolk. There is more yolk in a reptile's egg than in the egg of a frog or other amphibian. A tough, leathery shell forms around the egg before it is laid. Most reptiles' eggs are laid on dry land, and the shells keep them from drying out. Inside the shells, the embryos have enough food, in the yolk, to develop into little animals. They can get their own food as soon as they hatch.

Reptiles lay many fewer eggs than amphibians do. A turtle lays 6 to 12 eggs at a time. An alligator usually lays between 15 and 80 eggs at a time.

Some lizards and snakes do not lay eggs. Their eggs hatch inside the mother's body, and the young are born alive. Snakes have between 12 and 99 young at a time, either alive or as eggs.

Lizards have between 2 and 30 eggs or living young at a time.

Like newly hatched reptiles, those born alive are able to be on their own at birth. The eggs of reptiles may be laid in protected places. But reptile parents give little or no care to their eggs or young.

The Life Cycle of an Alligator

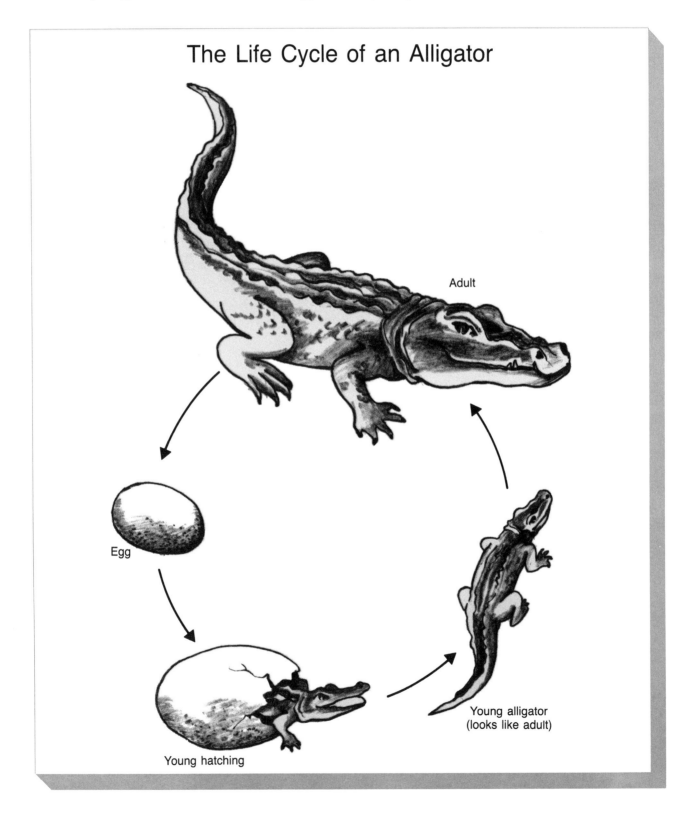

Adult

Egg

Young hatching

Young alligator
(looks like adult)

To Do Yourself   What Is the Life Cycle of a Frog?

You will need:

Small fishbowl, hand lens, frog eggs, aged
tap water

1. Collect some frog eggs from a pond in
   early spring. Place them in a clear glass
   bowl. Keep the bowl in a cool place.
2. Use a hand lens to observe the development of the eggs. Record the changes
   you observe, and record the time each
   change takes place.

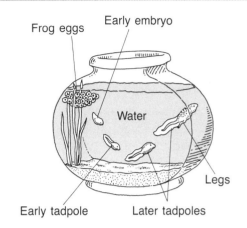

Questions

1. How long does it take for eggs to hatch? _____

2. What are the main stages in a frog's metamorphosis? _____

Review

I. Fill each blank with the word that fits best. Choose from the words below.

herpetologists   tadpoles   jelly   shells   metamorphosis
amphibians   reptiles

The fishlike young of a frog are _____ . Frogs' eggs are

covered by _____ . The eggs of reptiles are covered by

_____ . The eggs of _____ are laid on

dry land. The change of body form in a frog is _____ .

II. Circle the word that makes each statement true.

   A. Fertilization in reptiles is (internal/external).

   B. The young that hatches from a (frog's/turtle's) egg looks like the adult.

   C. Animals that breathe with lungs are (tadpoles/snakes).

   D. An alligator's egg has more (yolk/jelly) than a frog's egg.

III. Reptiles lay many fewer eggs than fish or amphibians do. Why are the young
   of reptiles more likely to survive than are the young of fish and amphibians?

How Do Birds Reproduce?

Exploring Science

Stay-at-Home Father. Mother has to go out to sea and hunt food. Who will stay home and mind the egg? Why, father, of course. He holds the egg on top of his feet. A fold of his skin covers and warms the egg. After two months, the egg hatches. Then both parents take turns holding and feeding the chick.

The parents in this story are emperor penguins (PEN-gwins). They are the largest and strangest of the penguins. Until a few years ago, scientists knew little about their family life. Now we know much more about them, because the birds have been bred at Hubbs-Sea World, in San Diego, California. Scientists there have watched how, after the egg is laid, the female passes it to the male.

In the wild, the father does not eat while the chick inside the egg on his feet develops. After it hatches, mother again takes over, part time. Then father must go to sea for food, or he may starve. At Hubbs-Sea World, scientists feed the father even while he is egg-sitting. They don't want to risk losing him.

● Why does a penguin, unlike a fish, frog, or snake, produce only one egg at a time?

An Emperor penguin warms an egg, until it hatches.

The Life Cycle of a Chicken

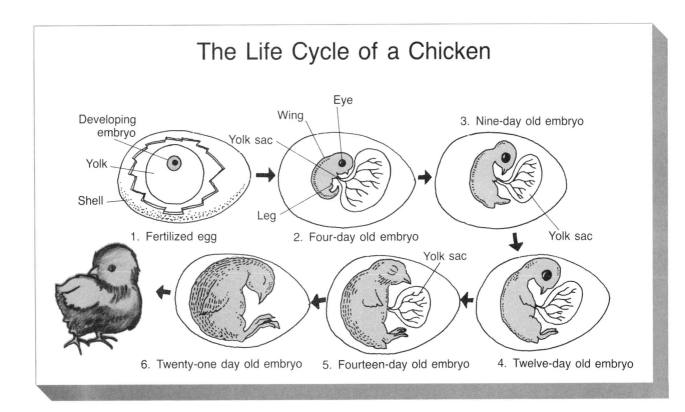

1. Fertilized egg — Developing embryo, Yolk, Shell, Yolk sac

2. Four-day old embryo — Wing, Eye, Yolk sac, Leg

3. Nine-day old embryo — Yolk sac

4. Twelve-day old embryo

5. Fourteen-day old embryo — Yolk sac

6. Twenty-one day old embryo

The Life Cycle of a Bird

Penguins belong to the group of vertebrates called **birds.** Most birds have wings and can fly. Birds are covered with feathers and breathe with lungs. Birds are also warm-blooded. The body temperature of a **warm-blooded** animal stays at a high level and more or less the same. It does not change if the outside temperature changes. Mammals, including you, are another group of warm-blooded animals.

Fish, amphibians, and reptiles are all **cold-blooded.** That means their body temperature changes when the outside temperature changes.

Birds have internal fertilization. The ovary of a female bird, such as a chicken, produces eggs. The tiny eggs pass into the top of the egg tube. The male's testes produce sperm. During mating, the male places sperm inside the bottom of the egg tube. The sperm swim up the tube to the eggs and fertilize them.

Each fertilized egg, or zygote, becomes an embryo as it moves down the egg tube. Along the way, the egg yolk and egg white are depos-

How an Egg Forms

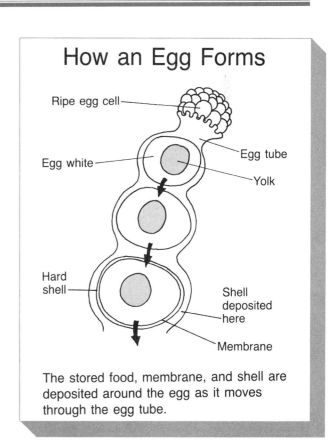

Ripe egg cell, Egg white, Egg tube, Yolk, Hard shell, Shell deposited here, Membrane

The stored food, membrane, and shell are deposited around the egg as it moves through the egg tube.

ited around the embryo. Finally, a shell is added and the egg is laid.

All birds, such as penguins, chickens, and robins, keep their eggs warm, or **incubate** (IN-kyuh-bayt) them. A chicken egg is incubated for 21 days, and then it hatches. During incubation, the embryo grows and develops, using both the yolk and the white for food. All bird parents continue to care for their young for a time after hatching.

To Do Yourself   What Are the Parts of a Bird Egg?

You will need:

Chicken egg, dish, hand lens

1. Carefully crack open a fresh egg into a dish. Locate the shell membrane, the white, and the yolk. Find the rope-like part of the white that holds the yolk in place. Draw what you observe.
2. Use a hand lens to observe the pores in the egg shell.
3. Examine the yolk to find a white speck the size of a pinhead. This is where the embryo begins to develop.

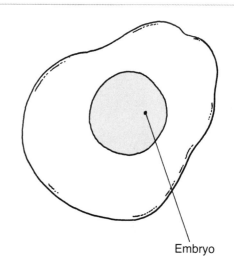

Embryo

Questions

1. What is the purpose of the egg yolk? _____

2. What is the purpose of the egg white? _____

3. What is the purpose of the pores in the egg shell? _____

4. Why was there no embryo in the egg you observed? _____

Review

I. Fill in each blank with the word that fits best. Choose from the words below.

ovary   egg tube   cold-blooded   warm-blooded   testis   incubate

A _____ animal's body temperature stays about the same. A

bird's egg cell is produced in the _____ . Egg yolk and

white form around the embryo inside the _____ . Parent

birds keep warm or _____ their eggs.

II. An ostrich has feathers, lays eggs, and is warm-blooded. But this animal has no wings and, therefore, cannot fly. A bat has hair, gives birth to live young, has wings, and can fly. Which animal is a bird? Explain your answer.

How Do Mammals Reproduce?

Exploring Science

Test-Tube Babies. The birth of Louise Brown in 1978 made history. She was the world's first test-tube baby. No, Louise was not "born" from a test tube. She was born from her mother's body, like other human babies. But her life began in a glass dish. Reporters called the dish a "test-tube," and the name remained. Why did Louise's life have to start in a dish?

A human egg is fertilized inside an egg tube in the mother. But sometimes the sperm cannot reach the egg because the egg tubes are blocked. Then the parents cannot have children. For these people, doctors may take an egg from the mother and place it in a dish. Sperm from the father are placed in the same dish. There, a sperm fertilizes the egg. A tiny embryo grows in the dish for a few days. It is then placed in the mother's body. If all goes well, 9 months later a baby is born.

It is no longer headline news when a test-tube baby is born. Many children have started life the way Louise did. One of these children is Louise's younger sister, Natalie.

The world's first test-tube baby, Louise Brown, with her sister, Natalie.

● A newspaper headline reads "Test-Tube Calf Born." How do you think the calf's life began?

How Mammals Reproduce

Humans are members of the group of vertebrates called **mammals.** The mammals also include animals like dogs, cats, monkeys, and whales. All mammals have hair or fur on their bodies and are warm-blooded. Mammals have **mammary** (MAM-uh-ree) **glands,** which produce milk for feeding their young. Most mammals give birth to one or more live young. (But there are two mammals that lay eggs. These are the duckbill platypus and the spiny anteater.)

A male mammal's main reproductive organs are the testes. In the human male, the testes are covered with skin and hang outside the body. A sperm tube from each testis carries sperm cells, which are made in the testes, into the **urethra.** Through the urethra, sperm pass outside the body.

In a female mammal, the organs that produce eggs are the ovaries. A human ovary usually releases one egg about every 28 days. The egg moves into an egg tube. While the egg is inside the tube, it can be fertilized.

During mating, sperm enter the female's body. The sperm swim through the womb, or *uterus* (YOO-tur-us), into the egg tubes. Millions of sperm may go into the tubes, but only one sperm can fertilize one egg. The fertilized egg, or **zygote,** moves down the egg tube as it

The Human Reproductive System

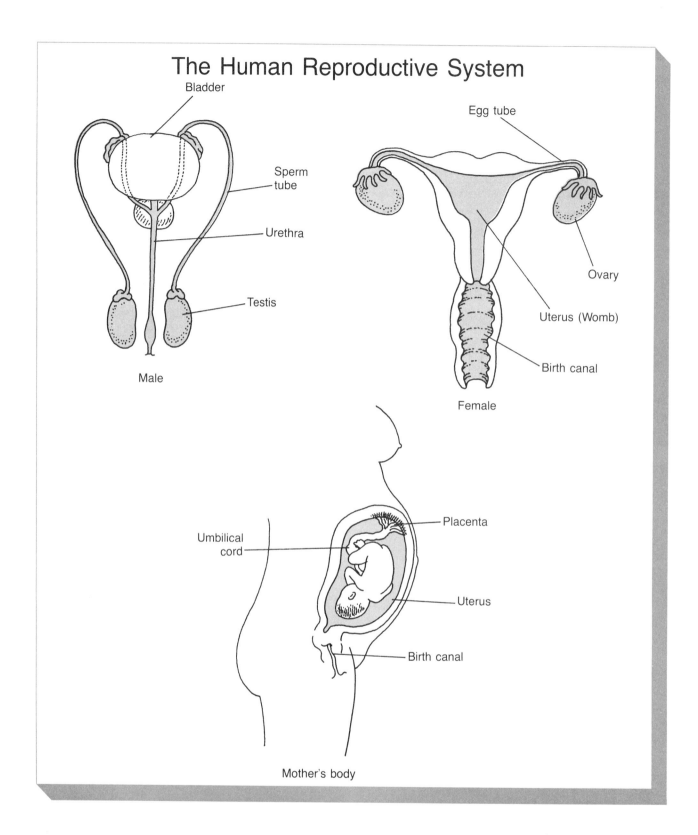

Bladder

Sperm tube

Urethra

Testis

Male

Egg tube

Ovary

Uterus (Womb)

Birth canal

Female

Umbilical cord

Placenta

Uterus

Birth canal

Mother's body

starts to develop. While still a tiny embryo it moves into the uterus. The embryo attaches itself to the wall of the uterus.

As the human embryo continues to develop, a flat structure called the **placenta** forms inside the uterus. Blood vessels in the placenta bring food and oxygen to the embryo. These vessels also carry wastes away from the embryo. The embryo is joined to the placenta by the ropelike **umbilical cord.** Food, oxygen, and wastes all move between embryo and placenta through the umbilical cord.

After about two months, a human embryo is called a **fetus** (FEE-tus). The fetus develops and grows until it is a baby, ready to be born.

When the time of birth comes, the muscles in the walls of the uterus contract, as **labor** begins. The contractions of labor push the baby through the **birth canal** and out into the world.

During the period of time between fertilization and birth, the mother is **pregnant** (PREG-nunt). The time of pregnancy for humans is about 9 months. For some other mammals, pregnancy may be shorter or longer. For a rat, there are 3 weeks between fertilization and birth. For an elephant, the time is 22 months.

Mammals provide more care for their young than do any other animals.

Many mammals give birth to a litter—several babies at one time.

Review

I. Fill in each blank with the word or term that fits best. Choose from the words below.

umbilical cord   **placenta**   **egg tube**   **urethra**   **sperm tube**   **uterus**
mammary glands   **fetus**   **birth canal**

Milk for a mammal's young is produced in the _____ .

Sperm pass from the sperm tubes into the _____ . An egg

can be fertilized while it is in an _____ . The

_____ connects the embryo to the placenta. After about

two months an embryo is called a _____ . During labor, the

_____ contracts and pushes the baby through the

_____ .

II. Circle the word that makes each statement true.

    A. Mammals are (warm-blooded/cold-blooded).

    B. The fertilized egg is the (ovary/zygote).

    C. Sperm cells are produced in the (testes/placenta).

    D. A human egg is produced about once every (9 months/28 days).

III. Scientists have found that when a pregnant mother drinks alcohol, the baby can be harmed. In a few sentences, explain how the alcohol gets into the baby. Use these terms: uterus, placenta, umbilical cord.

How Do Insects Reproduce?

Exploring Science

Why Jumping Beans Jump. Have you ever seen any "Mexican jumping beans?" They aren't really beans. They are seed pods of a Mexican arrow plant. When the pods are warmed, they jump and hop about. Some of the "beans" open and throw out seeds. But other "beans" just fall from the plant to the ground. These are sold to tourists as "jumping beans," or, more correctly, hopping pods. What makes them hop?

The pods that hop don't contain seeds at all. If you open one, you find a tiny caterpillar inside. A layer of silk lines the inside of the pod. When the desert sun heats the pod, the caterpillar digs its feet in the silk and jerks its body. This jerking causes the pod to hop. When the pod lands in the cool shade, it stops hopping.

Soon, even if placed in the sun or heated, the pod no longer moves at all. If you open the pod now, you find that the caterpillar has changed. It is wrapped in a covering and seems to be at rest. If you keep an unopened pod long enough, you may see the end of the caterpillar's "rest." Through a tiny hole in the pod, out comes a moth!

Why a moth? As you read on, you will find out.

● Why are no seeds found inside the bean pods that hop?

What makes a jumping bean jump?

Life Cycles of Insects

Moths, ants, flies, and other insects are **invertebrates.** That means they have no backbones. But insects do have skeletons on the outside of their bodies. An insect's tough "skin" is its outside skeleton.

Insects reproduce sexually. Male and female mate, and the eggs are fertilized internally, or inside the female. In the egg, the embryo lives on the yolk. The eggs are laid near a food supply that is used after the eggs hatch. After hatching, most insects go through a change of body form. This change is called metamorphosis. It may be complete or incomplete.

COMPLETE METAMORPHOSIS. There are four stages in the **complete metamorphosis** of an insect: egg, larva, pupa, and adult. Like all butterflies and moths, the "jumping bean" moth has complete metamorphosis. This moth lays its eggs in the flowers of the Mexican arrow plant. After the flower forms seeds, the eggs hatch

Complete Metamorphosis

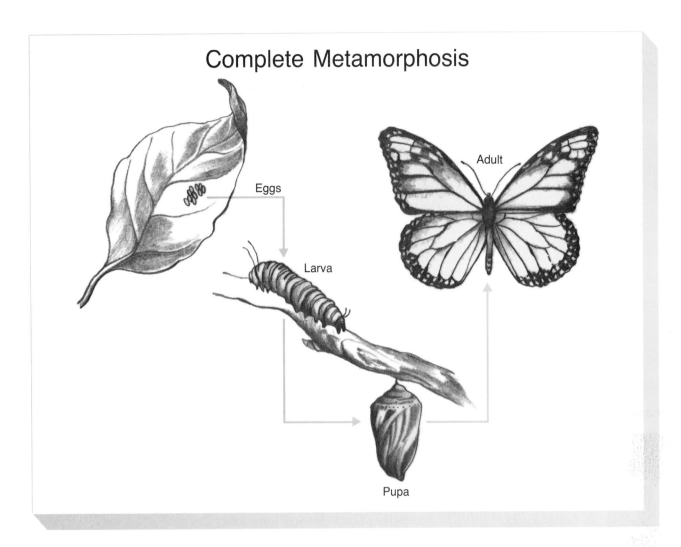

Eggs

Larva

Adult

Pupa

into caterpillars, which are the wormlike **larvas** (LAR-vuhs) of the moth. Other insect larvas also look like worms. Those we call caterpillars are the larvas of butterflies or moths. The larva of a fly is a maggot, and the larva of a beetle is a grub.

Insect larvas eat and grow fast. The "jumping bean" larvas eat the seeds inside the arrow plant's pods. Luckily for the plant, not all of its flowers are visited by the moth. Some of the seeds survive and keep the species from dying out. Larvas of other insects often do great damage to food crops and trees.

As a larva grows, it sheds its outside skeleton, or **molts,** several times. Each new skin is larger than the one before.

When a larva stops growing, it stops eating. Then it becomes a **pupa** (PYOO-puh) inside a hard "skin," or case. A moth larva (caterpillar) spins itself a silky shell, or **cocoon** (kuh-KOON). Then it becomes a pupa inside the cocoon. We get silk from the cocoons of silkworm moths.

During the pupa stage, the insect seems to be at rest. In fact, many body changes go on in the pupa. Still, the pupa is called the resting stage. In time, the pupa's "skin" breaks open, and out comes the **adult.** It has wings and other body parts completely unlike the larva.

Adult moths or butterflies may eat little or nothing. Many live only long enough to mate and lay eggs. Then the life cycle begins again.

INCOMPLETE METAMORPHOSIS. Some insects go through **incomplete metamorphosis.** In their life cycles there are just three stages: egg, **nymph,** and adult. The egg of a cockroach, a grasshopper, or a dragonfly hatches into a nymph. The nymph looks like a small adult, but without wings.

As the nymph eats and grows, it molts several times. With each molt, the wings grow larger. After the last molt, the wings are full grown and the animal can produce eggs or sperm. When the adults mate, the life cycle begins again.

Incomplete Metamorphosis

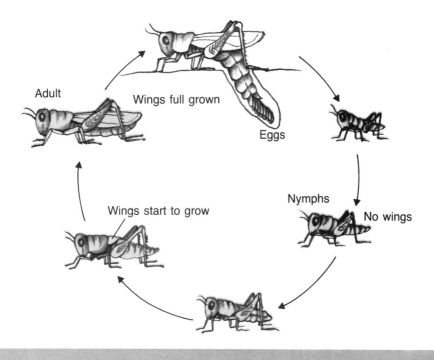

Adult

Wings full grown

Eggs

Nymphs

No wings

Wings start to grow

To Do Yourself How Do Some Insects Reproduce?

You will need:

Caterpillar, jar, lid with air holes, soil, twig, leaves, hand lens

1. Put 2 centimeters of moist soil in a jar. Place a twig in the soil.
2. Place a caterpillar in the jar. Add some leaves from where the caterpillar was found.
3. Observe the caterpillar. Record your observations. Draw the changes you see; record the time each takes.
4. If your caterpillar becomes a butterfly or moth, release it outside.

Lid with holes

Twig with foliage

Caterpillar

Moist soil

Questions

1. How many stages did you observe in the development from egg to adult? _____

2. What stage were you not able to observe? _____

3. At what stage is the insect most destructive? _____

4. Is this a complete or an incomplete metamorphosis? _____

Review

I. Fill in each blank with the word that fits best. Choose from the words below.

metamorphosis   adult   pupa   invertebrates   larva   nymph
molts   embryo   egg

Insects are _____ because they have no backbones. The

wormlike stage of a moth is the _____ . A just-hatched

grasshopper that looks like a little adult is a _____ . During

growth, a young insect sheds its skin, or _____ . A change

of body form is called _____ . The "resting" stage of a

moth is the _____ . The stage of an insect that lays eggs is

the _____ .

II. If the statement is true, write **T**. If it is false, write **F**. Then correct the underlined word.

A. _____ An insect's egg is fertilized <u>internally</u>.

B. _____ A grasshopper goes through <u>complete</u> metamorphosis.

C. _____ The stages of a butterfly's life cycle are egg, <u>larva</u>, pupa, and adult.

D. _____ The pupa stage of a moth is covered by a silk case called a <u>nymph</u>.

E. _____ The stages of a cockroach's life cycle are egg, <u>larva</u>, adult.

III. A centipede looks like a caterpillar in some ways. Both are wormlike and seem to have many legs. A centipede lays eggs that hatch into little centipedes. Do you think the centipede, like a caterpillar, is the larva of a moth or butterfly? Explain your answer.

Caterpillar

Centipede

A. Hidden in the puzzle below are the names of seven stages in the life cycles of different animals. Use the clues to help you find the names. Circle each name in the puzzle. Then write each name on the line next to its clue.

```
A L A R V A D F
F G J O Q D M N
E S U Z X U A Y
T A D P O L E M
U V I E F T T P
S B R E L Y D H
K N B G W C P C
E Z W G P U P A
```

Clues:

1. What a frog's egg hatches into. _____

2. Two-month-old human embryo. _____

3. May contain much yolk. _____

4. Wingless grasshopper or roach. _____

5. Produces eggs or sperms. _____

6. A maggot or a grub. _____

7. May have a cocoon. _____

B. Write the word (or words) that best completes each statement.

1. _____ Testes are organs that produce   **a.** yolk   **b.** eggs   **c.** sperm

2. _____ The vertebrates that produce the most eggs are   **a.** fishes   **b.** birds   **c.** mammals

3. _____ A toad, a crocodile, and a snake are all   **a.** amphibians   **b.** reptiles   **c.** herps

4. _____ After a zygote has divided once, it is an embryo with   **a.** one cell   **b.** two cells   **c.** a ball of cells

5. _____ Warm-blooded animals include   **a.** rats   **b.** salamanders   **c.** lizards

6. _____ An animal that goes through metamorphosis is the   **a.** alligator   **b.** frog   **c.** penguin

7. _____ A frog's eggs are protected by   **a.** egg white   **b.** shells   **c.** jelly

8. _____ Mammary glands are found in a   **a.** platypus   **b.** turtle   **c.** grasshopper

9. _____ The vertebrates that provide the most parental care are **a.** mammals **b.** amphibians **c.** reptiles

10. _____ When a caterpillar molts it sheds its **a.** legs **b.** skeleton **c.** wings

C. Apply What You Know

1. Study the drawings of the embryos of a trout, a robin, and a pig. Label the numbered parts. Choose from these labels. A label may be used more than once.

embryo   **umbilical cord**   **shell**   **uterus**   **yolk**   **yolk sac**

placenta

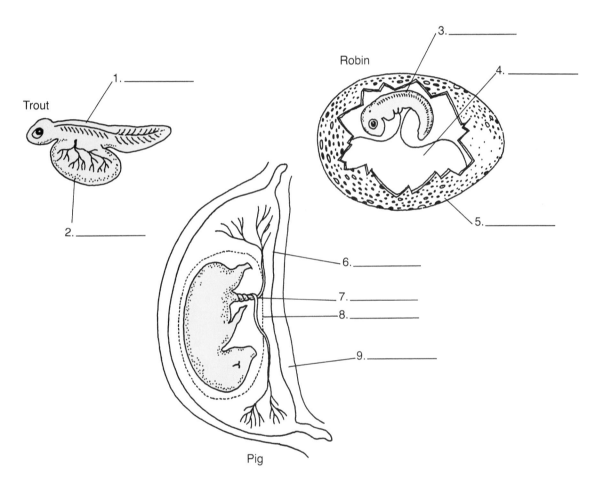

2. Each statement below refers to one or more of the animals whose embryos are shown. On the line after each statement, write one or more of the following: trout, robin, pig.

a. The egg it develops from was fertilized internally. _____

b. Its food supply comes from the mother's blood. _____

c. It will be incubated while it develops. _____

d. Its food supply was stored in the egg. _____

e. It is a cold-blooded animal. _____

3. Study the drawings below of the life cycle of a milkweed bug.

Life Cycle of the Milkweed Bug

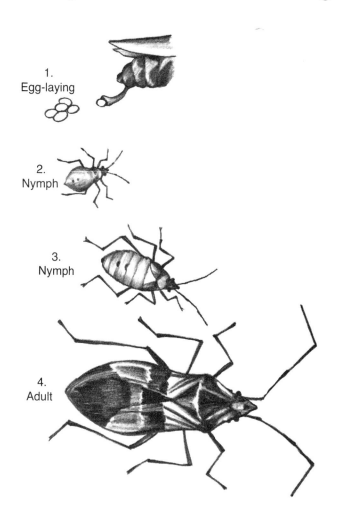

1.
Egg-laying

2.
Nymph

3.
Nymph

4.
Adult

For each statement about the bug that is true, write T in the blank. For each false statement write F. Then correct the underlined term.

a. _____ The bug belongs to a group of <u>vertebrates</u>.
b. _____ Between stages 2 and 3, the bug <u>molts</u>.
c. _____ At stage 4, the bug is a <u>nymph</u>.
d. _____ The bug's metamorphosis is <u>complete</u>.

D. Find Out More

1. Read about reproduction in social insects. Some examples are ants, bees, and termites. How are they like and unlike the insects you have studied?
2. Get some snails in an aquarium store. Each snail contains both sexes. You can observe their mating and egg-laying. The eggs are large enough to see. Two weeks after laying, the eggs hatch. Make drawings of all your observations.

Careers in Life Science

Zoos to the Rescue. Why do we have zoos? Wild animals educate and entertain us. In a zoo, we can get near them and enjoy their beauty. In recent years, zoos have taken on a new purpose. It is to help save endangered species. For many animals, zoos may be their last hope for survival.

Do you care deeply about animals? Can you handle them more easily than most people can? Do you have a feeling of kinship with wild creatures? If so, a career in a zoo might be for you.

Zoo Keepers. Zoo keepers feed, care for, and observe the behavior of animals. Some keepers are experts on the breeding of the animals in their charge. When animal mothers cannot or will not raise their own babies, zoo keepers become foster parents.

Most zoo keepers have two or more years of study in zoology or animal husbandry before they land a job in a zoo. Some keepers begin as zoo volunteers while still in high school. All learn most of their job as apprentices to experienced keepers.

Zoo Veterinarians. A veterinarian, or "vet," is an animal doctor. If you have a pet, you may have taken it to a vet. Zoo vets plan diets for the animals, treat their illnesses, and perform surgery. Many zoo vets and other scientists do re-

This zoo keeper acts as a "surrogate mother" for a young gorilla.

search on the reproduction of endangered species. Left in the wild, many species would die out. Some of these species are now increasing their numbers inside zoos.

Zoo vets start the way all vets do, with four years of college. At least three more years of study in a school of veterinary medicine are then required.

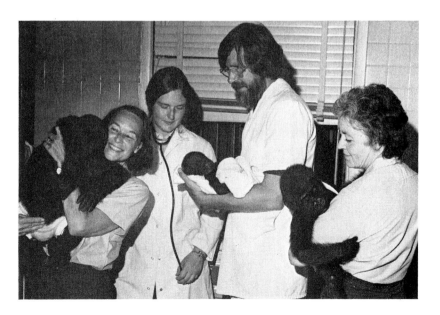

A zoo veterinarian's main job is to keep the animals in the zoo healthy.

HEREDITY AND CHANGE THROUGH TIME

How Do Parents Pass Traits To Offspring?

Exploring Science

The Jim Twins. "I looked into his eyes and saw a reflection of myself. I wanted to scream or cry. But all I could do was laugh." That's what Jim Springer said when he first met Jim Lewis, his twin brother.

Both Jims knew they had been born twins. But Springer thought that his twin brother had died as a baby. Lewis knew that he and his twin were adopted at birth by different families. At age 39, Lewis, who lived in Lima, Ohio, began to search for Springer. Lewis found Springer in Dayton, Ohio, a nearby city.

The Jim twins are identical. This means they look almost exactly alike. As they talked, the Jims found they were also alike in other ways. At school, both loved math and hated spelling. Both studied carpentry and mechanical drawing. Both had a dog named Toy. Both had a first wife named Linda and a second wife named Betty. One of the Jim twins named his first son James Alan. The other Jim named his first son James Allan!

Scientists have studied many sets of identical twins who were raised apart. Most of those twins have some amazingly similar life experiences. But they also have differences. Both Jim twins worked part time as law officers. But they had different main jobs. Springer was a records clerk, while Lewis was a security guard. Studying twins like the Jims helps scientists learn about what parents pass to offspring at birth.

● Some sets of twins are not identical. They look no more alike than ordinary brothers and sisters. Suppose a pair of unlike twins are raised apart. Do you think they have as many of the same experiences as identical twins do? Give a reason for your answer.

The Jim Twins were not only identical in appearance; they also had identical likes and dislikes, even though they grew up separately.

From Parents to Offspring

What do you look like? Is your hair brown, red, black, or blond? Is it curly or straight? What color are your eyes and your skin? These are some of your characteristics (kar-ik-tuh-RIS-tiks) or **traits** (TRAYTS). So are your height and the shape of your nose. For the Jim twins, and all identical twins, traits like these are the same, or nearly so. For most people, their traits identify them as individuals.

Where do you get your traits? You receive many traits from your parents. Traits passed from parents to offspring are **inherited** (in-HER-ih-tid).

How can you inherit your "father's eyes" or your "mother's nose"? The answer is in the center, or nucleus, of your cells. In the nucleus of every cell there are threadlike parts called chromosomes (KROY-muh-sohms). Each chromosome is made up of thousands of tiny **genes** (JEENS). It is the genes that determine the traits that you inherit.

Almost all cells, such as bone, skin, and muscle, are called **body cells. Sex cells** are the only ones that are not called body cells. In each body cell, the chromosomes are paired. One chromosome in each pair comes from the father. The other chromosome in the pair comes from the mother.

Every kind of living thing has a certain number of chromosomes in its body cells. For humans, the number is 23 pairs, or 46. For fruit flies, the number is 4 pairs, or 8.

In the sex cells, chromosomes are not paired. An egg cell or a sperm cell has just half the number of chromosomes as a body cell. For humans, there are 46 chromosomes in a body cell. So there are 23 chromosomes in an egg or a sperm. For fruit flies, there are 8 chromosomes in body cells. How many chromosomes are there in a fruit fly's egg or sperm? For corn, the number of chromosomes in a body cell is 20. How many are there in an egg or a sperm of the corn plant?

You began life when the nucleus of a sperm joined with the nucleus of an egg. The sperm cell, from your father, had 23 chromosomes. The egg cell, from your mother, had 23 chromosomes. So the fertilized egg had 46 chromosomes, or 23 pairs. This is how body cells get chromosomes in pairs, one in each pair coming from each parent.

The genes that make up chromosomes come in pairs, too. You get half of your chromosomes from each parent. That means you get half your genes from each parent. It also means you get half your heredity from each parent.

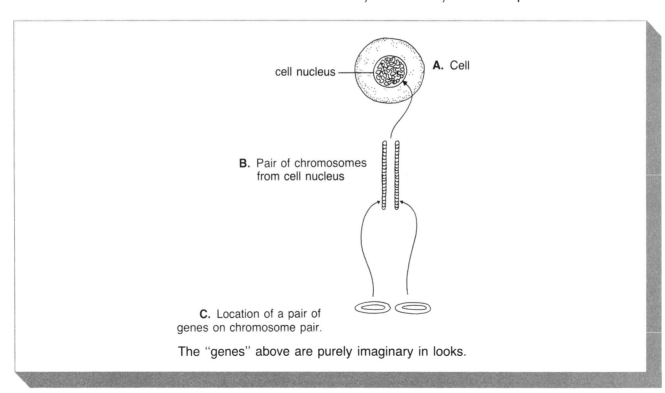

cell nucleus —

A. Cell

B. Pair of chromosomes from cell nucleus

C. Location of a pair of genes on chromosome pair.

The "genes" above are purely imaginary in looks.

To Do Yourself   What Is An Inherited Trait?

You will need:

1 strand of hair each from 2 parents and 1 offspring, scissors, microscope, slide and cover slip, forceps, dropper, water

1. Get a set of hair strands from your teacher or from members of your family.
2. Cut the strands so that you can place them side by side on the microscope slide. Label each. Place a drop of water and a cover slip on the slide.
3. Examine each hair strand under the microscope.
4. Compare the parents' hair with that of the offspring. Write your comparisons in the chart below:

Slide	Color	Texture	Shine	Curly or straight
Parent 1				
Parent 2				
Offspring				

Questions

1. Can you determine which hair characteristics were inherited from the mother?

   From the father? _____

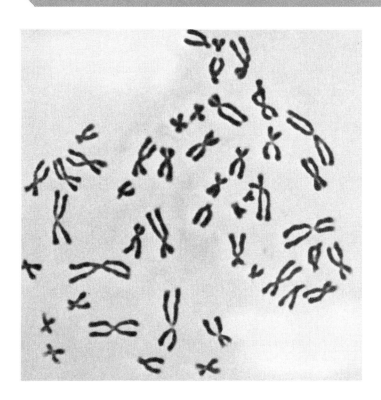

Count the chromosome pairs in this photo. Using this number, determine what species these chromosomes belong to.

Review

I. Fill each blank with the word (or words) that fits best. Choose from the words below.

identical   body cells   genes   traits   chromosomes   sex cells
inherited

Brown hair and blue eyes are examples of _____ . A trait

passed from parent to offspring is _____ . There are 46

_____ in your body cells. There are thousands of

_____ in each chromosome. Cells in which chromosomes

are *not* in pairs are _____ .

II. Circle the word (or words) that makes each statement true.

A. The numbers of chromosomes in a human egg and a human sperm are (*the same/different*).
B. A body cell of a pea plant has 26 chromosomes. Therefore, a sex cell of the pea has (*26/13*) chromosomes.
C. A fertilized egg has (*half/twice*) the number of chromosomes as a sex cell.
D. The (*body cells/sex cells*) of a cat have chromosomes in pairs.

III. Anything you have to learn (that is, any behavior that you were not born with) is not inherited. Give some examples of things you do that are not inherited traits. _____

_____

_____

_____

What Happens When Cells Divide?

Exploring Science

Growing Up Short . . . Or Not So Short. Each boy in the picture is 12 years old. Each boy at the left is about 1.5 meters, or average height. The boy at the right is about 1.2 meters, or shorter than average.

Some youngsters are short because they do not have enough growth hormone, called GH. When these boys and girls grow up, they will still be shorter than average. To help some short children grow taller, doctors give them shots of GH.

Not long ago, there was just one way for doctors to get GH for the shots. The GH was taken from the pituitary glands of people who had died. (Remember that the growth hormone is made in the pituitary gland.) It takes 50 to 100 human pituitaries to help one boy or girl grow only a little taller. The supply of the glands is not enough to meet the demand. Many short children still grow up short.

Now there is a new way to get GH. A certain human gene "tells" the pituitary to make GH. Scientists have learned how to attach this human gene to the gene material in bacteria. The bacteria follow the gene's instructions. They start making GH. And as they reproduce, the bacteria pass the human GH gene to their offspring. Soon there are millions of bacteria making GH.

Using bacteria to produce GH and other scarce chemicals is one way that scientists are solving many genetic problems.

● When bacteria reproduce, do the genes in the bacteria also reproduce? Explain why you answer as you do.

Growth hormone can help the youngster on the left grow a few more centimeters.

When Cells Divide

GENES, CHROMOSOMES, AND DNA. How do bacteria copy a human GH gene? The same way your cells do.

The genes of all living things are made of the chemical **DNA.** If you could look at DNA under a super-powerful microscope, what would it look like? It would look like a long, twisted ladder.

In the diagram, you can see that four kinds of rungs are found in the DNA ladder. Different genes result from different arrangements of the rungs. Billions of arrangements are possible.

The diagram also shows how DNA can reproduce, or copy, itself:

1. The DNA ladder untwists.
2. Each rung of the ladder splits in two.
3. Each half of the original ladder makes a copy of itself.
4. The four halves combine to make two ladders. Now there are two copies of the original DNA ladder.

DNA makes up genes. And genes make up chromosomes. Chromosomes are much, much larger than genes. Under a microscope, it is possible to watch chromosomes copy themselves. This copying happens because the DNA copies itself.

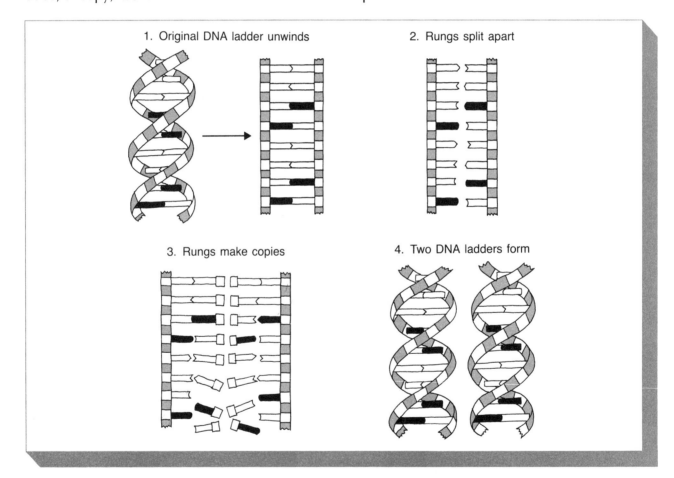

1. Original DNA ladder unwinds

2. Rungs split apart

3. Rungs make copies

4. Two DNA ladders form

MITOSIS. The process in which a body cell nucleus divides to become two nuclei is called **mitosis** (my-TOH-sis). Remember that any cell except a sex cell is a body cell. At the start of mitosis, each chromosome copies itself. Then the nucleus divides into two. One copy of each chromosome goes into each new nucleus. Each new body cell is just like the original cell. It has all the same kinds of genes in it.

As you grow, body cells divide to make new cells. Mitosis takes place during these cell divisions. Cells in your body may wear out or become damaged, such as when you cut yourself. Mitosis helps make new body cells to replace the old cells.

How Mitosis Works

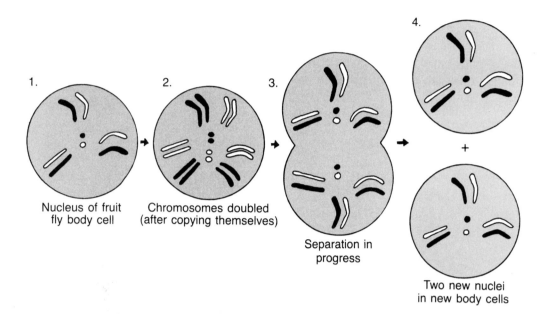

1. Nucleus of fruit fly body cell

2. Chromosomes doubled (after copying themselves)

3. Separation in progress

4. Two new nuclei in new body cells

MEIOSIS. When sex cells form, the nucleus divides in a different way. Remember that body cells have chromosomes in pairs. When a cell in an ovary or a testis divides to make sex cells, the pairs of chromosomes separate. One chromosome from each pair goes into each new nucleus. So each egg or sperm has just half the number of chromosomes as a body cell. This kind of division is called **meiosis** (my-OH-sis).

In a fruit fly, there are 8 chromosomes in a body cell. After mitosis, there are still 8 chromosomes in a body cell. But after meiosis, there are just 4 chromosomes in each sex cell that forms, one chromosome from each pair. In your body cells, there are 46 chromosomes. After mitosis, there are still 46 chromosomes in a body cell. After meiosis, there are just 23 chromosomes in each sex cell, egg or sperm, that forms.

How Meiosis Works

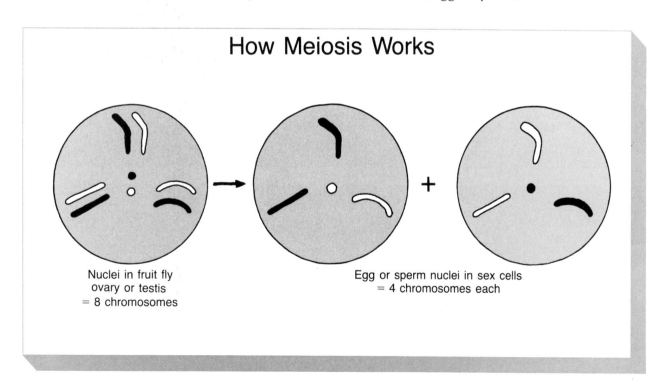

Nuclei in fruit fly ovary or testis = 8 chromosomes

Egg or sperm nuclei in sex cells = 4 chromosomes each

FERTILIZATION. What happens to chromosomes at fertilization, when an egg and a sperm join? A fruit fly egg cell has 4 chromosomes. A fruit fly sperm cell has 4 chromosomes. When the sperm fertilizes the egg, the zygote (fertilized egg) that forms has 8 chromosomes.

The same thing happens when a human sperm fertilizes a human egg. The human egg and sperm each have 23 chromosomes. When they join, there are 46 chromosomes in the zygote.

The zygote of a fruit fly, human, or any other living thing is a body cell. It has pairs of chromosomes. In a human zygote, there are 23 pairs, or 46 chromosomes. When this zygote divides, each cell in the embryo that develops is a body cell. All the divisions of the zygote into other body cells are by mitosis.

How Fertilization Works

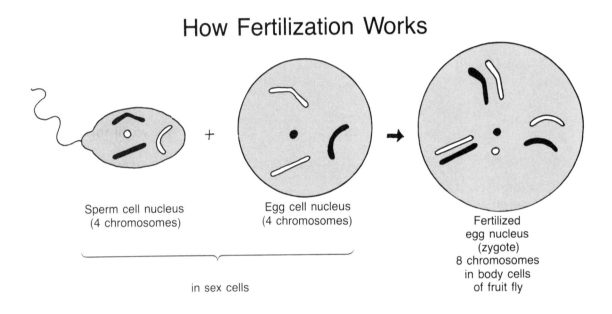

Sperm cell nucleus
(4 chromosomes)

Egg cell nucleus
(4 chromosomes)

in sex cells

Fertilized
egg nucleus
(zygote)
8 chromosomes
in body cells
of fruit fly

The fruit fly is widely used in the study of heredity.

Review

I. Fill each blank with the word (or words) that fits best. Choose from the words below.

    DNA   **chromosomes**   **zygote**   **mitosis**   **sex cells**   **fertilization**

The chemical that makes up genes is _____ . The nucleus

of a cell that forms body cells divides by _____ . Because

DNA can copy itself, _____ can also copy themselves. Sex

cells join at _____ .

II. Circle the word that makes each statement true.

    A. Sperm cells form as a result of (mitosis/meiosis).

    B. Skin cells form as a result of (mitosis/meiosis).

    C. The number of chromosomes in a cell is the same after (fertilization/mitosis) takes place.

    D. An egg cell with just half as many chromosomes as a body cell forms during (meiosis/fertilization).

    E. A process in which the number of chromosomes is doubled is (meiosis/fertilization).

III. Each body cell of a corn plant has 20 chromosomes. How many chromosomes are there in a sperm cell of corn? In an egg cell? How many are there in a zygote of corn? Explain. _____

_____

_____

_____

What Are Dominant and Recessive Genes?

Exploring Science

Speckled Corn and Jumping Genes. Have you seen Indian corn? Its grains can be purple, yellow, or speckled. The same ear can have grains of different colors. Some people use Indian corn to decorate their homes.

Scientist Barbara McClintock had another use for Indian corn. She studied the way its colors are inherited. She began her work with corn in the 1920s. One October day in 1983, she heard, on the radio, that she had won the Nobel prize. This prize is the highest honor a scientist can receive. McClintock said her work is "asking the corn plant to solve problems and then watching its responses." What did she ask the corn? And what did the corn "say" back to her?

One of McClintock's questions had to do with the speckled color. The corn's answer was that some of its genes can jump. When a gene jumps from one chromosome to another, specks may appear on the corn grain.

At first, other scientists paid no attention to McClintock's discovery of jumping genes. Many years later, they found jumping genes in some disease germs. This new knowledge may help doctors to fight those germs. It turned out that McClintock's discovery was very important.

● Do you think it is possible that some human genes "jump"? Explain.

Barbara McClintock received the Nobel Prize for her work on "jumping genes."

Dominant and Recessive Genes

The laws of heredity were first stated in the 1800s, by the Austrian scientist Gregor Mendel. Like McClintock, Mendel made his discoveries with plants.

Mendel worked with garden peas. Some pea plants grow tall. Others grow short. Height is an inherited trait in peas. Each pea plant has two genes for height, one from each parent. A plant that has two genes for tallness is pure for that trait. It is called **pure tall.** A plant that has two genes for shortness is **pure short.**

Mendel observed that when both pea-plant parents are pure tall, all their offspring are tall. When both parents are pure short, all the offspring are short. He used the capital letters **TT** to stand for the two tallness genes in a pure tall. The small letters **tt** stand for the two shortness genes in a pure short. All the offspring of two **TT** parents are also **TT,** or pure tall. All the offspring of two **tt** parents are **tt,** or pure short.

What would happen if one parent was pure tall (**TT**) and the other was pure short (**tt**)? Mendel took pollen, which contains the plant's sperm, from some pure talls. He placed this pollen on the pistils of pure short plants. The pistils contain the plant's eggs.

He also placed pollen from pure short plants onto pistils of pure tall plants. We say he **crossed** the pure talls with the pure shorts. Then he waited for the offspring to grow.

Each parent plant in Mendel's crosses was pure for height. The tall plants had two genes for tallness (**TT**). The short plants had two genes for shortness (**tt**). When a pea plant has one gene for tallness and one gene for shortness, it is called a **hybrid** (HY-brid). We write **Tt** to stand for a hybrid. The offspring of Mendel's crosses were hybrids. Each offspring had one gene for tallness from one parent. And it had one gene for shortness from the other parent.

What do you think the hybrids looked like? Were they tall, short, or in-between? Mendel was surprised. They were all tall! Only the genes for tallness showed up. The genes for shortness seemed to disappear.

This is how Mendel explained what happened. Tallness in pea plants is a **dominant** (DOM-uh-nunt) **trait.** A dominant trait is one that shows up in a hybrid. The trait that does not show up in a hybrid is **recessive** (rih-SES-iv). For pea plants, shortness is recessive.

Next, Mendel crossed two hybrid tall plants (**Tt**). What would the offspring be like this time? Mendel was surprised again. Most of the offspring were tall. But some were short. On the average, one offspring out of four was short.

Mendel reasoned that shortness was hidden by the tallness in the hybrids. But when two hybrids (**Tt**) are crossed, some of the offspring are pure short (**tt**). In a hybrid (**Tt**) a dominant gene hides the recessive gene. But the recessive gene is still there, and it can show up in the offspring of the hybrid.

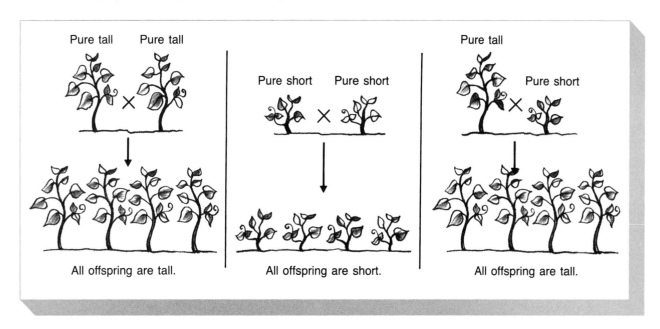

Pure tall   Pure tall

Pure short   Pure short

Pure tall   Pure short

All offspring are tall.   All offspring are short.   All offspring are tall.

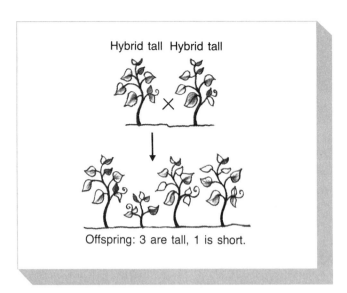

Hybrid tall   Hybrid tall

×

Offspring: 3 are tall, 1 is short.

To Do Yourself   **How Are Genes From Parents Combined in Offspring?**

You will need:

20 red beans, 20 white beans, 2 jars

You will make a model of the way dominant and recessive genes are inherited.

1. Place 10 red beans and 10 white beans into each of 2 jars.
2. Shake each jar. Close your eyes and pick one bean from each jar. Record your selection in a table.
3. Repeat step 2 until all the beans have been picked.

Each red bean will stand for a dominant gene. Each white bean will stand for a recessive gene.

Red combines with red to produce red offspring (pure)

Red combines with white to produce red offspring (hybrid)

White combines with red to produce red offspring (hybrid)

White combines with white to produce white offspring (pure)

Jar 1

(One parent)

Jar 2

(One parent)

Questions

1. Why was one bean selected from jar 1 and one from jar 2? _____
   _____

2. Why were the two beans "combined?" _____

3. What does this activity show about genes? _____
   _____

Review

Fill each blank with the word (or words) that fits best. Choose from the words below.

pure tall   **pure short**   **Mendel**   **hybrid**   **dominant**   **McClintock**
recessive

The first scientist to state laws of heredity was _____ . In

peas, a _____ plant has two genes for shortness. A plant

with one gene for tallness and one gene for shortness is _____ .

In peas, tallness is a _____ trait and shortness is a

_____ trait.

II. Mendel crossed peas pure for green seeds with peas pure for yellow seeds. All the offspring had yellow seeds. Which seed color (in peas) is dominant? Which is recessive? Explain. _____

_____

_____

_____

III. In humans, curly hair is dominant over straight hair. Is it possible for two curly-haired parents to have a straight-haired child? Explain. _____

_____

_____

_____

Can Heredity Be Predicted?

Exploring Science

Arch, Loop, or Whorl: What's Your Type? Make a print of your thumb. Or look at your thumb with a magnifying glass. Compare what you see with the pictures below. One type of fingerprint is an arch, one is a loop, and one is a whorl. Which type is yours?

Compare your print with those of your classmates. Find one that is the same type as yours. Can you see lines that are not the same in the two prints? Even for identical twins, no two prints are exactly the same.

You know one use for fingerprints. Detectives use them to track down criminals. Hospitals use babies' footprints to identify them. Prints are also used by genetic counselors. A **genetic counselor** is a doctor or other expert trained to predict heredity. Prints of fingers, hands, and feet are clues to some traits that can be inherited.

But prints alone do not tell all. Other tools of a genetic counselor are blood tests and family histories. In tracking down inherited traits the genetic counselor, like other detectives, uses clues of many kinds.

● Have you heard the expression "skip a generation"? It is used in talking about some human traits—like red hair, for example. What do you think the expression means?

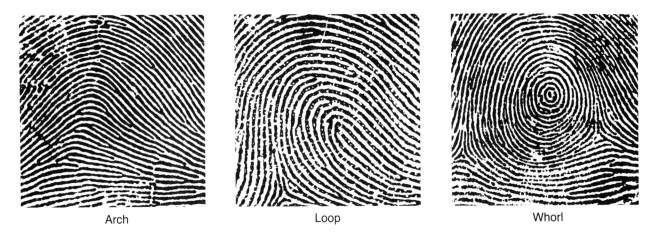

Arch   Loop   Whorl

The arch, the loop, and the whorl are the three main kinds of fingerprints.

Predicting Heredity

If a parent has a certain gene, a child may, or may not, inherit that gene. Some human genes are either dominant or recessive. Others are neither. Let's see how both kinds of genes are passed on.

DOMINANT AND RECESSIVE GENES. Suppose that two people with brown eyes marry. Can they have a child with blue eyes? The gene for brown eyes is dominant. And the gene for blue eyes is recessive. A capital **B** stands for the brown-eye gene. A small **b** stands for the blue-eye gene. For a person with two brown genes we write **BB.** For a person with two blue genes we write **bb.** For a person with one brown gene and one blue gene we write **Bb.**

The person with **BB** is called pure brown. The person with **bb** is called pure blue. And the person with **Bb** is a hybrid. The sex cells of a pure brown are all **B.** The sex cells of a pure blue are all **b.** And the sex cells of a hybrid have a 50-50 chance of being **B** or **b.**

How can the sex cells of two hybrid brown-eyed parents combine? To show this, we use a chart called a **Punnett** (PUN-et) **square.** A Punnett square shows the different ways that two parents' sex cells can combine. For each number below, look at the same number in the diagrams.

(1) We draw a square with four boxes in it. For two hybrid parents, write **B** and **b** for the father's genes across the top. We write **B** and **b** for the mother's genes down the side.

(2) In the first box, we write what would happen if the first sperm (**B**) combined with the first egg (**B**). The result would be **BB,** a pure brown. A child with this combination will have brown eyes.

(3) In the second box, we write how the second sperm (**b**) would combine with the first egg (**B**). The result is **Bb,** a hybrid brown. A child with this combination will have brown eyes.

(4) In the third box, we write how the first sperm (**B**) would combine with the second egg (**b**). Again, the result is hybrid brown, **Bb.**

(5) In the fourth box, we write how the second sperm (**b**) and the second egg (**b**) would combine. This child has **bb,** or pure blue eyes.

Can two brown-eyed parents have a blue-eyed child? Yes, if both parents are hybrid (**Bb**) for eye color. The *chance* of their having a blue-eyed child is 1 in 4, as shown by the Punnett square.

Let's look at another example of how eye color might be inherited. One parent is hybrid brown (**Bb**). The other parent is pure blue (**bb**).

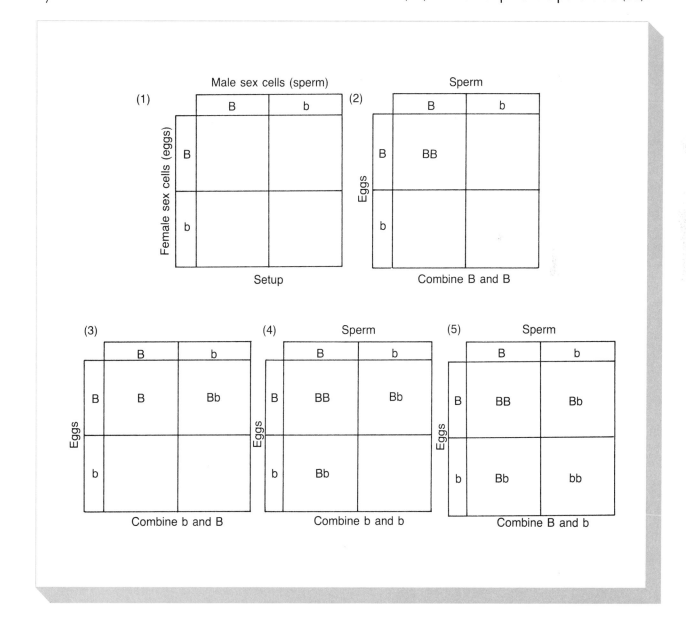

As the Punnett square shows, the chance of a child having blue eyes is 1 in 2. Its chance of having brown eyes is also 1 in 2.

BLENDING TRAITS. The genes for some traits are neither dominant nor recessive. In four-o-clock flowers, the genes for color can be red (**R**) or white (**W**). When a pure red flower (**RR**) is mated with a pure white flower (**WW**), all the offspring are pink (**RW**). In this kind of gene combination, traits are mixed, or **blended.**

Blending takes place in much of human heredity. Genes for dark and light skin color are neither dominant nor recessive. There also are several pairs of genes that help determine human skin color. Thus, many different shades of human skin color are possible.

Some people have neither brown nor blue eyes. Hazel, green, and gray eyes may be due to blending or to the work of several pairs of genes.

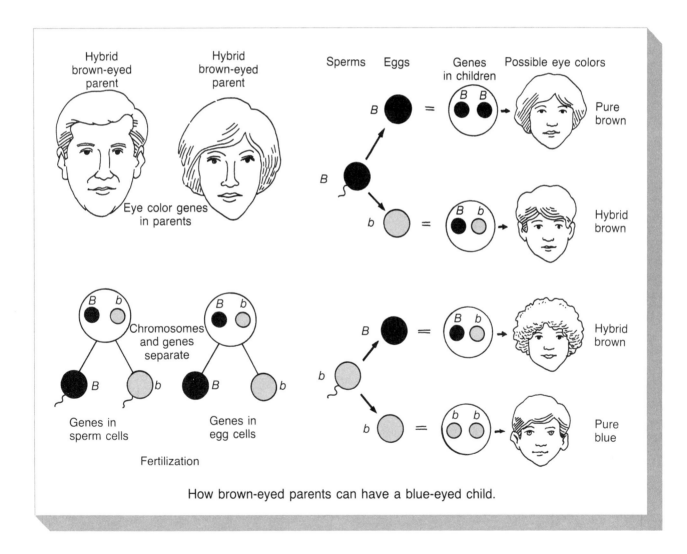

How brown-eyed parents can have a blue-eyed child.

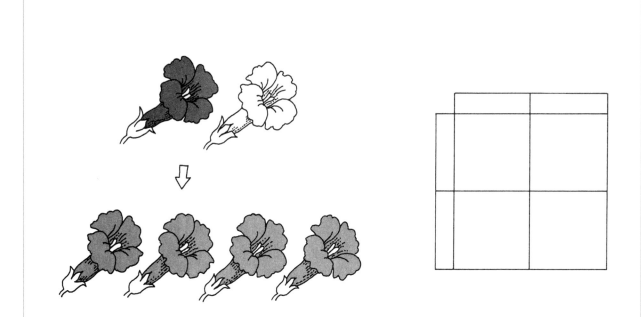

In some flowers, when one parent is red and the other is white, the offspring are all pink.

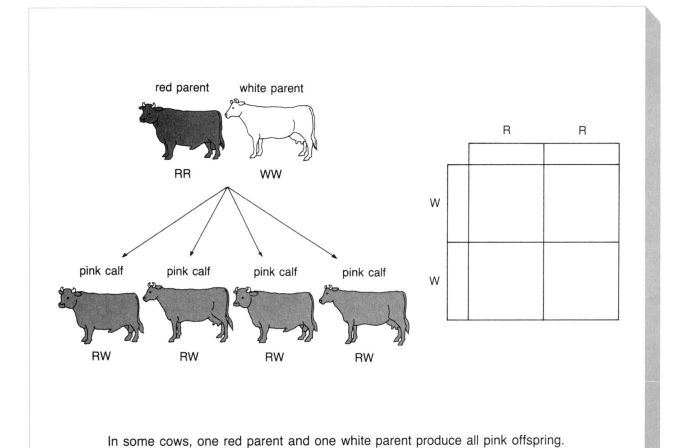

In some cows, one red parent and one white parent produce all pink offspring.

227

To Do Yourself   How Can Crossbreeding Produce New Kinds of Organisms?

You will need:

Tangerine, grapefruit, tangelo, plastic knife, paper plates, napkins

1. Make a table to record the following traits in each of the fruits: size, color, seed size, juiciness, taste, sweet or sour, flavor, smell.
2. Observe the grapefruit and the tangerine for each of the traits in step 1. Record the traits in your table.
3. Determine which of the traits are favorable and which are unfavorable.
4. Then examine the tangelo for the traits in step 1. Repeat steps 2 and 3. The tangelo is a cross between the grapefruit and the tangerine. Record the traits in the table.

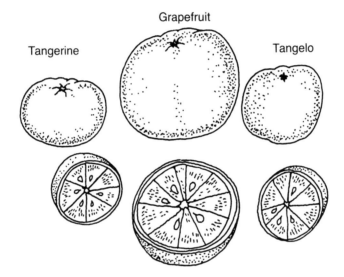

Questions

1. What were the favorable traits in the grapefruit? In the tangerine? In the tangelo?

   _____

2. What were the unfavorable traits in the grapefruit? In the tangerine? In the tangelo? _____

3. Why are fruits such as the tangelo developed? _____

   _____

Review

I. Circle the word that makes each statement true.

    A. In a Punnett square for eye color, the letter **b** stands for a gene for (*brown/blue*).

    B. The letters **BB** in the square stand for a person who has (*brown/blue*) eyes.

    C. A hybrid offspring in the square would be written (**Bb/bb**).

    D. Among the offspring of two hybrid brown-eyed parents, the chance of a blue-eyed child is 1 in (*3/4*).

II. In the Punnet square, show what offspring may result from a pure blue-eyed father and a hybrid brown-eyed mother. Then answer these questions:

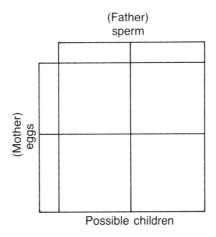

    A. Can any of the children have brown eyes? If so, what are the chances?

    B. Can any of the children have blue eyes? If so, what are the chances?

    C. Suppose the parents have just one child. Will the child have brown eyes or blue eyes? Explain your answer.

    D. Suppose there are four children. Will two have brown eyes and two have blue eyes? Explain your answer.

III. In the Punnet square, show what offspring result from a cross between hybrid (**RW**) pink four-o-clocks. Then answer these questions:

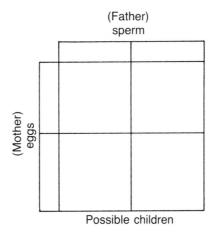

    A. Can any of the offspring be red? If so, what are the chances?

    B. Can any be pink? If so, what are the chances?

    C. Can any be white? If so, what are the chances?

How Is Sex Inherited?

Exploring Science

His and Her Brains. Are boys smarter in math than girls? What do scientists say? It depends on which scientists you ask. Some say "yes." Others say "no." What are the facts?

On national math tests, most of the top scores were made by boys. Some scientists think this means most boys are born smarter in math than most girls. Other scientists disagree. They say the reason is not that boys are born smarter in math. They say girls are brought up to *think* they can't do well in math. So they don't do as well on the tests.

How could being male or female affect your brain? Even before birth, the male and female sex organs produce hormones. In males, the hormone **testosterone** (teh-STOS-tuh-rohn) is made by the testes. This hormone, say some scientists, causes male and female brains to be different. More research is needed before we know for sure. Meanwhile, the debate goes on.

● What might influence girls to think that they cannot do math?

Both sexes are equally able to perform math problems.

Heredity and Sex

"Is it a boy or a girl?" This is the first thing everyone wants to know about a new baby. We don't know for sure how the brains of boys and girls are different. But we do know why some babies are born male and others female. The reason is in the chromosomes.

You know you have 46 chromosomes in your body cells. All the chromosomes in a body cell can be lined up into 23 pairs. Whether you are male or female depends on one of these pairs, called the **sex chromosomes.**

Sex chromosomes come in two shapes. One shape is an **X chromosome.** The other shape is a **Y chromosome.** A female body cell has two **X chromosomes (XX).** A male body cell has one **X**

chromosome and one **Y** chromosome (**XY**).

Every egg cell has one **X** chromosome. But only half of the sperms have an **X** chromosome. The other half have a **Y** chromosome. When a sperm with an **X** chromosome fertilizes an egg, the zygote has two **X** chromosomes (**XX**). When a sperm with a **Y** chromosome fertilizes an egg, the zygote has one **X** chromosome and one **Y** chromosome (**XY**). Which zygote will develop into a female? That's right—the one with **XX** chromosomes. And the one with **XY** chromosomes will develop into a male.

For each baby in a family, what are the chances that it will be male or female? The chances are even. To show why, we use a Pun-

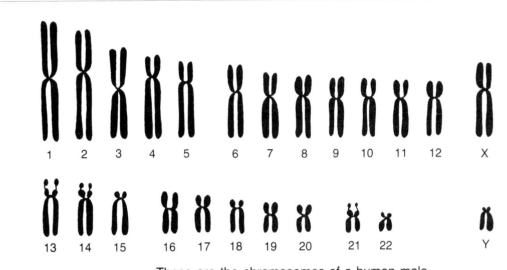

These are the chromosomes of a human male.

nett square. We see that half of the possible egg-sperm combinations will result in male offspring. The other half will result in female offspring. A Punnett square only shows the *chances* of having boys or girls. In any one family, most, or even all, of the children can be of one sex. But in the whole population, the numbers of boys and girls are about equal.

We can use what we know about **X** and **Y** chromosomes to answer some other questions. Why are identical twins always the same sex?

And why are nonidentical, or **fraternal** (fruh-TUR-nul), twins sometimes of different sexes and sometimes of the same sex?

As you know, after a sperm fertilizes an egg, an embryo forms. Sometimes, an embryo splits in half soon after fertilization. Each half becomes a separate embryo and, eventually, a separate individual. But because they came from the same sperm and egg, both embryos contain all the same chromosomes. That means they are always of the same sex. The original

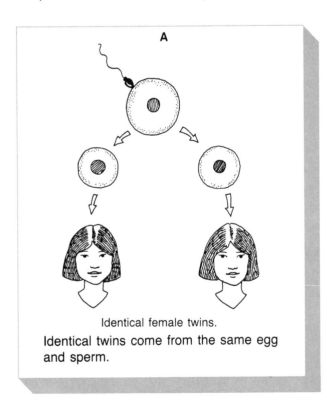

A

Identical female twins.

Identical twins come from the same egg and sperm.

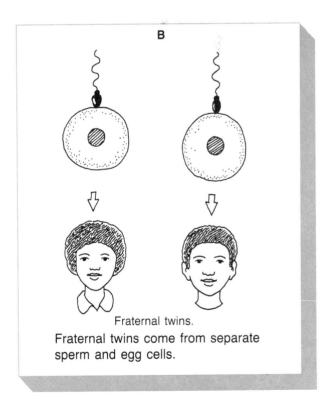

B

Fraternal twins.

Fraternal twins come from separate sperm and egg cells.

embryo had either **XX** or **XY** sex chromosomes. If it had **XX**, what sex are the twins? If it had **XY**, what sex are they?

Having all the same chromosomes means that the twins have all the same genes, too. Because of this, twins that develop from one fertilized egg are **identical** (eye-DEN-tih-kul). And because identical twins have all the same genes, they have all the same traits.

Sometimes, two eggs are fertilized at the same time. Each egg is fertilized by a different sperm. Then two-egg, or fraternal, twins form. Suppose one egg is fertilized by a **Y** sperm and the other by an **X** sperm. Then the twins are a boy and a girl. Can you explain why? Of course, both eggs could be fertilized by **X** sperms, or both by **Y** sperms. What sex would the twins be in each case? Why can they be of the same sex but still not be identical—that is, not have all the same traits?

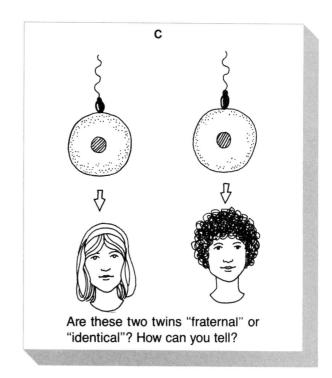

Are these two twins "fraternal" or "identical"? How can you tell?

To Do Yourself   **What Are the Chances of Producing a Male or a Female?**

You will need:

15 red beans, 5 white beans, 2 jars

We will make a model of how X and Y chromosomes pass from parents to offspring. Each red bean stands for an X chromosome. Each white bean stands for a Y chromosome.

1. Place 10 red beans in jar 1.
2. Place 5 red beans and 5 white beans in jar 2.
3. Close your eyes and select one bean from jar 1 and one bean from jar 2. Make a table to record your selections.
4. Repeat step 3 until no more beans remain. Record your results.

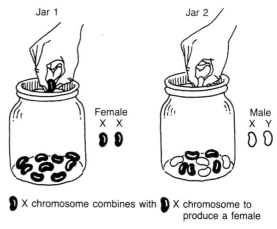

X chromosome combines with X chromosome to produce a female

X chromosome combines with Y chromosome to produce a male

Questions

1. How many females and males were produced? _____

2. If you made the same selections 100 more times, what do you think the results would be? _____

3. What does this tell about the chances of producing a male or a female? _____
_____

Review

I. Fill each blank with the word or words that fits best. Choose from the words below.

identical   **male**   **fraternal**   **female**   **Y**   **hormone**
sex chromosomes   **sex cells**   **X**

Your body cells contain 23 pairs of chromosomes including one pair

of _____ . The chromosome pair **XX** is found in

_____ body cells, and the pair **XY** in _____

body cells. A sperm cell may have either an _____ or

a _____ chromosome. An egg cell always has

a(n) _____ chromosome. Twins that come from one egg are

_____ . Twins that come from two eggs are

_____ .

II. John and Jane are brother and sister. They are also twins.

A. Are they identical or fraternal? Explain. _____

_____

B. Which twin came from a sperm with a **Y** chromosome? _____

C. Which twin came from a sperm with an **X** chromosome? _____

III. A family has two boys and one girl. They are expecting another child. What are the chances that it will be a boy or a girl? Explain.

_____

_____

_____

IV. A famous set of quintuplets, the Kienasts, are three girls and two boys. Each has other traits that are different. Can you explain how they were formed?

_____

_____

_____

What Are Genetic Disorders?

Exploring Science

Dr. Ferguson and the Sickle Cell. A healthy person's red blood cells are round. But people with certain defective genes have another kind of red blood cell. Their red blood cells are shaped like curved blades, or sickles. They are called **sickle cells.** People with these odd-shaped red blood cells have sickle-cell disease.

Unlike normal red blood cells, sickle cells break easily. As a result, people with sickle-cell disease do not have enough red cells. That means that not enough oxygen can get to their body cells. The victims feel tired. They may have swollen joints and general poor health.

Dr. Angella Ferguson does special research on sickle-cell disease. Her work has helped many patients to cope with the disease. She can help them feel better and live longer.

As yet, there is no cure for sickle-cell disease. But, as you will soon see, scientists can tell whether or not people might have a child with the disease.

To test for some defective genes, scientists take cells from the person. What part of the cells do they study? Explain.

Dr. Angella Ferguson is noted for her research on sickle cell disease.

Normal cells.

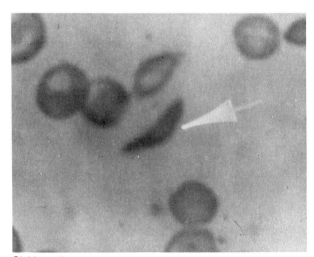

Sickle cells

In sickle cell disease, many red blood cells are shaped like a sickle.

Genetic Disorders

Over 2,000 genetic disorders are known. A **genetic** (juh-NET-ik) **disorder** is a disease that a person can inherit from his or her parents. Some genetic disorders mainly affect certain groups of people. Sickle-cell disease occurs more frequently among blacks. Some other genetic diseases are most common among whites. And some are more common among males than females. We can use Punnett squares to show how some of these disorders are inherited.

SICKLE-CELL DISEASE. Sickle-cell disease is caused by a recessive gene. A small letter **s** stands for the gene. To have the disease, a person must have a pair of the genes (**ss**). A person who is hybrid for the disease has one recessive, defective gene (**s**). That hybrid also has one dominant, normal gene (**S**). This hybrid (**Ss**) is healthy, but has the sickle-cell trait and is called a **carrier.**

Look at the Punnett square. It shows how the genes of two hybrid parents (**Ss**) can be passed to their children. There is one chance in four that a child will have sickle-cell disease. What are the chances that a child will be a carrier (**Ss**) but not have the disease?

People who think they may have the sickle-cell trait can be tested. They can learn if they have a defective gene (**s**).

HUNTINGTON'S DISEASE. This is a rare disease that affects the brain. It destroys the victim's mind and body. Then the victim dies. There is no cure. It is a truly terrible disease.

Huntington's disease is caused by a dominant gene (**H**). A person who is hybrid also has a normal, recessive gene (**h**). In the case of Huntington's, a hybrid (**Hh**) has the disease. This is because the defective gene is dominant and thus shows up.

A Punnett square shows how Huntington's disease may be passed to children from one hybrid (**Hh**) and one normal (**hh**) parent. Study the diagram. It shows that there is one chance in two that a child of this cross will have the disease.

The signs of Huntington's disease rarely show up early in life. The disease usually does not strike before the age of 40. By that time, a person who has the gene may have already had children and passed on the deadly gene to them.

For a long time, there was no way to test for the gene before the disease developed. Now,

Inheritance of Sickle Cell Disease

Genes in father's sperm

	S	s
S	SS	Ss
s	Ss	ss

Genes in mother's eggs

There is one chance in four that these parents will have an affected child.

Inheritance of Huntington's Disease

Genes in father's sperm

	h	h
H	Hh	Hh
h	hh	hh

Genes in mother's eggs

There is an even chance that the parents will have an affected child.

How Hemophilia Is Usually Inherited

Father has normal set of genes.

Mother carries recessive gene in X chromosome.

X   Y   X   X°

XX — This daughter is normal.

XX° — This daughter is a carrier; she does not have hemophilia.

XY — This son is normal.

X°Y — This son has hemophilia.

Hemophilia occurs in males; it is rare for a female to have hemophilia.

scientists have a test they can use. People with a family history of Huntington's disease can be tested. They can learn if they have the gene. If they do, there is an even chance that they will pass it on to children.

HEMOPHILIA. **Hemophilia** (hee-muh-FIL-ee-uh) is a disease in which the victim's blood does not clot normally. People with hemophilia are sometimes called "bleeders." Their blood does not contain a protein needed for blood clotting. These people take shots of the protein. Without the shots even tiny cuts will not stop bleeding.

The gene for hemophilia is attached to an **X** chromosome. It is a recessive gene. A female who has the gene on one of her two **X** chromosomes is normal. But this gene makes her a carrier for the disease. If a female has hemophilia, she has the defective gene on both of her **X** chromosomes.

A male, remember, has just one **X** chromosome. If he has the hemophilia gene on his **X** chromosome, he has the disease. There is no second, normal gene to "hide" the hemophilia gene.

To make a Punnet square for hemophilia, we write **X°** for an **X** chromosome that has the hemophilia gene on it. We write **X** for a normal **X** chromosome. And we write **Y** for a **Y** chromosome. A male who has the disease is **X°Y**. A normal male is **XY**. A female who is a carrier is **XX°**. A normal female who is not a carrier is **XX**. A female hemophilia victim is rare. But when that does happen, her chromosomes are **X°X°**.

Study the diagram. The Punnett square shown is the most usual way in which a person inherits hemophilia. Most bleeders are males whose mothers were carriers. Can you explain why there are fewer females than males who have hemophilia?

Some Other Genetic Disorders

Disease	Some Effects of the Disease
Tay-Sach's disease	nerve damage, early death
PKU disease	mental retardation
Cystic fibrosis	abnormal breathing, digestion
Down's disease	mental retardation
Muscular dystrophy	wasting away of muscles
Turner's syndrome	dwarfism, heart defects

Inheritance of Hemophilia

		Father's chromosomes (Normal = No disease)	
		X	Y
Mother's chromosomes (Carrier on one of her two X's.)	X°	X°X	X°Y
	X	XX	XY

The Punnett square shows that two of the children can be normal, one can be a carrier, and one can be affected.

Review

I. Circle the word (or words) that makes each statement true.

    A. The gene for sickle-cell disease is (dominant/recessive).

    B. A person who has the sickle-cell trait has (one gene/two genes) for the disease.

    C. To have sickle-cell disease, a person must have (one gene/two genes) for the disease.

    D. The gene for Huntington's disease is (dominant/recessive).

    E. A person who has Huntington's disease needs to get the gene from (just one parent/both parents).

    F. The gene for hemophilia is found on the (**X/Y**) chromosome.

    G. Most bleeders are males whose (fathers/mothers) were carriers of hemophilia.

II. Cystic fibrosis is a common genetic disease among whites. It affects breathing and digestion and shortens life. This disease is caused by a recessive gene. Can two healthy parents have a child with cystic fibrosis? Draw a Punnett square to explain your answer. Use **c** for the gene for the disease and **C** for a normal gene.

III. If a man with hemophilia (**X°Y**) marries a normal woman (**XX**), will the sons have hemophilia? Will the daughters have it? Will the daughters be carriers? Draw a Punnett square to explain your answers.

How Have Living Things Changed?

Exploring Science

Bigfoot: Monster or Myth? Who, or what, is Bigfoot? People say Bigfoot is a giant hairy creature that lives in the woods. It looks like some sort of ape. But it does not seem to belong to any known species. For more than 100 years, people in many places have said they have seen Bigfoot. In the Pacific Northwest, the Indians call this creature Sasquatch. In China, it is known as the Wild Man. In the Florida everglades, its name is Skunk Ape. (People say it smells awful!) Its huge feet have also earned it the name of Bigfoot.

This photo supposedly shows Bigfoot.

The best photo of Bigfoot anyone has made is fuzzy. But scientist Grover Krantz has collected many footprints said to be Bigfoot's. He thinks some of the prints are real. However, most scientists think Bigfoot is a myth.

Krantz thinks the clues we have are valid. But he does agree that more evidence is needed. Someday, someone may catch one of the creatures. Or someone may find some of its bones. Meanwhile, the mystery remains.

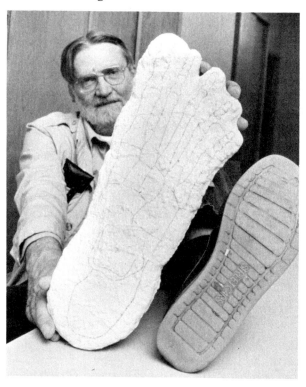

Grover Krantz compares Bigfoot's print to the size of his own shoe.

● Some of the footprints Krantz has studied look "human." But he thinks they can't be. How do you think the prints are not like a human's?

Change Through Time

If any Bigfoots are alive, there are probably very few of them. Their kind may already have died out, or become **extinct** (ik-STINGKT). Life has existed on the earth for millions of years. During that time, large numbers of species have become extinct.

Traces or remains of living things from long ago are called **fossils** (FOS-uls). Many fossils do not look like any living kinds of animals or plants. So we know they belong to species that are extinct.

Some fossils are prints of parts such as feet, shells, and leaves. The prints were made in soft material that later turned to rock. Scientists have made models of ancient tree ferns from fossils of extinct kinds of plants. The model in the picture is how a North American forest looked 300 million years ago.

When the climate changed, the fern forests died out. In time, layers of dead mosses and ferns became beds of coal. Prints of ancient tree ferns are often seen in coal.

The hard parts of dead organisms can also become fossils. Bones, teeth, and wood may remain after soft body parts decay. These hard parts may turn into stone. If they become stone, they may last millions of years.

In a few cases, a whole animal has been preserved as a fossil. An insect sometimes became stuck in tree sap. The sap hardened into clear **amber** (AM-bur). The insect was preserved inside the amber.

Wooly **mammoths** (MAM-uths)—huge mammals related to elephants—sometimes were frozen. Whole mammoths or large parts of them have been found in ice. Fossils in amber and ice have been preserved for many thousands of years.

By studying fossils, scientists can learn how some kinds of animals have changed through time. Sixty million years ago, the horse was about the size of a small dog. Its foot had four toes. Scientists think this was the ancestor of today's horses.

Over millions of years, the horse became larger. Its middle toe became a hoof. Today's horse stands about five times as tall as the horse of 60 million years ago. The process of change through time that results in new kinds of living things is called **evolution** (ev-uh-LOO-shun).

Among the most fascinating animals that ever lived were the **dinosaurs** (DYE-nuh-sawrs). We know them from their fossils. These animals were reptiles, related to such present-day reptiles as lizards. The dinosaurs became extinct millions of years before humans appeared on earth. Why did they die out? Scientists aren't sure. There are many ideas. Perhaps the climate changed. Perhaps the earth was struck by an object from space. We only know that they ceased to exist.

This is how a coal-forming forest looked 300 million years ago in North America.

The Evolution of the Horse

Time		Leg
3 million years ago		
25 million years ago		
60 million years ago		

To Do Yourself   How Can You Make a Fossil Print?

You will need:

Clay, small bowl, plaster of Paris, spoon, water, shell, hand lens

1. Press a shell into clay to make a print, then remove the shell carefully. You have made a cast.
2. Observe the cast with your hand lens and note the details.
3. Place 4 to 5 spoonfuls of plaster of Paris in a small bowl. Carefully add several spoonfuls of water and mix.
4. When the mixture is smooth and thick, pour some of it in the cast. Let the plaster harden.
5. When the plaster is hard, remove it carefully from the cast. This is a mold. Observe the details with your hand lens. Compare these to the cast.

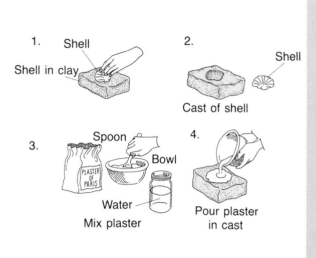

Questions

1. What part of the activity is like a fossil? _____

2. How are fossils used to identify organisms? _____

Review

I. Fill each blank with the word that fits best. Choose from the words below.

horses   extinct   fossils   evolution   dinosaurs   mammoths

insects

A species that has died out is _____ . The remains or

traces of life long ago are called _____ . Change through

time that results in new types of living things is _____ .

Today's elephants may be related to extinct woolly _____ .

Lizards are present-day relatives of extinct _____ .

II. Circle the word that makes each statement true.

   A. The earliest ancestor of the horse had (two/four) toes.
   B. Forests that lived long ago and turned to coal were (ferns/redwoods).
   C. Most fossils are preserved (hard/soft) body parts.
   D. Tree sap that turned into (stone/amber) sometimes contained fossils of insects.

III. Fossils of ancient sea shells have been found on mountains in Kentucky. What might this tell us about how the earth has changed through time?

What is Natural Selection?

Exploring Science

Now You See It, Now You Don't. Imagine you are a moth. You like to rest on tree trunks. How do you protect yourself from hungry birds? You can be the same color as the tree. Or, you can hold still and keep quiet. In other words, you would look like part of the tree. Then the birds cannot see you, and you are safe.

More than 100 years ago, light-colored peppered moths were common in England. The moths were a perfect match for the light-colored trees on which they lived. Once in a while, a change occurred in a moth's genes for color. Then a dark moth was born. When the dark moth rested on a light tree, it was easily seen. A bird quickly ate it. The few dark moths that were born did not live long enough to reproduce. They could not pass the dark genes to offspring. So almost all the peppered moths were light.

Then many factories were built in England. As soot from the factories filled the air, the tree trunks turned dark. The light moths became the ones easily seen and eaten. They became the ones that did not live long enough to reproduce. The few dark moths were now protected. They survived, reproduced, and passed their dark genes to their offspring. More and more dark moths—and fewer and fewer light ones—were born.

After a number of years, most of the peppered moths in England were dark. Few light moths were left.

● Which hare is more likely to live long enough to reproduce: a white hare that lives in the snow or a brown hare in the snow? Explain.

(Left) Light-colored peppered moth could not be seen easily by birds. (Right) When soot darkened trees, light-colored moths could be easily seen by birds and were eaten. Dark-colored moths survived.

Natural Selection

The English population of peppered moths changed from one of mostly light moths into one of mostly dark moths. This change is an example of evolution at work.

A theory to explain how new forms of living things come to be, and how old forms die out, was first proposed by Charles Darwin. In 1831, the *Beagle* set sail from England. Darwin was aboard as the ship's naturalist. For five years, the *Beagle* traveled around the world. It stopped in South America, in Australia, and at many islands.

During the voyage, Darwin studied many forms of life. He collected many fossils and living things. He took these back to England for further study. He was struck by the great variety of species of both the present and the past. In 1858, Darwin put forth the idea that present species evolved from species of the past. He called his theory of how this happens **natural selection** (sih-LEK-shun). Darwin's theory has five parts:

(1) Most living things produce more young than can grow up. A fish may lay millions of eggs. A plant may produce thousands of seeds.

(2) Such large numbers of young must compete for food and space. Only some of the young survive. The rest lose the struggle and die.

(3) No two living things are exactly alike. Traits differ, or *vary*, even in the same species. Look at the people around you. Each has some different traits. Among peppered moths, individuals vary in color.

(4) The traits of some organisms help them to be better fitted, or **adapted,** to their environment. Well-adapted individuals are better able to survive.

(5) Organisms that survive will live long enough to reproduce. Through heredity, the traits that helped them survive will pass to their offspring.

Darwin knew that offspring could inherit traits from parents. But he did not know about genes. In the 1900s, the genes were found to be the carriers of heredity. Sometimes, a gene goes through a change, or **mutation** (myoo-TAY-shun). During reproduction, the changed gene passes to offspring. Mutations in genes for color caused the dark moths to be born.

Study the pictures of how giraffes may have evolved. Do you see how natural selection may account for the long necks of today's giraffes?

Millions of years ago, giraffes had necks of different lengths. These differences were hereditary.

Natural selection led to survival of offspring with long necks.

Today, only long-necked giraffes have survived.

To Do Yourself   What Is the Survival Rate of Some Organisms?

You will need:

Seeds (pea, bean, or radish), soil, cut-off milk carton, water, plastic spoon

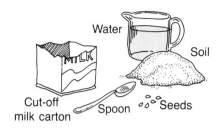

Water
Soil
Cut-off milk carton   Spoon   Seeds

1. Plant 9 seeds in some soil in the bottom half of a milk carton. Label with the date and number of seeds planted.
2. Water to moisten the soil, but do not soak. Place the carton in sunlight and keep the soil moist.
3. After one week, count how many of the seeds sprouted. Record your results.
4. Let the seedlings grow for another week and count the plants that survive. Again record your results. Keep the soil moist, as seedlings grow.
5. Compare your results with the class's results.

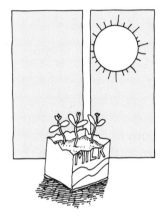

Questions

1. How does the seed experiment compare to Darwin's theory? _____

2. How does producing many seeds help a plant species to survive? _____

Review

I. Fill each blank with the word that fits best. Choose from the words below.

vary   selection   struggle   mutations   adapted   evolution
reproduce   heredity

Darwin's idea of how species evolve is called natural _____ .

A _____ for existence occurs because large numbers of young compete. Among individuals of a species, traits differ or

_____ . Some traits make a living thing better fitted, or

_____ , to the environment. Organisms better fitted to

survive will live long enough to _____ . Changes

or _____ in genes can adapt a species to a changed environment.

II. Suppose a thousand tadpoles (young frogs) hatch at the same time in a small pond.

A. Can all of them survive? Explain.
B. Which ones do you think are more likely to grow up to adult frogs?

A. Unscramble the groups of letters to form science words. Write the words in the blanks.

   1. B H D Y I R (has one dominant and one recessive gene for a trait)

   _____

   2. L T F R A E N A R (non-identical twins) _____

   3. S S I M O E I (division that forms sex cells) _____

   4. T I E V L O O N U (change that results in new species) _____

   5. L O I S F S (trace of a living thing from long ago) _____

   6. H I I T E N E R D (passed from parents to offspring) _____

B. Write the word (or words) that best completes each statement.

   1. _____ A sperm cell has the same number of chromosomes as **a.** an egg cell **b.** a body cell **c.** a zygote

   2. _____ One out of 4 pea-plant offspring are short when both parents are **a.** pure tall **b.** pure short **c.** hybrid

   3. _____ After a cell with 8 chromosomes divides by mitosis, each new cell will have **a.** 4 chromosomes **b.** 8 chromosomes **c.** 16 chromosomes

   4. _____ The sex chromosomes of a human male are **a. XX b. YY c. XY**

   5. _____ Blood does not clot normally in a person who has **a.** hemophilia **b.** Huntington's disease **c.** sickle-cell disease

   6. _____ Pink four-o-clock flowers are due to genes that are **a.** dominant **b.** recessive **c.** blending

   7. _____ The number of chromosomes in a human sperm is **a.** 13 **b.** 23 **c.** 46

   8. _____ A person with the genes **BB** for eye color is called **a.** pure blue **b.** pure brown **c.** hybrid

   9. _____ Prints of ancient fern trees are found in **a.** ice **b.** amber **c.** coal

   10. _____ The scientist who proposed the theory of natural selection was **a.** Mendel **b.** McClintock **c.** Darwin

C. Apply What You Know

   1. In humans, dark hair is dominant and light hair is recessive. Suppose a light-haired man marries a dark-haired woman. The man's body cells contain two genes for light hair, **dd.** The woman's body cells contain one gene for dark hair and one for light hair, **Dd.** On the diagram below, fill in the boxes that show what genes for hair color will be in their sex cells. Then complete the Punnett square that shows what hair-color genes their children can have.

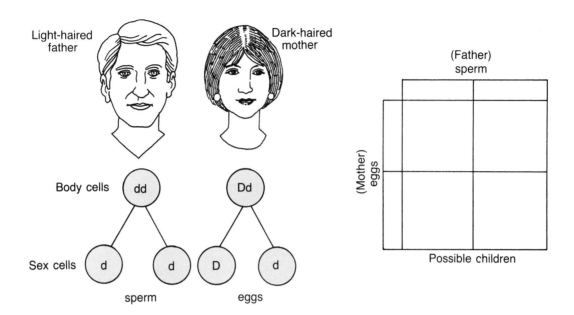

2. Circle the word (or words) that makes each statement about the couple and their children true:
   a. The mother is (hybrid/pure) for dark hair.
   b. The father is (hybrid/pure) for light hair.
   c. The chance that a child will have light hair is one in (two/four).
   d. A pair of parents with (**DD** and **dd**/**Dd** and **Dd**) could also have a light-haired child.
3. A certain kind of chicken can have black, white, or gray feathers. Its color is determined by blending genes. A black chicken's body cells have two genes for black feathers, **BB.** A white chicken's body cells have two genes for white feathers, **WW.** A gray chicken's body cells have one gene for black and one for white, **BW.** Suppose a black rooster mates with a white hen. On the diagram fill in the boxes for the genes for color in their sex cells. Then complete the Punnett square for the genes their offspring can have.

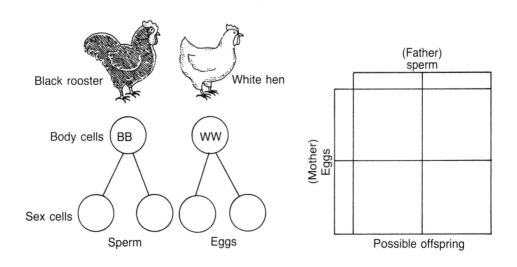

4. Suppose a gray rooster is mated with a gray hen. Complete the boxes in the next diagram for the chickens' body cells and their sex cells. Then complete the Punnett square for their offspring.

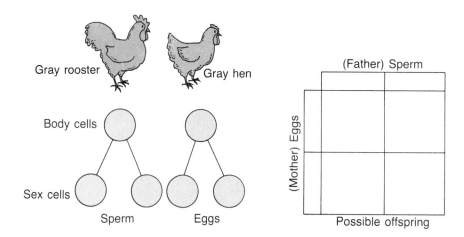

5. Circle the word (or words) that makes each statement about the chickens true.
   a. The offspring of a black chicken and a white chicken are all (black/gray).
   b. Two black chickens (could/could not) have gray offspring.
   c. When two gray chickens mate, the chances are that (half/all) of their offspring will be gray.
   d. If a white chicken mates with a gray chicken, (none/half) of the offspring may be black.

D. Find Out More

In humans, color-blindness is caused by a defective gene attached to the **X** chromosome. Make a Punnett square, using the letters below. They stand for the possible combinations of the **X** and **Y** chromosomes for both normal and color-blind individuals:

XX = normal female X^CX = carrier female X^CX^C = color-blind female
XY = normal male X^CY = color-blind male

Draw Punnett squares to show each of the following:
1. The possible children of a carrier female and a normal male.
2. The possible children of a color-blind male and a normal female.

A. Study the drawing of a garden-pea flower. Label each part. Use the following labels:

stamen   sepal   petal   ovary   pistil

Circle the word that makes each statement about the garden-pea plant and its flowers true:

1. In a food pyramid, the garden pea would be at the (top/bottom).
2. After pollination, a pollen tube grows into the (sepals/ovary).
3. If a pure-tall pea plant is crossed with a pure-short pea plant, the offspring are all (tall/short).
4. The part of the pea plant that carries on photosynthesis is the (root/leaf).

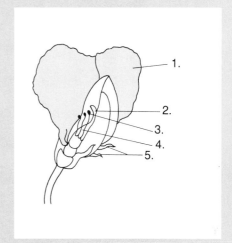

1.
2.
3.
4.
5.

B. On the drawing below, write labels for each numbered part. Use these labels:

kidneys   spinal cord   cerebellum   adrenals   biceps   pancreas

lungs   salivary glands

Each number below refers to one of the parts shown. The number of the statement is the same as the number of the part. Circle the word (or words) that makes each statement true.

1. The part of the brain that helps muscles work together is also the center for (sight/balance).
2. Messages go to and from the brain through a long nerve cord attached to the (cerebrum/medulla).
3. The contraction of the diaphragm and (rib muscles/windpipe) causes air to rush into the body.
4. Millions of tiny filters remove the (carbon dioxide/urea) from the blood.
5. The digestive juice in the mouth contains an enzyme that starts to break down (protein/starch).
6. When the upper-arm muscle nearest the chest (contracts/relaxes), the elbow bends.
7. When the body's "emergency" glands go into action, the heart (speeds up/slows down).
8. The same gland that makes a digestive juice makes the hormone (thyroxin/insulin).

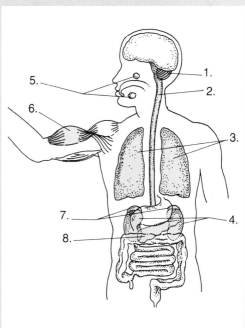

5.
1.
2.
6.
3.
7.
4.
8.

10

PROTECTING HEALTH

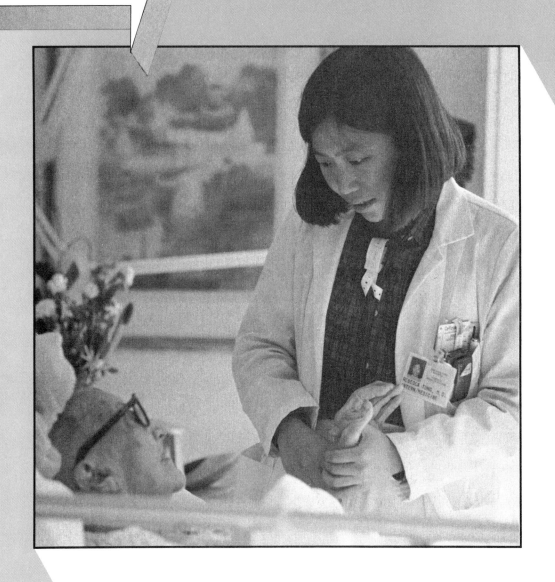

What Are Infectious Diseases?

Exploring Science

The Two "Bugs" of Lyme Disease. Old Lyme is a town in Connecticut. In 1975, its name was given to a new disease—Lyme disease. The first signs of the disease are skin rash, fever, chills, aches, and pains. Many of its victims were children. After a while, some of them got well. But some were left with arthritis, which causes pain in the joints.

At first, no one knew the cause of Lyme disease. Scientists usually have to find out what causes a disease before they can cure it. Like detectives, scientists who studied Lyme disease looked for clues.

One clue was that the victims all lived near each other. That meant that the disease might be "catching," or passed from person to person. Diseases that are passed from person to person are usually caused by some kind of microbe, or tiny "bug." Another clue was that the disease was found in a rural area. That could mean that some kind of insect or large "bug" might carry the tiny "bug."

In 1976, the large "bug" was found. It was a tick. Ticks are related to the insects. It was a tick that carried a microbe from a sick person to a healthy one. In 1983, scientists found a likely suspect for the other "bug." It was a bacterium, a kind of microbe, shaped like a spiral. By that time, Lyme disease had also been found in 13 other states. It has been found in Australia and Europe, too.

● What are two possible ways scientists might try to fight Lyme disease?

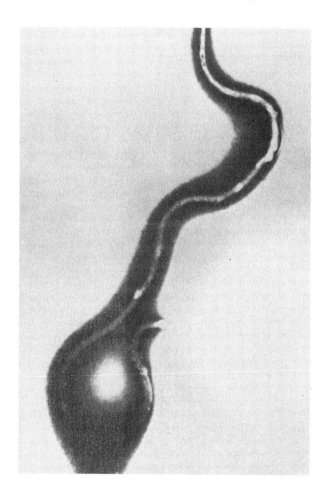

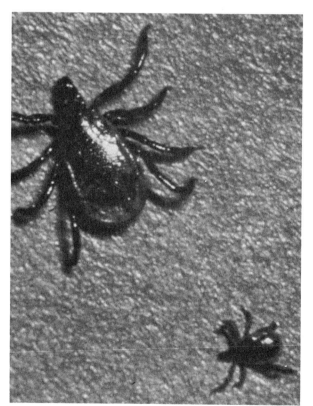

The bacteria that causes Lyme disease (left) are carried by the tick shown at right. The bacterium is a moneran; the tick is related to the insects.

Infectious Diseases

Microbes that cause diseases, such as Lyme disease, are called germs. Diseases that are carried from person to person are called **infectious** (in-FEK-shus) diseases. In most infectious diseases, or **infections** (in-FEK-shuns), the cause is a microbe. A few infectious diseases are caused by larger organisms, such as worms.

One group of microbes are the **bacteria.** Most bacteria are harmless and some are very helpful. But some cause disease. Disease bacteria are around us all the time. They can only make us sick if they get past the body's defenses. When bacteria do make us sick, they make poisons or **toxins** (TOK-sins). These toxins cause the signs, or **symptoms,** of disease. Some of the symptoms are pain and fever. Can you think of others? The table on the next page lists some common bacterial diseases.

Viruses also cause many common diseases. Some of these are listed in the table.

Some Organisms That Cause Infectious Diseases

A. Bacteria (grouped by shape)

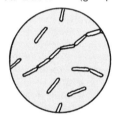
Bacilli Cause Tetanus

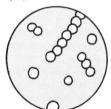
Cocci Cause strep throat

Spirilla Cause syphillis

B. Viruses

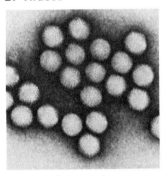
Influenza virus

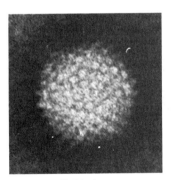
Cold virus

C. Protozoan

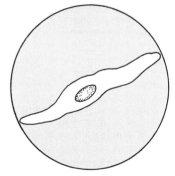
Malaria protozoan

D. Parasitic worms

Porkworm

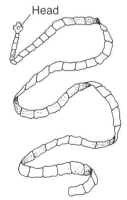
Head

Tapeworm

Bacterial Diseases	How Spread	Description
diphtheria	contact	deadly; affects respiratory organs
strep throat	contact	severe sore throat
tetanus (lockjaw)	deep wounds	paralysis; deadly
typhoid fever	food, water	affects digestive system; deadly
pneumonia (some kinds)	in the air	affects lungs, can be deadly
whooping cough	contact	respiratory; deadly
venereal diseases (VD) *gonorrhea* *syphilis*	direct sexual contact	affects sex organs; brain, nerve damage; can be deadly
botulism	improperly canned food, or food in swollen, dented, or damaged cans	deadly; affects nervous system
Virus Diseases		
cold	contact, or in the air	fever, sneezing, coughing, etc.
influenza ("flu")	contact, or in the air	respiratory; muscle aches
chicken pox	contact	rash, fever
mumps	contact	swollen neck glands
measles	contact	rash, fever
polio	contact	paralysis; nerve injury
virus pneumonia	direct contact, or in air	affects lungs
rabies	bite of infected dog or other mammal	nerve and brain injury; deadly
herpes (a type of VD)	direct sexual contact	affects sex organs
Protozoan Diseases		
malaria	bite of infected mosquito	fever, chills
amebic dysentery	food and water	affects intestines; liver
Fungus Diseases		
ringworm	contact	itching and ring-like sores on scalp
athletes foot	contact	itching and sores on toes
Worm Diseases		
porkworm (trichina)	undercooked, infected pork	affects muscles; pain, sometimes deadly
tapeworm	undercooked, infected pork, beef, or fish	affects intestines

Protozoans and fungi can also cause infectious diseases. Another group of diseases are those caused by **parasitic worms.** The table lists some of these, too.

A disease that is "catching" is called a **contagious** (kun-TAY-jus) disease. Contagious diseases are usually passed from person to person by touching, or direct contact. Microbes may sometimes be passed by touching things that a sick person has used, such as a dish. Some bacteria and viruses may be passed along through air, water, or food. Certain infectious diseases that affect the sex organs can be only "caught" by sexual contact. These are the **venereal** (vuh-NEER-ee-ul) **diseases,** called **VD.**

Some germs are passed to other people with the help of another organism. Lyme disease bacteria are carried by certain ticks. Malaria protozoans are carried by mosquitoes. Rabies viruses are carried by dogs or other animals.

To Do Yourself   What Are Some Ways That Diseases Are Spread?

You will need:

4 covered petri dishes with agar, glass marking pencil, dropper, dirty water, coin, tape

1. Open and leave a petri dish on a window sill for 10 minutes. Then cover and label the dish.
2. With a marking pencil, divide the outside of another petri dish into 3 equal parts.
3. Open the dish and place 2 fingers on the agar in one section. Place a coin on the second section, then remove it. Put a drop of dirty water on the third section. Cover and label the dish.
4. Cough or sneeze into the third petri dish. Close and label it.
5. Label the fourth petri dish "Control." Do not open it.
6. Seal the dishes with tape. Place the dishes in a dark, warm place for a week. Observe them every day and record your observations. CAUTION: *Do not open the petri dishes.*

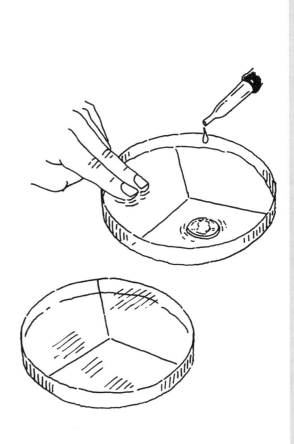

Questions

1. Where did the bacteria start to grow first? _____

_____

2. Where was the last place that the bacteria grew? _____

_____

3. Name several ways you found how bacteria could be spread. _____

_____

How a Virus Infects a Cell

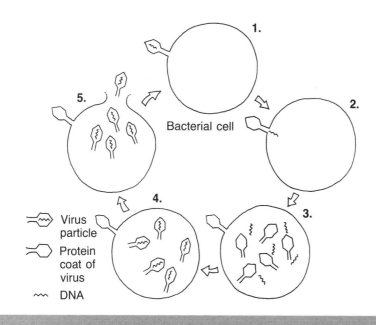

1. Virus attaches self to cell.
2. DNA of virus enters cell, leaving coat outside.
3. Virus makes more DNA and coats inside cell, which dies.
4. These virus parts are assembled.
5. Cell burst open releasing many new viruses.

Review

I. Fill each blank with the word that fits best. Choose from the words below.

**parasitic   infections   toxins   botulism   VD   symptoms
contagious**

Infectious diseases are caused by microbes or _____ worms.

Infectious diseases may also be called _____ . Bacteria

produce poisons, or _____ that can make us sick. Any

disease that can be "caught" is _____ . A group of diseases

that affect the sex organs are called _____ .

II. To answer the following, use the table of infectious diseases. Circle the word (or words) that makes each statement true.

A. Colds and flu are common (bacterial/virus) diseases.
B. Eating undercooked pork may result in infection by a (fungus/worm)
C. Gonorrhea is a disease passed to others by (sexual contact/mosquitoes).
D. Two kinds of germs that can cause pneumonia are viruses and (bacteria/worms).
E. Two diseases in which there is a rash and fever are (measles/mumps) and chicken pox.
F. Using food from a dented can is risky because the can may contain the toxin of (botulism/rabies).

III. People once thought infectious diseases were caused by evil spirits. How did the invention of the microscope help change that belief?

How Does the Body Fight Infection?

Exploring Science

Sean's First Banana. Sean Halloran was 15 months old when he had his first banana. "I've been wanting to give it to him for a long time," said his mother. "He didn't like it. But that didn't matter." Sean was not impressed with the banana. But for his parents it was a big event. Why?

Fruits like bananas have many bacteria on them. The body normally can fight such bacteria, so people do not get sick. But Sean was born with a defect called SCID. This meant his body could not fight any kind of infection.

At first, Sean was put in a **sterile,** or germ-free, environment. He lived in a special, super-clean room at the hospital. His mother had to scrub clean and put on a mask and gown before she could see him.

At the age of two weeks, Sean got a transplant of bone marrow from his father. You might ask, why bone marrow? Normally, cells in the bone marrow make other cells that can fight germs. The cells made by Sean's marrow could not fight germs. It was hoped that these cells from his father's marrow would find a home inside Sean's own marrow. There, they would make cells that could fight germs.

After 5 months, tests showed that the transplant was working. Sean's bone marrow had begun to make his own germ-fighting cells. So he was allowed to go home. His mother still had to give him sterile food. She had to keep the house super-clean. And the family all had to wear masks. But in time doctors allowed them

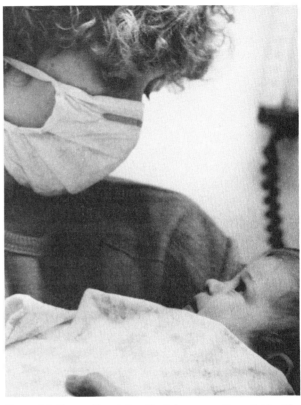

Sean Malloran lived the first few months of his life in a germ-free hospital room.

to go without masks. And, finally, Sean could eat some food that actually had germs on it!

● Why must doctors use a sterile environment for operations on people whose bone marrow *can* fight germs normally?

Body Defenses Against Infection

Microbes that could cause infections are everywhere. But most people stay free of infectious disease. Why is that? The body has two main **lines of defense** against germs. In Sean's case, it was the second line of defense that was defective.

Your skin is part of your body's **first line of defense.** So are your breathing passages and your stomach. As long as your skin remains unbroken, it keeps germs out. Your nose and your windpipe and bronchi (the tubes that branch from the windpipe) are lined with **cilia.**

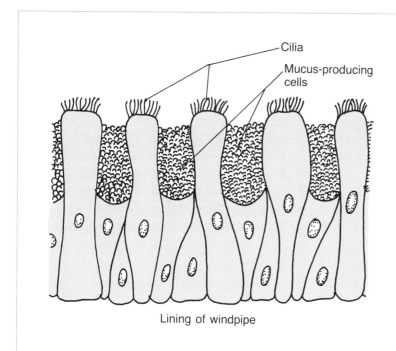

Cilia

Mucus-producing cells

Lining of windpipe

The cilia and mucus in the windpipe are part of the body's first line of defense.

These are hairlike parts that sweep out dirt, which carries germs. The sticky mucus that these breathing parts produce also traps germs. A cough or a sneeze forces mucus and trapped germs out of your body. Most germs that are in your food are killed by the acid in your stomach.

Sometimes disease germs get past the body's first line of defense. Then the **second line of defense** takes over. This defense is in the blood system. There are two kinds of white blood cells in the second line of defense. Both kinds come from cells made in the bone marrow. Normal bone marrow makes one kind of white blood cells that can eat bacteria and other germs. Another kind of white blood cell can make chemicals that attack germs. Sean's white cells could not do either of these things.

Some white blood cells can move out of the bloodstream into spaces between cells. There, they can flow around microbes, like amebas. In this way, the blood cells destroy the invaders by eating them.

Another kind of white blood cell makes chemicals called **antibodies.** For every type of microbe that invades the body, a special type of antibody is produced. The first time a germ gets

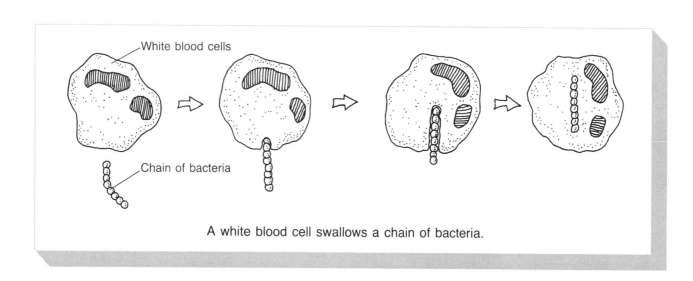

White blood cells

Chain of bacteria

A white blood cell swallows a chain of bacteria.

into your body, it may make you sick. If all goes well, your body makes antibodies for that kind of germ. The germs are destroyed. You get well, and some of the antibodies stay in your bloodstream. After that, if that kind of germ attacks again, your body remembers how to make the antibodies. It quickly makes more. Then you do not get sick. We say you are **immune,** or have **immunity** (ih-MYOO-nih-tee), to that kind of germ, or to the disease it causes.

You can get immunity to some diseases in two ways. One way is to have the disease. You may, for example, get sick with chicken pox, which is caused by a virus. After you get well, some of the antibodies against chicken pox virus stay in your blood.

Another way to become immune is by having shots called **vaccines** (vak-SEENS). A vaccine is made from weakened or dead viruses or bacteria. What vaccines have you had? You may remember having shots for polio, whooping cough, measles, and mumps. These shots are required of children before they enter school. The vaccine does not usually make you sick. But the white blood cells still react by making antibodies. After that, if you are attacked by living germs against that disease, you do not get sick.

To Do Yourself   What Is One Way the Body Traps Germs?

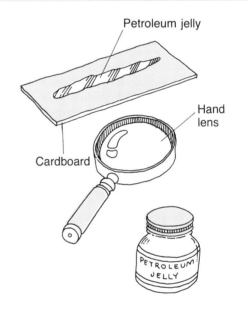

You will need:

Cardboard, petroleum jelly, sand, talcum powder, hand lens

To show the action of mucus in your nose and throat passages, make a model.

1. Cut a piece of cardboard 8 centimeters by 20 centimeters.
2. Spread a layer of petroleum jelly in the middle of the cardboard. Place some sand and powder about 5 centimeters in front of the jelly.
3. Close your eyes. Blow the sand and powder past the layer of petroleum jelly.
4. Clean up the excess sand and powder.

Questions

1. What does the petroleum jelly represent in the model? _____

2. What did you observe about the petroleum jelly? _____

_____

3. What is one use of the mucus that lines your air passages? _____

_____

Review

I. Fill each blank with the word (or words) that fits best. Choose from the words below:

vaccine   **white blood cells**   **defense**   **cilia**   **antibody**   **mucus**
bone marrow   **immunity**

The body has two main lines of _____ against infectious

disease. Coughing forces out germs caught in sticky _____ .

Germ-eating _____ destroy some microbes. For every type

of invading germ a special kind of _____ is produced.
Having antibodies in the blood against a germ gives you

_____ . A _____ is a kind of shot that
makes you immune to a certain disease.

II. If the statement is true, write *T*. If it is false, write *F*. Then correct the underlined word.

A. _____ The acid in your stomach is part of your <u>second</u> line of defense.

B. _____ Antibodies against measles can make you <u>immune</u> to measles.

C. _____ Cilia that help get rid of germs are found in the <u>bone marrow</u>.

D. _____ White blood cells that eat bacteria are part of your <u>first</u> line of defense.

III. Why would it have been useless for doctors to give vaccines to Sean before he had a bone marrow transplant?

What is Heart Disease?

Exploring Science

Stormie's Valentine. February 14 is Valentine's Day. It's a day for heart-shaped gifts called valentines. Some valentines are flowers. Some are cards with pictures of hearts on them. Saint Valentine lived many years ago. He was supposed to be a protector of those in love.

On Valentine's Day in 1984, Stormie Jones got a new heart—a transplanted one. She also got a new liver. At the age of 6, she was the first person ever to get both a new heart and a new liver.

Why did such a young girl need two new organs? Stormie was born with a defect in her liver. It caused her blood to have too much **cholesterol** (kuh-LES-tuh-rohl). The body needs small amounts of this fat. But too much cholesterol can damage the heart.

Stormie's heart was badly damaged. She also needed a new liver that would keep down the cholesterol. Without a double transplant she would not live long. From another little girl who died in an accident, she got her double transplant. Her valentine was the gift of life itself. Six months later, she was back at school, working and playing with her friends.

● Do you think Stormie's heart disease was caused by a germ, or was it genetic? Why?

Stormie Jones was the first person to receive both a heart transplant and a liver transplant.

Heart and Blood Vessel Disease

Did you know that more Americans die from heart diseases than from any other cause? Many also die from blood vessel diseases. At age 5, Stormie Jones had a heart attack. Without her transplant, she would have died. The same process that led to Stormie's attack also happens in older children and adults. But because of Stormie's liver defect, it happened faster in Stormie.

For people with normal livers, there may be too much fat in the diet. This could lead to too much fatty cholesterol in the blood. There may also be other reasons that the blood cholesterol level is high. In these people, fat slowly coats the inner walls of the arteries. The thicker the fatty coat becomes, the less blood can get through the arteries.

Fat-clogged arteries can lead to **heart attack.** This is how it happens. A tiny blood clot may form inside an artery. If the artery is clogged by fat, the space inside is narrow. A small clot blocks the artery. No blood can get through.

Remember that arteries carry blood to all parts of the body. Arteries called the **coronary arteries** "feed" the heart's own muscle. Suppose the blood supply to a part of the heart muscle is shut off. The muscle dies for lack of

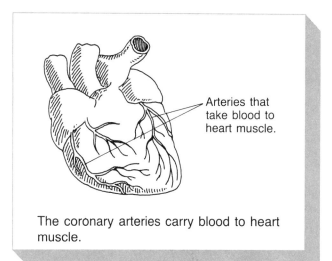

Arteries that take blood to heart muscle.

The coronary arteries carry blood to heart muscle.

Table 1 Warning Signs of Heart Attack

- Lasting "heavy" pain or discomfort in center of chest.
- Pain may spread to arm, shoulder, neck, or jaw.
- Sweating may come with the pain.
- Nausea and vomiting may also occur.
- Along with other signs, shortness of breath.

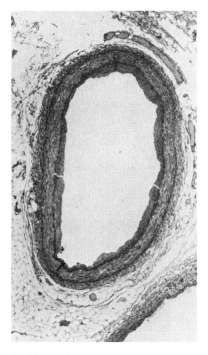

1. Normal artery

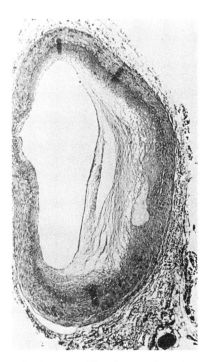

2. Artery with atherosclerosis

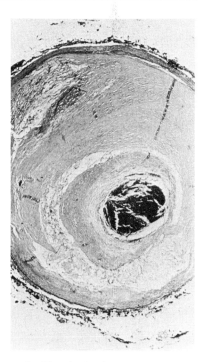

3. Blood clot in an artery with atherosclerosis

food and oxygen. The result is a heart attack.

Often, the amount of heart muscle that is damaged is small. The patient can recover with rest and medical care. But sometimes there is so much damage to heart muscle that a heart attack victim dies. Everyone should know the warning signs of heart attack. Anyone with any of these signs should call a doctor without delay.

Have you heard of anyone who has **high blood pressure?** This means that the blood pushes harder than normal on the walls of the arteries to pass through. Doctors aren't sure what causes most high blood pressure. A high salt diet, smoking, and stress seem to make the chance of having it greater.

High blood pressure is dangerous. It can lead to blood vessel disease. **Stroke** is a blood vessel disease that affects the brain. A stroke may happen in two ways. One kind of stroke is caused by a blocked artery. A blood clot may block a narrowed artery in the brain. Another kind of stroke happens when an artery in the brain bursts. Often the reason it bursts is high blood pressure.

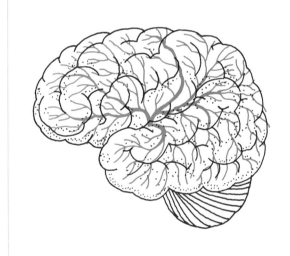

A stroke occurs when a blood clot blocks a narrow artery in the brain.

Either kind of stroke shuts off the blood that feeds part of the brain. What happens to the victim depends on the part of the brain that is affected. The stroke victim may have a loss of memory. The person may be unable to speak, or to move some parts of the body. In all cases of stroke, some nerve cells die. If too many nerve cells die, the person dies. Table 2 lists the warning signs of stroke.

Table 2 Warning Signs of Stroke

- Sudden, temporary weakness or numbness of one side of the face, or one arm, or one leg.
- Temporary loss of speech, or trouble speaking or understanding speech.
- Temporary dimness or loss of sight, especially in one eye.
- A period of double vision.
- Dizziness or unusual headaches.
- Change in personality or mental ability.

Scientists have done much research on how to prevent heart and blood vessel diseases. Their findings have led to the following advice:

- Eat less animal fat (which includes cholesterol). That means cutting down on meat, eggs, butter, and whole milk. Drink low-fat milk and eat low-fat cheese.

- Eat less salt. Over-salting food is only a habit.

- If you smoke, stop. If you don't smoke, don't start.

- Exercise regularly. Jogging, swimming, and bicycle riding are among the types of activity that help keep the heart and blood vessels in shape. *Caution:* before you start any exercise program, get your doctor's approval.

- Keep your weight normal. Extra pounds can strain the heart. (Eating less fat and exercising are two ways to keep your weight down.)

To Do Yourself   How Can an Artery Become Blocked?

You will need:

2 plastic straws, 2 medicine droppers, 2 jars, pipe cleaner, lard, a partner

1. To make a model of a blocked artery, push each end of one straw into lard.
2. Use the pipe cleaner to push the lard into the straw. Do this until the straw is lined with lard.
3. Fill both droppers with water. Hold one straw over one jar, while your partner does the same with the other straw.
5. Both of you squeeze the water into straws. Record what happens. Try it several times.

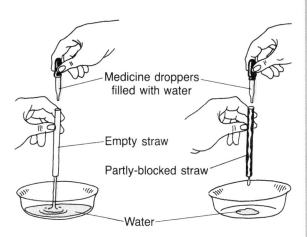

Medicine droppers filled with water

Empty straw

Partly-blocked straw

Water

Questions

1. Which straw does the water pass through fastest? The slowest? _____

2. What does the lard represent in the body? _____

3. What does the straw represent in the body? _____

Review

I. Fill each blank with the word (or words) that fits best. Choose from the words below.

liver   cholesterol   arteries   heart attack   veins   stroke

blood pressure   coronary

Too much _____ in the blood may lead to fat-clogged

_____ and make their walls become thicker. A condition

that may lead to heart or blood vessel disease is high _____ .

If a _____ artery is blocked, some heart muscle dies.

Either _____ or _____ may result from a blood clot in an artery.

II. Circle the word (or words) that makes each statement true.

A. Pain in the chest is a sign of (stroke/heart attack).
B. A broken blood vessel in the (brain/heart) can cause stroke.
C. A diet that is (high/low) in salt may help prevent high blood pressure.
D. Loss of speech is one sign of (heart attack/stroke).
E. A diet that is (high/low) in fat may help prevent heart attack.

What is Cancer?

Exploring Science

Turn Back the Clock. Imagine the way people lived in the year 1900. Many things that are part of your daily life were unknown then. There were no radios, TVs, or movies. There were no airplanes or space ships. There were no computers. Cars were scarce; most people traveled by horse cart. Telephones were not yet part of most homes.

In 1900, freezers and refrigerators were also unknown. Partly for this reason, the diet of most people was also different than it is now. No one wants to "turn back the clock" to 1900. We want to keep our TVs, airplanes, computers, and freezers. Yet, we should return to some of the eating habits of 1900. Scientists who study the causes of cancer believe so.

In the 1980s, the National Academy of Sciences gives us this advice: like people in 1900, we should eat:

—Less fat: cut down on fatty meat, dairy products, eggs.

—More fiber: whole grains, fruits, and vegetables.

—More "cabbage-family" foods: cabbage, broccoli, brussel sprouts, cauliflower, kale.

Scientists suggest that we should eat more like people did at the beginning of the century.

But unlike people in 1900, we should eat:

—Less smoked, salt-cured, and salt-pickled food. (Why do you think people ate even more of these foods in 1900 than now?)

Scientists do not yet know all the causes of cancer. But a "turn-back-the clock" diet does seem to help prevent it.

—In what way is a diet for preventing heart disease like the diet for preventing cancer?

Many "cabbage-family" foods are frozen today.

Cancer

How can what we eat help prevent cancer? Even for scientists, this is a hard question. Cancer is a puzzle. Scientists have found some of the pieces. One piece shows that there is a link between diet and cancer.

Just what is cancer? There are actually over 100 different diseases called cancer. All **cancers** are alike in one way. The growth and reproduction of cells gets out of control. Cancer is cell growth gone wild. The new cells do not do their jobs. For example, cancerous liver cells do not act as normal liver cells.

Normally, cells divide and grow in an orderly way. As each living thing develops, new cells form until the body parts reach normal size. Then the division of cells stops. After that, cells divide only to replace those that wear away or die.

But sometimes cells divide without stopping. Then a growth forms, called a **tumor** (TOO-mur). Most moles, warts, and other tumors stop growing. They do not get above a certain size. They do not spread to other parts of the body. Tumors of this kind are **benign.** Most benign tumors are harmless. But sometimes they should be removed.

Other kinds of tumors do not stop growing. They can spread to other parts of the body. This kind of tumor is **malignant** (muh-LIG-nunt). Malignant tumors are also called cancers. A malignant tumor can be very dangerous. Why? As it grows and spreads, it crowds out and de-

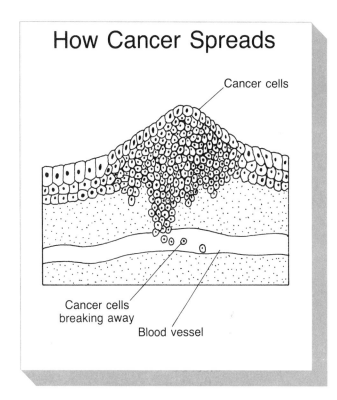

How Cancer Spreads

Cancer cells

Cancer cells breaking away

Blood vessel

stroys healthy tissue. Unless the growth is stopped, the person who has cancer will die.

Cancer can occur anywhere in the body. Leukemia is cancer of bone marrow. In this disease, too many white blood cells are made. Red blood cells are crowded out and their work is interfered with. In the same way, stomach cancer interferes with digestion.

The reason cancers start is not the same in every case. Too much or not enough of certain foods seems to be involved in some kinds of cancer. Chemicals called **carcinogens** (kar-SIN-uh-juns) are part of the cause of some cancers. A few of the chemicals known to cause cancers in animals or humans are listed in the table. Somehow, a carcinogen changes normal cells into cancer cells. **Radiation** (ray-dee-AY-shun) from X rays, the sun, or nuclear sources can also start the growth of some cancers.

Cancers that are detected early enough can be treated. Many can be cured. One method of treatment is to cut away the cancer, by **surgery.** If this is done before the cancer spreads, the cancer may be cured. **Radiation** from X rays or radioactive chemicals can also kill cancer cells. They must be used carefully. **Chemotherapy** (kem-uh-

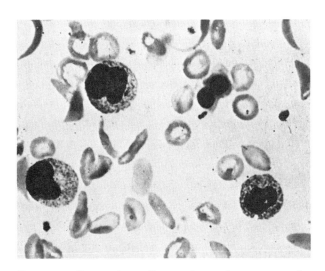

Cancer cells, such as those shown here, are cells that "have gone wild."

THER-uh-pee), the use of medicines, is another treatment doctors use. All treatments have the best chance of success when the cancer is detected early. Everyone should know the early warning signs of cancer.

Table 1 Some Carcinogens

Chemical	Sources	Enters Body Through
asbestos	heatproofing, fireproofing, insulating materials	breathing particles from the air
EDB	insect-killer (on wheat)	eating breads, cereals, etc.
nitrites	curing meat	eating bacon, hot dogs, etc.
PCB	industrial uses	breathing or eating particles in air, water
tobacco	cigarettes, cigars	smoking cigarettes, breathing smoke of other people's cigarettes

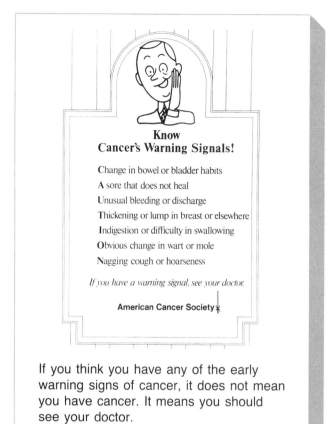

**Know
Cancer's Warning Signals!**

Change in bowel or bladder habits
A sore that does not heal
Unusual bleeding or discharge
Thickening or lump in breast or elsewhere
Indigestion or difficulty in swallowing
Obvious change in wart or mole
Nagging cough or hoarseness

If you have a warning signal, see your doctor.

American Cancer Society

If you think you have any of the early warning signs of cancer, it does not mean you have cancer. It means you should see your doctor.

To Do Yourself What Is in Burning Tobacco?

You will need:

Heat-proof test tube, test-tube holder, burner, cotton ball, water, cigarette tobacco

1. Place a few grams of tobacco into a test tube.
2. Plug the top with a wad of cotton.
3. Hold the tube, as shown, over a flame.
4. Move the bottom of the tube over the flame for about 3 minutes. Observe the cotton in the test tube.
5. Cool the tube. Remove the cotton and observe the brown tar on it.

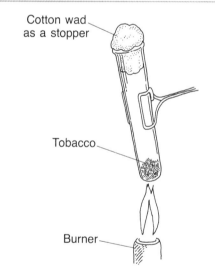

Cotton wad as a stopper

Tobacco

Burner

Questions

1. If the burning tobacco were breathed into the body, where would the tar collect?

_____

2. What might happen when too much tar gets into the body? _____

_____

Review

I. Fill each blank with the word that fits best. Choose from the words below.

division   surgery   chemotherapy   carcinogen   malignant   benign
tumor   radiation

A cancer-causing chemical is a _____ . Three methods of

treating cancer are _____ , _____ , and

_____ . An abnormal growth of cells is called a

_____ . Growths that are _____ are

cancers.

II. Write the kind of tumor, either **benign** or **malignant**, that each statement describes.

A. Does not spread to other parts of the body._____

B. Grows out of control._____

C. Is usually harmless._____

D. Destroys healthy tissue._____

E. Can be very dangerous._____

F. Leukemia is one example._____

G. Includes most moles and warts._____

III. What two health rules help prevent both heart disease and cancer?

_____

_____

_____

What is Drug Abuse?

Exploring Science

Think Before You Drink. The huge Long Island Railroad diesel is on a late-night run. Engineer Thomas Cavanagh keeps his eyes on the track ahead. Suddenly, he sees a yellow van. The safety gate is down, but the van is trying to get around it. Cavanagh slams on his brakes. But it is already too late. The train crashes into the van, and nine teenagers are dead. Blood tests showed that all had been drinking.

True stories like this are starting many people to think. There are now over 3 million members of a group called SADD—Students Against Driving Drunk. It has members in high schools in 22 states. It was founded by Paul Anastas, a teacher-coach in Massachusetts. Anastas lost two teen athletes in accidents in which the driver had been drinking.

Members of Students Against Driving Drunk conduct active campaigns against drinking and driving. They invite guest speakers to talk at school assemblies. Some groups have sold bumper stickers to get their message across.

Deirdre Cormack is president of SADD in Mineola, New York. (It was in Mineola that the train struck the van.) She says: "Many students think drinking and driving is a macho thing. They think they are really cool after a couple of beers. Well, we want to get the point across that it is very uncool to get in a car with someone who has been drinking."

● Drunk drivers of all ages can have fatal crashes. But there are many more among younger drivers. Why do you think this is so?

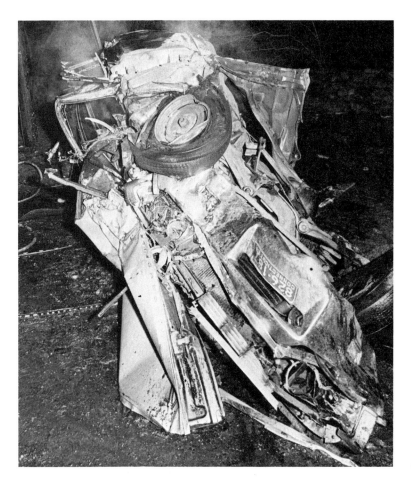

An accident caused by a drunk driver.

266

Drug Abuse

Alcohol, which is the chemical present in beer, whiskey, wine, and gin, is a drug. It is the alcohol in such drinks that makes you drunk. Does it surprise you that alcohol is a drug? Just what is a drug?

Any substance, except food, that causes a change in the body can be a **drug.** Used properly, many drugs are medicines. Some examples are aspirin and penicillin. These drugs may be ordered by doctors to help you fight diseases. But even those drugs that are medicines can be used in the wrong way. The improper use of a drug is known as **drug abuse** (uh-BYOOS). Using a drug in the wrong amounts is drug abuse. Using a drug for the wrong reason is also drug abuse.

How does drug abuse get started? Often, young people start abusing a drug to "feel good." They may abuse drugs to escape problems. They may abuse drugs to be accepted by others.

Drug abusers often develop a need for drugs. The need for a drug is called **drug dependence** (dih-PEN-duns). Drug-dependent people are called **addicts** (AD-ikts). Drugs that are abused affect the mind, the body, or both. For some drugs, the dependence is emotional. The addict needs the drug for its effect on the mind. For other drugs, the dependence is physical. The addict needs the drug for its effect on the body. The dependence produced by some drugs is both emotional and physical.

Different drugs have different effects. A **depressant** (dih-PRES-unt) is a downer. A **stimulant** (STIM-yuh-lunt) is an upper. A **hallucinogen** (huh-LOO-suh-nuh-jen) is a vision-producer. Drug usage can have an effect on even normal, or routine, behavior. The pictures below show how barbiturates—a type of depressant—affected a spider making a web. The table on page 268 lists some other drugs of each type.

Web on right was made by spider under influence of barbiturates; the spider's normal web is on left.

Table 1 Addictive Drugs

Type	Some Effects	Examples & Street Names	Type of Dependence
Depressants (Downers)	slow down nervous system; slow heart and breathing rates; make user sleepy; often cause depression	alcohol (beer, whiskey, wine, vodka, etc.)	emotional (can become physical, too)
		heroin (horse, duge, smack, junk, H)	emotional and physical
		codeine (schoolboy)	emotional and physical
		barbiturates (barb, blues)	emotional and physical
		morphine (M)	emotional and physical
Stimulants (Uppers)	speed up nervous system; make user anxious, excited, restless, wakeful	cocaine (coke, snow)	emotional
		amphetamines (speed, pep pills)	emotional
		benzedrine (bennies, cartwheels)	emotional
		dexedrine (dexies)	emotional
		nicotine (cigarettes, fags, cigars)	emotional and physical
Hallucinogens	user sees, hears things that do not exist (hallucinations); user loses coordination, behaves strangely; may cause depression or panic.	LSD (acid, sugar)	emotional
		marijuana (grass, pot, weed)	emotional
		PCP (angel dust)	emotional
		mescaline (cactus)	emotional

Review

I. Fill each blank with the word (or words) that fits best. Choose from the words below:

emotional   hallucinogens   aspirin   addict   physical   drug abuse

stimulants   depressants

Any improper use of a drug is _____ . A need for a drug's effect on the mind is a(n) _____ dependence. A person who needs a drug is an _____ . "Uppers" are drugs that are _____ . "Downers" are drugs that are _____ . "Vision-producers" are _____ .

II. Use the table of addictive drugs to answer the following. Circle the word (or words) that makes each statement correct.

   A. A depressant is a drug that *(speeds up/slows down)* the nervous system.
   B. A drug user who sees something that does not exist might have been taking *(angel dust/speed)*.
   C. Grass is another name for *(cocaine/marijuana)*.
   D. Alcohol is a *(stimulant/depressant)*.
   E. The addict's dependence on LSD (or acid) is *(emotional/physical)*.

III. Smoking is a cause of both heart disease and cancer. Why is it better not to start smoking than to try to stop after you have started?

Review What You Know

A. Use the clues below to complete the crossword.

Across
1. Shots to prevent diseases
5. "Bug" that carries Lyme disease microbe
9. Can carry rabies germs
10. Can be passed to other people

Down
1. Spread by sexual contact
2. Cancer-causing chemical
3. Shuts off blood supply to part of brain
6. Drug-dependent person
7. Cause ringworm and athlete's foot
8. Improper use of drug

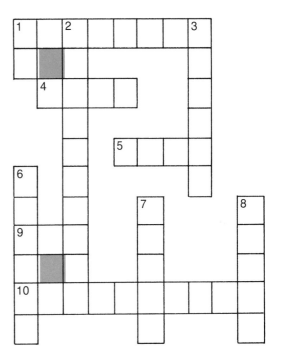

B. Write the word or phrase that best completes each statement.

1. _____ A vaccine can give immunity to **a.** heart attack
   b. cancer **c.** polio

2. _____ High blood pressure may lead to **a.** pneumonia
   b. stroke **c.** venereal disease

3. _____ Most warts and moles are **a.** malignant tumors
   b. cancers **c.** benign tumors

4. _____ Alcohol is a drug that is **a.** a depressant **b.** a
   stimulant **c.** an upper

5. _____ Smoking is unhealthy because it may help to
   cause **a.** only cancer **b.** only heart disease **c.** both cancer and heart
   disease

C. On the line below each picture, write the label that describes it. Choose from these labels:

porkworm   **polio virus**   **windpipe cell**   **red blood cell**
Lyme disease bacterium

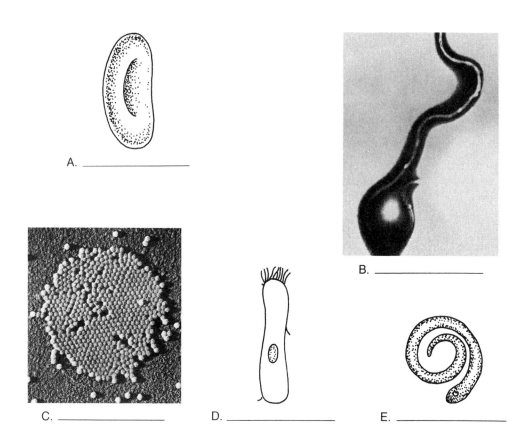

A. _____

B. _____

C. _____   D. _____   E. _____

For each of the following, write the letter of each drawing that matches it.

1. May be present in undercooked meat. _____

2. Its cilia sweep out germs. _____

3. Carried to other people by a tick. _____

4. Carries oxygen to cells. _____

5. Causes an infectious disease. _____

D. Find Out More

1. In the library, find out how many people died from infectious disease in 1900 and in 1980. Then find out how many people died from heart disease and cancer in both years. Make a graph of your findings. What accounts for the changes in the numbers? State your own ideas, then read further to check them.

2. Collect labels from over-the-counter drugs sold as medicine, reducing pills, vitamins, or other uses. Do the labels warn against overuse? Do they warn about side effects? What other information do the labels give?

A. Study the drawing of life in a pond. Circle the word (or words) that makes each statement about the scene true.

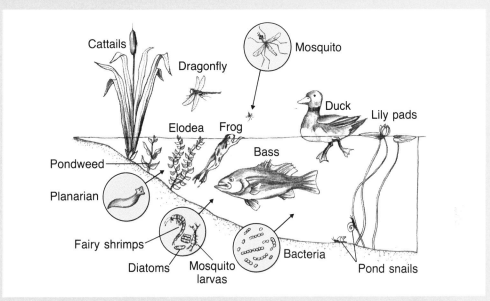

1. The air, water, and soil are all parts of the pond (community/ecosystem).
2. All the lily pads in the pond make up a (population/food web).
3. Photosynthesis is carried on by the (bacteria/cattails).
4. The (mosquito larva/frog) is at a young stage of its life cycle.
5. The (bass/duck) is warm-blooded.
6. The (diatom/elodea) is classified in the protist kingdom.
7. The dragonfly is (a vertebrate/an invertebrate).
8. All (shrimp/planarian) can reproduce by regeneration.
9. The most eggs are laid by the (duck/bass).
10. Because the snail eats dead organisms it is a (predator/scavenger).

B. Column A lists diseases or disorders. In column B are some ways to prevent or treat diseases or disorders. In each blank, write the letters of each item in column B that matches an item in column A.

A	B
1. _____ Night blindness	a. Eat foods rich in calcium
2. _____ Cancer	b. Cut down on animal fats
3. _____ Sickle-cell disease	c. Eat foods rich in vitamin A
4. _____ Heart attack	d. Avoid carcinogens
5. _____ Diabetes	e. Exercise regularly
6. _____ Whooping cough	f. Visit a genetic counselor
7. _____ Weak bones (rickets)	g. Take insulin
8. _____ Hemophilia	h. Have shots of a vaccine

C. The statements below refer to the human body. If the statement is true, write **T** in the blank. If the statement is false, write **F**. Then correct the underlined word or words.

1. _____ The <u>pituitary</u> gland produces growth hormone.

2. _____ Most digestion takes place in the <u>stomach</u>.

3. _____ The blood <u>platelets</u> help in the clotting process.

4. _____ A <u>ball-and-socket</u> joint is found in the knee.

5. _____ The organs that filter urea from the blood are the <u>ureters</u>.

6. _____ Helpful bacteria live in the <u>large intestine</u>.

7. _____ The testes belong to both the reproductive and <u>endocrine</u> systems.

8. _____ A human embryo develops inside the womb or <u>ovary</u>.

9. _____ <u>White</u> blood cells help to fight infections.

10. _____ Hormones are produced by the <u>nervous</u> system.

11. _____ Insulin is produced in the <u>spleen</u>.

12. _____ Clotting in the blood vessels can cause a <u>stroke</u>.

13. _____ Goiter is a disease that affects the <u>thyroid</u> gland.

14. _____ Blood platelets are produced in the <u>pancreas</u>.

15. _____ The largest bone in the human leg is the <u>ulna</u>.

Careers in Life Science

Health Care—On the Scene and Behind the Scenes. Do you think you would like to work in health care? It may surprise you that there are over 200 different jobs for you to choose from. Of course there are doctors, nurses, and others who have direct contact with sick people. Without these "on-the-scene" workers, we could not have hospitals. But hospitals—and other health-care settings such as doctors' offices and clinics—also have many "behind-the-scenes" workers. They may never see the people they serve, but their work is necessary and important.

Medical Laboratory Assistants and Technicians. Do you enjoy working with microscopes and test tubes? The "hands-on" part of studying life science is also part of working in a medical laboratory. Some high schools offer courses that prepare you for a job as a laboratory assistant after graduation. Or you may qualify as an assistant by a year of on-the-job training. Two or more years of further study are needed to become a medical technician.

Nurse Aides and Nurses. Working as a hospital volunteer or "candy-striper" may help you to find out if you would enjoy a career as a nurse. After high school, you can then become a nurse aide with a few weeks of on-the-job training. A

Lab assistants and technicians help in testing a patient's blood.

year of training after high school would prepare you to become a licensed practical nurse, or L.P.N. To become a registered nurse, or R.N., you need two or more years of study after high school.

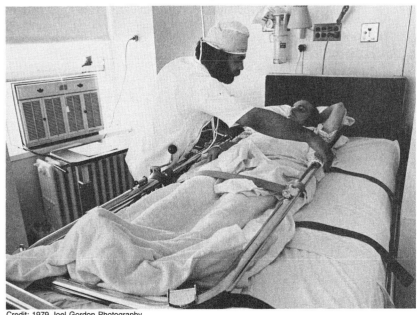

Credit: 1979 Joel Gordon Photography

Many men who were medical corpsmen in the armed services later become LPN's when they return to civilian life.

GLOSSARY

Glossary

Adapted (uh-DAPT-ud) Well-fitted for survival in an environment.

Addict (AD-ikt) Person who abuses a drug and becomes dependent upon the drug.

Adrenalin (uh-DREN-ul-in) Hormone that gives the body extra energy during times of excitement, fear, or anger.

Adult (uh-DULT) Stage in an animal's life cycle that is able to produce sperm or eggs, and so to reproduce.

Air sacs (SAKS) Tiny structures in lungs from which oxygen goes from the air into the blood, and carbon dioxide from the blood into the air.

Algae (AL-jee) Simple, plant-like organisms that are producers of food.

Amino acids (uh-MEE-noh AS-ids) Chemicals that are the building blocks of proteins.

Amphibians (am-FIB-ee-uns) Group of cold-blooded vertebrates, most of which spend part of their life cycle in water and part on land.

Antibodies (AN-tih-bod-ees) Chemicals, made by white blood cells, that fight germs.

Anus (AY-nus) Opening through which solid waste that remains after digestion passes out of the body.

Aorta (AY-or-tuh) Largest artery in the body.

Appendix (uh-PEN-diks) Worm-shaped useless sac attached to the large intestine.

Arteries (AR-tuh-rees) Blood vessels that carry blood away from the heart.

Asexual (ay-SEK-shoo-ul) **reproduction** Reproduction from one parent.

Atrium (AY-tree-um) An upper chamber of the heart, which receives blood from the veins and sends it to a ventricle.

Bacteria (bak-TEER-ee-uh) (Singular: **bacterium**) Simple, one-celled organisms, some of which are helpful and some are harmful.

Behavior (bih-HAYV-yur) All the actions of a living thing.

Benign tumor (bih-NYN TOO-mur) Harmless growth of cells that does not spread.

Biceps (BY-seps) Muscle in upper arm that, when it contracts, bends the elbow.

Bile (BYL) Juice, made by the liver, that helps break down fats.

Biology (by-OL-uh-jee) The study of living things.

Biome (BY-ohm) A large area of land that has the same climate and has a certain kind of climax community.

Biosphere (BY-uh-sfeer) The part of the earth in which life exists.

Bladder (BLAD-ur) Elastic sac that stores urine until it passes through the urethra and outside the body.

Blending inheritance (BLEN-ding in-HER-ih-tuns) Inheritance in which the genes are neither dominant nor recessive but both show in the offspring.

Brain (BRAYN) Center of control in the nervous system, made up of the cerebrum, cerebellum, and medulla.

Bronchus (BRONG-kus) (pl. **bronchi** [BRONG-ky]) Tube through which air passes from the windpipe into the lung.

Budding (BUD-ding) Asexual reproduction that produces two cells of different sizes.

Bulb (BULB) Short, thick underground stem with leaves that store food and can reproduce the plant.

Calorie (KAL-uh-ree) A measure of food energy.

Cambium (KAM-bee-um) Growth tissue in woody stem of a plant.

Cancer (KAN-sur) Malignant tumor or other growth of cells that spreads and crowds out or destroys healthy tissue.

Capillaries (KAP-uh-ler-ees) Microscopic blood vessels that connect arteries with veins.

Carbohydrates (Kar-boh-HY-drayts) A group of nutrients that includes starches and sugars.

Carbon dioxide (KAR-bun dy-OK-syd) A gas given off by animals as a waste and used by plants to make food.

Carcinogens (Kar-SIN-uh-juns) Chemicals that cause cancer.

Cardiac muscle (KAR-dee-ak) Involuntary muscle tissue of the heart.

Carnivore (KAR-nuh-vohr) Consumer that eats meat.

Cartilage (KAR-tuh-lij) Flexible tissue that forms parts of the skeleton, such as the outer ear and tip of the nose.

Cells (SELS) Tiny units of which living things are made.

Cell membrane (MEM-brayn) The outer skin of a cell.

Cell wall (SEL WAWL) Stiff covering of a cell of a plant or of a plant-like microbe.

Cellulose (SEL-yuh-lohs) Non-living woody matter in the cell walls of plants.

Cerebellum (ser-uh-BEL-um) Part of brain that controls balance and the working together of muscles.

Cerebrum (SER-uh-brum) Part of the brain that has

control centers for thought, the senses, and voluntary muscles.

Cholesterol (kuh-LES-tuh-rohl) An animal fat needed in small amounts, but which may be unhealthy in larger amounts.

Chlorophyll (KLOHR-uh-fil) Green substance that cells use to make food.

Chloroplasts (KLOHR-uh-plasts) Green cell parts that contain chlorophyll.

Chromosomes (KROH-muh-sohms) Thread-like parts in cell nucleus made up of DNA and genes.

Cilia (SIL-ee-uh) Hairlike parts of cells in breathing passages, which sweep out dirt and germs.

Circulatory (SUR-kyuh-luh-tohr-ee) **system** The transport system, which circulates blood through the body.

Class (KLAS) A group of similar orders of organisms.

Climate (KLY-mit) The pattern of weather in a place over a long period of time.

Climax community (KLY-maks kuh-MYOO-nih-tee) A stable community at the end of a succession.

Climax (KLY-maks) **plants** The plants that remain as dominants in a stable community.

Clot (KLOT) Net of threads and trapped red blood cells that helps stop bleeding from a cut.

Cocoon (kuh-KOON) Silky shell spun by the larva of an insect and which protects it during the pupa stage.

Cold-blooded (KOHLD-BLUD-id) Having a body temperature that changes when the outside temperature changes.

Community (kuh-MYOO-nih-tee) All the populations that live together in a certain place and interact with one another.

Compound (KOM-pound) Kind of matter made up of two or more elements joined together chemically.

Conditioned (kun-DISH-und) **response** A learned response in which one stimulus takes the place of another.

Conifer (KOH-nuh-fur) One of a class of cone-bearing plants.

Coniferous (koh-NIF-ur-us) Referring to conifers, or cone-bearing trees.

Consumer (kun-SOO-mur) Organism that feeds on other living things.

Contagious (kun-TAY-jus) **disease** Disease that can be passed to other people by contact or other means.

Contract (KON-trakt) To shorten or squeeze together.

Cutting (KUT-ing) Cut-off stem or leaf that can be used to reproduce the plant.

Cycle (SY-kul) Series of steps that lead a material or living thing back to where it started.

Cytoplasm (SY-tuh-plaz-um) The material in a cell that is inside the cell membrane and outside the nucleus.

Deciduous (dih-SIJ-oo-us) Referring to trees that shed their leaves in the winter.

Decomposer (dee-kum-POH-zur) Consumer that breaks down wastes or dead organisms to get food.

Deficiency (dih-FISH-un-see) **disease** Disease caused by a lack of a vitamin or a mineral.

Depressants (dih-PRES-unts) Drugs that slow down the heart beat, breathing rate, and nervous system.

Diaphragm (DY-uh-fram) Muscle below the lungs that is used in breathing.

Digestion (dih-JES-chun) The process of breaking large food molecules into small molecules that the body can use.

Digestive (dih-JES-tiv) **system** Group of organs that break down, or digest, food into molecules the body can use.

DNA (dee-en-ay) Chemical that makes up genes in all organisms.

Dominant gene (DOM-uh-nunt JEEN) Gene that always shows itself.

Dominant (DOM-uh-nunt) **plants** The most numerous plants in a community.

Drug (DRUG) Any substance other than food that causes a change in the body.

Drug abuse (uh-BYOOS) The improper use of drugs.

Drug dependence (dih-PEN-duns) The need for a drug.

Eardrum (EER-drum) Tissue between outer ear and middle ear that vibrates when struck by sound waves.

Ecologist (ih-KOL-uh-jist) Biologist who studies ecology.

Ecology (ih-KOL-uh-jee) The study of the relationship of living things to the environment.

Ecosystem (EK-oh-sis-tum) A living community and its nonliving environment.

Egg cell (EG SEL) Female reproductive cell of a plant or an animal.

Element (EL-uh-munt) One of the basic kinds of matter that combine to form compounds.

Embryo (EM-bree-oh) A young, undeveloped plant or animal.

Endangered species (en-DAYN-jurd SPEE-sheez) Living thing in danger of becoming extinct.

Endocrine (EN-duh-krin) **system** Group of organs that produce chemical messengers called hormones.

Environment (en-VY-run-munt) Everything that is around a living thing.

Enzymes (EN-zyms) Chemicals that help digest foods.

Esophagus (ih-SOF-uh-gus) Tube that carries food from the mouth to the stomach.

Evaporate (ih-VAP-uh-rayt) To go into the air as a gas, or vapor.

Evolution (ev-uh-LOO-shun) The process of change through time that results in new types of living things.

Excretion (ik-SKREE-shun) Getting rid of wastes.

Exhale (eks-HAYL) To let air out of the body.

External (ik-STUR-nul) **fertilization** Fertilization outside the body of a female animal.

Extinct (ik-STINGKT) Referring to a species that has died out.

Family (FAM-uh-lee) A group of similar genera of organisms.

Fats (FATS) Group of nutrients that supply fuel for energy.

Fatty acids (FAT-ee AS-ids) Substances formed as a result of the digestion of fats.

Feces (FEE-seez) Solid waste that forms in the large intestine.

Fertilization (fur-tuh-lih-ZAY-shun) The joining of the nuclei of an egg and a sperm.

Fetus (FEE-tus) Human embryo after two months of development.

Fiber (FY-bur) Complex carbohydrate the body cannot digest, but is needed for healthy digestion.

Fission (FISH-un) Asexual reproduction by splitting that produces two cells of equal size.

Food chain (FOOD CHAYN) A way of showing the order in which food energy passes from one organism to another.

Food pyramid (PIR-uh-mid) A way of showing how much food each organism in a food chain eats.

Food web (FOOD WEB) A way of showing how two or more food chains are linked together.

Formula (FOR-myuh-luh) A way to write the symbols for a compound.

Fossils (FOS-uls) Traces or remains of living things from long ago.

Four-food groups (FOOR-food GROOPS) Groups of foods needed for a balanced diet.

Fraternal (fruh-TUR-nul) **twins** Nonidentical, two-egg twins, that do not have all the same genes.

Fruit (FROOT) Ripened ovary, containing seeds, of a plant.

Fungi (FUN-jy) (singular: **Fungus**) Non-green, plant-like simple organisms.

Gallbladder (GAWL-BLAD-ur) Bag under the liver that stores bile.

Gastric (GAS-trik) **juice** Digestive juice made by, and in, the stomach.

Genes (JEENS) Parts of chromosomes that control the inheritance of traits.

Genetic (juh-NET-ik) Referring to genes or heredity.

Genus (JEE-nus) (pl: **genera** [JEN-ur-uh]) A group of species that are alike in many ways and are closely related.

Germs (JURMS) Microbes that cause infectious diseases.

Glycerol (GLIS-uh-rohl) Substance formed as a result of the digestion of fats.

Grafting (GRAF-ting) Reproducing a plant by joining its cut-off stem to the stem of another plant that is rooted.

Habitat (HAB-ih-tat) The place where a species lives.

Hallucinogens (huh-LOO-suh-nuh-jens) Drugs that cause people to see, hear, smell, or taste things that do not exist or in strange ways.

Hemophilia (hee-muh-FIL-ee-uh) Genetic disorder in which blood does not clot normally.

Herbivore (HUR-buh-vohr) Consumer that eats plants.

Herp (HURP) Any amphibian or reptile.

Hormones (HOR-mohns) Chemical messengers that control activities in the body.

Hybrid (HY-brid) Organism that has two unlike genes for a trait.

Hypothesis (hy-POTH-ih-sis) A guess or a possible answer to a scientific question.

Identical (eye-DEN-tih-kul) **twins** Twins from one fertilized egg that have all the same genes.

Immune (ih-MYOON) Having resistance, or immunity, to a disease germ.

Immunity (ih-MYOO-nih-tee) The body's ability to resist a disease.

Incubate (IN-kyuh-bayt) To keep eggs warm while the embryos in them are developing.

Infectious (in-FEK-shus) **diseases** Diseases caused by germs or parasitic worms.

Inhale (in-HAYL) To take air into the body.

Inherited (in-HER-ih-tid) Passed from parents to offspring.

Insulin (IN-suh-lin) Hormone that controls the use of sugar in the body.

Internal (in-TUR-nul) **fertilization** Fertilization inside the body of a female animal.

Invertebrates (in-VUR-tuh-brayts) Animals without backbones.

Involuntary (in-VOL-un-ter-ee) Not under control of the will.

Joint (JOYNT) Place where bones meet.

Kidneys (KID-nees) Organs that filter wastes from the blood and make urine.

Kingdom (KING-dum) One of the five largest groupings of organisms.

Large intestine (in-TES-tin) Part of the digestive system in which solid wastes are formed and water is absorbed into the blood.

Larva (LAR-vuh) The worm-like second stage in the life cycle of an insect that has complete metamorphosis.

Lens (eye) (LENZ) Part of eye that focuses light on the retina.

Lens (microscope) (LENZ) Curved glass that focuses light.

Life functions (FUNGK-shuns) All the things living things do to stay alive.

Ligaments (LIG-uh-munts) Bands of tissue that tie bones together at joints.

Limiting factor (LIM-ih-ting FAK-tur) Anything in the environment that puts limits on where an organism can live or on its numbers.

Malignant (muh-LIG-nunt) **tumor** A cancerous growth.

Mammal (MAM-ul) Warm-blooded animal with hair and mammary glands.

Mammary (MAM-uh-ree) **glands** Organs in mammals that produce milk for feeding their young.

Marrow (MAR-oh) The center of long bones, where blood cells are made.

Medulla (mih-DUL-uh) Part of the brain that controls breathing, heartbeat, and many involuntary, reflex actions.

Meiosis (my-OH-sis) Division of cells that forms sex cells.

Metamorphosis (met-uh-MOR-fuh-sis) Change in body form during an animal's life cycle.

Microbe (MY-krohb) Organism so small that it can be seen only with a microscope.

Minerals (MIN-ur-uls) Nutrients that help the body work properly and that build bones, teeth, and blood.

Mitosis (my-TOH-sis) Process in which a body cell nucleus divides into two nuclei.

Molt (MOHLT) In insects, to shed an outside skeleton during growth.

Motor nerve (MOH-tur NURV) Nerve that carries messages from the spinal cord and brain to other parts of the body.

Mucus (MYOO-kus) Sticky substance produced in the windpipe and bronchi.

Mutation (myoo-TAY-shun) Change in a gene that produces changes in the offspring.

Natural selection (sih-LEK-shun) A theory of how present species have evolved from those of the past.

Nerve (NURV) Bundle of fibers of nerve cells that carry messages.

Nervous system (NUR-vus SIS-tum) Group of organs whose job is to control and carry messages through the body.

Niacin (NY-uh-sin) One of the group of B-vitamins.

Niche (NICH) The way an organism fits into its habitat.

Nitrates (NY-trayts) Compounds of nitrogen with oxygen and other elements.

Nitrogen (NY-truh-jun) Basic element that makes up part of living things.

Nonvascular (non-VAS-kyuh-luh) **plants** Plants that lack tubes to carry water.

Nucleus (NOO-klee-us) A cell's center of control.

Nutrients (NOO-tree-unts) Materials in foods that the body needs.

Nutrition (noo-TRISH-un) The science of how the body uses food.

Nymph (NIMF) Young stage in life cycle of an insect with incomplete metamorphosis.

Offspring (AWF-spring) New organism that results from reproduction.

Omnivore (OM-nuh-vohr) Consumer that eats both plants and animals.

Order (OR-dur) A group of similar families of organisms.

Organ (OR-gun) Group of tissues that work together to do a special job.

Organism (OR-guh-niz-um) A living thing.

Ovary (OH-vuh-ree) Female reproductive organ in a plant or an animal.

Oxygen (OK-sih-jun) Element in the air that living things use to get energy from food.

Pancreas (PAN-kree-us) Gland that produces both a digestive juice and a hormone, insulin.

Parasites (PAR-uh-syts) Living things (including many bacteria, viruses, protozoans, and worms) that live off other living things.

Parasitic worms (par-uh-SIT-ik WURMS) Worms that cause infectious diseases.

Penicillin (pen-ih-SIL-in) Drug, made from a mold, used to treat bacterial diseases.

Petals (PET-uls)   The colored outer parts of a flower that help protect its inner parts and that attract insects.

Phloem (FLOH-em)   Tissue in plants that moves food through stems from leaves to roots.

Photosynthesis (foh-tuh-SIN-thih-sus)   Process by which green cells put together, in the presence of light, carbon dioxide and water to make sugar and oxygen.

Phylum (FY-lum) (pl. **phyla** [FY-luh])   A group of similar classes of organisms.

Pioneer (py-uh-NEER) **plants**   The first plants to grow on bare land.

Pistil (PIS-til)   A female reproductive part of a flower.

Pith (PITH)   Soft tissue in a plant stem that stores food.

Pituitary (pih-TOO-ih-ter-ee) **gland**   "Master gland" that makes growth hormone and other hormones that help control other glands.

Placenta (pluh-SEN-tuh)   Organ in a mammal mother that gives food to the embryo.

Plasma (PLAZ-muh)   The liquid part of the blood.

Platelet (PLAYT-lit)   Pieces of cells in the blood that help form clots.

Pollen (POL-un)   Powder made up of pollen grains, which contain sperm cells.

Pollination (pol-uh-NAY-shun)   The transfer of pollen from a stamen to a pistil.

Pollute (puh-LOOT)   To add something harmful to the environment.

Population (pop-yuh-LAY-shun)   All the members of one species that live in an area.

Pore (POOR)   Tiny opening of a sweat gland in the skin.

Predator (PRED-uh-tur)   Animal that eats other animals.

Prey (PRAY)   The animal that a predator eats.

Producer (pruh-DOO-sur)   Green plant or other green organism that makes food.

Proteins (PROH-teens)   Nutrients that contain nitrogen and that build and heal tissues.

Protozoans (proh-tuh-ZOH-uns)   One-celled animal-like organisms classified as protists.

Pulse (PULS)   Beating of arteries as the heart beats.

Punnett (PUN-et) **square**   A chart used to predict the heredity of a trait.

Pupa (PYOO-puh)   The noneating stage of an insect with complete metamorphosis.

Pupil (PYOO-pul)   Part of the eye through which light enters the eye.

Pure (PYOOR)   Having two like genes for a trait.

Recessive gene (rih-SES-iv JEEN)   Gene that is hidden when a dominant gene for the same trait is present.

Reflex (REE-fleks)   Involuntary action in response to a stimulus.

Regeneration (rih-jen-uh-RAY-shun)   The growing back of lost parts.

Reproduce (ree-proh-DOOS)   To produce more of one's own kind.

Reptiles (REP-tils)   Group of cold-blooded vertebrates that includes snakes, lizards, alligators, and crocodiles.

Respiration (res-puh-RAY-shun)   The "burning" of food in which sugar combines with oxygen to produce carbon dioxide and water, with the release of energy.

Respiratory (RES-per-uh-tohr-ee) **system**   Group of organs that take air into and out of the body.

Response (rih-SPONS)   A reaction to a stimulus.

Retina (RET-uh-nuh)   Part of the eye on which images of objects seen are formed.

Saliva (suh-LY-vuh)   Liquid in the mouth produced by the salivary glands and containing an enzyme that helps digest starch.

Scavenger (SKAV-in-jur)   Animals that eat other animals that they find dead.

Sensory (SEN-suh-ree) **nerve**   Nerve that carries messages from the sense organs to the spinal cord and brain.

Sepals (SEE-puls)   Leaf-like flower parts that protect the flower bud before it opens.

Sex chromosomes (SEKS KROH-muh-sohms)   The X and Y chromosomes, that control inheritance of sex.

Sexual (SEK-shoo-ul) **reproduction**   Reproduction from two parents.

Sickle-cell disease (SIK-ul-sel dih-ZEEZ)   Genetic disorder in which red blood cells have the shape of a sickle.

Skeletal (SKEL-ih-tul) **muscle**   Voluntary muscle, attached to the skeleton, as in the arms and legs.

Small intestine (in-TES-tin)   Part of the digestive system where most of digestion takes place.

Smooth muscle (SMOOTH MUS-ul)   Involuntary muscle, as in the stomach and intestines.

Species (SPEE-sheez)   A group of organisms that have all the same structures.

Sperm (SPURM)   Male reproductive cell of a plant or an animal.

Spinal cord (SPYN-ul KORD)   Nerve cord that relays messages between the brain and other parts of the body.

Spores (SPOHRS) Reproductive cells of a mold.

Stamen (STAY-mun) A male reproductive part of a flower.

Stimulants (STIM-yuh-lunts) Drugs that speed up the heart beat, breathing rate, and nervous system.

Stimulus (STIM-yuh-lus) (pl. **stimuli** [STIM-yuh-ly]) Message received from the environment, or a change in the environment, to which an organism responds.

Stroke (STROHK) Blocking of an artery in the brain.

Succession (suk-SESH-un) A series of changes in a living community.

Sweat glands (SWET GLANDS) Tiny parts in the skin that form sweat.

Symptom (SIMP-tum) Sign, such as pain or fever, of a disease.

System (SIS-tum) Group of organs that work together to do a special job.

Tendon (TEN-dun) Band of tissue that connects a muscle to a bone.

Testis (TES-tis) (pl. testes [TES-teez]) Male reproductive organ in an animal.

Theory (THEE-uh-ree) An explanation of a scientific idea that has been thoroughly tested and accepted.

Thyroid (THY-roid) **gland** Gland that produces the hormone thyroxin.

Thyroxin (thy-ROK-sin) Hormone that controls the rate at which the body produces energy.

Tissue (TISH-oo) Group of similar cells that do a special job.

Toxin (TOK-sin) Poison that may be produced by disease bacteria.

Traits (TRAYTS) Characteristics, which may be inherited, that identify organisms as individuals.

Triceps (TRY-seps) Muscle in upper arm that, when it contracts, straightens the elbow.

Tuber (TOO-bur) Fleshy underground stem that can reproduce the plant.

Umbilical cord (um-BIL-ih-kul KORD) Cord containing blood vessels that attach a mammal embryo to the placenta.

Urea (yoo-REE-uh) Waste formed when amino acids break down and found in urine and sweat.

Ureters (yoo-REE-turs) Tubes that carry urine from the kidneys to the bladder.

Urethra (yoo-REE-thruh) Tube through which urine (and, in males, sperm) leaves the body.

Urine (YOOR-in) Liquid waste produced by the kidneys.

Vaccine (vak-SEEN) Weakened or dead viruses or bacteria, used to prevent disease.

Vacuoles (VAK-yoo-ohls) Bubble-like cell parts that store water, food, and wastes.

Valve (VALV) Structure in a vein or the heart that prevents blood from flowing backwards.

Vascular (VAS-kyuh-lur) **plants** Plants that have tubes for carrying water.

Vegetative propagation (VEJ-ih-tay-tiv prop-uh-GAY-shun) Asexual reproduction of plants from growing parts.

Veins (VAYNS) Blood vessels that carry blood toward the heart.

Venereal (vuh-NEER-ee-ul) **diseases** Diseases of the sex organs that are passed to others by sexual contact, often called VD for short.

Ventricle (VEN-trih-kul) Chamber of the heart that sends blood out of the heart into the arteries.

Vertebra (VUR-tuh-bruh) (pl. **vertebrae**) One of the small bones that make up the backbone of an animal.

Vertebrates (VUR-tuh-brayts) Animals that have backbones.

Villi (VIL-eye) (singular: **villus**) Tiny parts in the walls of the small intestine that absorb digested foods into the blood.

Viruses (VY-rus-is) Particles smaller than bacteria that in some ways are like living things and in other ways unlike living things and which cause many diseases.

Vitamins (VY-tuh-mins) Nutrients needed by the body to help it work properly and to prevent certain diseases.

Voluntary (VOL-un-ter-ee) Under control of the will.

Warm-blooded (WORM-BLUD-id) Having a body temperature that stays more or less the same and does not change if the outside temperature changes.

Windpipe (WIND-pyp) Tube through which air goes from nose and throat into the bronchi.

Xylem (ZY-lum) Tissue that moves water and minerals up through stems from roots to leaves.

Yolk (YOHK) Stored food supply for an animal embryo.

Zygote (ZY-goht) Cell that results from the fertilization of an egg by a sperm.

INDEX

Tontlewicz, Jimmy, 116
Toothless mammals, 51
Touch, sense of, 139
Toxins, 250
Traits, 212
Transfusions, 98
Transport system, 100–103
Trial-and-error learning, 149, 150
Triceps, 127
Trichina, 251
Tropical rain forest, 21, 22
Trunk-nosed mammals, 52
Tuber, 169
Tuberculosis, 100
Tumor, 263
Tundra, 21, 22
Turner's syndrome, 237
Turning point, 124
Twigg, Rebecca, 118
Twins, 211, 231–232
Typhoid fever, 251

U

Umbilical cord, 200, 201
Uppers, 267, 268
Urea, 118
Ureter, 119
Urethra, 119, 199, 200
Urine, 117
Uterus, 199, 200

V

Vaccines, 256
Vacuoles, 36
Valve, 102
Vascular plants, 46, 47
VD, 251, 252
Vegetables, 73, 82
Vegetative propagation, 169
Veins, 100, 101
Venereal diseases, 251, 252
Ventricle, 102, 103, 105
Venus fly trap, 12
Vertebrae, 48, 123
Vertebrates, 48, 50
Veterinarian, 209
Villi, 97
Virus, 45, 250
Virus diseases, 250–251
Virus pneumonia, 251
Vitamin A, 75
Vitamin B, 75
Vitamin C, 76
Vitamin D, 76
Vitamin E, 75, 77
Vitamin K, 75, 77
Vitamins, 73, 75–77
Voluntary action, 145
Voluntary response, 136
Voyager I, 138

W

Warm-blooded animals, 197
Wastes, bodily, 3, 118–119
Water, 73, 82
Water cycle, 10
White blood cells, 98, 255
Whoopers, 26
Whooping cough, 251
Whooping cranes, 26, 27
Wildlife, 8
Windpipe, 113, 114, 153
Woody stems, 69
Wooly mammoth, 239
Worm diseases, 251, 252

X

X chromosome, 230–232
Xylem, 69

Y

Y chromosome, 230–232
Yeast, 163
Yolk, 185
Yolk sac, 190

Z

Zoo keepers, 209
Zoo veterinarians, 209
Zoos, 209
Zygote, 186, 199, 218

CREDITS

Credits

versity; © Manfred Kage/Peter Arnold, Inc.; © Courtesy Sickle Cell Anemia Association. p. 238, © D. Kirkland, SYGMA; © Rene Dahinden.

Unit 10:

p. 248, © James A. McInnis. p. 249, © CDC. p. 250, © CDC. p. 254, © Artemis/Hartigan. p. 258, © Ed Lallo/People Weekly, © 1984 Time, Inc. p. 259, © American Heart Association. p. 262, © The Bettmann Archive; © James A. McInnis. p. 263, © American Cancer Society. p. 264, © American Cancer Society. p. 266, © Syd Greenberg/Photo Researchers, Inc. p. 267, © Peter Witt. p. 273, © 1981 Erika Stone/Photo Researchers, Inc.; © 1979 Joel Gordon Photography.